Daniel Brookshier
Darren Govoni
Navaneeth Krishnan
Juan Carlos Soto

JXTA: Java P2P Programming

SAMS

800 East 96th Street, Indianapolis, Indiana 46240

JXTA: Java P2P Programming

International Standard Book Number: 0672323664

Library of Congress Catalog Card Number: 2001097507

Printed in the United States of America

First Printing: March 2002

05   04   4   3

Trademarks

Warning and Disclaimer

Associate Publisher
Michael Stephens

Acquisitions Editor
Todd Green

Development Editor
Tiffany Taylor

Managing Editor
Charlotte Clapp

Project Editor
Natalie Harris

Copy Editor
Pat Kinyon

Indexer
Erika Millen

Proofreader
Jody Larsen

Technical Editors
Sebastien Baehni
Dave Savage

Interior Designer
Dan Armstrong

Cover Designer
Alan Clements

Page Layout
Cheryl Lynch

Contents at a Glance

Table of Contents

Foreword

Project JXTA was set up to operate as an open-source effort from its inception. This innovative and controversial approach was based on a few beliefs by the project originators at Sun Microsystems. First was the belief that the best innovation often happens outside of your team. Thus, we wanted a way to engage other Sun and non-Sun developers. Next was that JXTA had to be an open standard to become successful in a relatively short time. This is a view consistent with Sun's history; the company actively collaborates on open standards and develops implementations that are interoperable with solutions from other vendors. Finally was the belief that an ambitious effort like JXTA could not be done by any single company, especially if it relied on becoming an open standard. This meant that we needed an environment where no one entity, including Sun, had all the power.

The Project JXTA open-source community has seen tremendous growth in a short time. In its first 6 months, almost eight thousand developers signed up, and the technology and documentation had been downloaded over three hundred thousand times. The jxta.org Web site has become a meeting place for many bright people from different backgrounds and different motivations but with a common goal to develop solutions that enable cooperation by peers of all types. I think the early success of the jxta.org community validates the decision to be open source. This book, a collaboration of authors from the JXTA community, is a reflection of approach.

The comparison between Project JXTA and this book extends to many of the characteristics of an open-source project. For example, this book was written by a number of authors working remotely and who, in most instances, have never met in person. Like any project on jxta.org, not all participants contributed the same amount. In general, each author contributed as much as they were able, while a lead author or project owner oversaw maintaining a coherent vision. The writing of this book implemented the open-source concept of "meritocracy" where the more you've done, the more you are able to do. This is very much how JXTA software is developed today.

Open source development is not without risk. For example, in the case of Project JXTA, there remains uncertainty about the direction for the technology with many points of view. Should JXTA use its own protocols or adopt protocols currently used by Web Services, such as SOAP? Are the current protocols the correct ones? Of course, there are non-technical risks. If the JXTA technology is open-source, will there be enough opportunities to make money? Should I start now? Or, should I wait until the future is a little clearer? Perhaps less obvious is that by doing a project in the open, others have better "intelligence" on what you are working on and your status. Is it worth the risk that others beat you to the market? These risks translate to writing a book about JXTA. Mitigating them requires anticipating new opportunities, making intelligent bets, and adapting as new information is gathered to deliver a timely resource.

New technology opportunities are seldom easy to find and exploit and usually come to those who seek them out at the frontiers of innovation. With the explosion of connected devices, each capable of not just consuming, but also providing valuable resources to the network. Peer-to-peer technology is one such frontier in the evolution of distributed computing whose time has arrived. JXTA provides the infrastructure and foundation to rapidly develop innovative new solutions that are interoperable with others. jxta.org provides the forum to tap into the efforts of other forward-thinking developers, researchers, scientists, entrepreneurs, and business people who are members of the JXTA community.

I think you will find this book to be very helpful to gain an understanding of Project JXTA's goals, technology, and implementation status. The thought-provoking descriptions will provide you insights on how you can use the technology to build exciting new peer-to-peer applications. This book is the result of a lot of hard work by a group of dedicated authors who, just like Project JXTA, persevere despite many challenges and uncertainty. The authors worked collaboratively to learn a new technology area while enduring countless changes in the early versions of JXTA. They relied on each other and the interaction of many members of the community at jxta.org to get things right and describe JXTA in a way that developers understand. The result is a book that provides a current and practical window into Project JXTA.

I invite you to join the JXTA community—both the community created by the authors and reviewers who bring you the best book possible and the extended community centered at jxta.org. Welcome to Project JXTA!

Juan Carlos Soto

jxta.org Community Manager and Group Marketing Manager, Project JXTA, Sun Microsystems

January 2002, San Francisco, California

About the Authors

Daniel Brookshier is a world-class Java consultant, author, and speaker with 20 years of experience. Mr. Brookshier's knowledge of software development covers many industries, including transportation, telecom, wireless, healthcare, B2B, petroleum engineering, law, insurance, software tools, and aerospace. He is an international consultant with contract assignments in the United States, Norway, the United Kingdom, and China. Mr. Brookshier is the founder of two Java user groups in Dallas, Texas, the writer of several Java programming books, and he has published numerous articles about Java in industry magazines. Daniel is a recognized expert on Java software development, Java standards, Java Management, enterprise software, and JavaBeans component development. Daniel can be reached at `turbogeek@cluck.com`.

Darren Govoni is a Distinguished Engineer at Cacheon, Inc. in San Francisco where he is responsible for product architecture and technology roadmapping. Darren is an active writer and speaker on Java technologies, P2P systems, Web Services, and adaptive computing. In 1999, Darren founded Metadapt Design Systems with an emphasis on design metaphors for complex adaptive systems. His research forms the basis for Cacheon technology and products.

Navaneeth Krishnan is currently Senior Product Engineer at Aztec Software and Technology Solutions where he has designed and developed several e-commerce solutions and reusable frameworks primarily based on the J2EE architecture. His current focus is on Web Services and peer-to-peer technologies. He has been involved in JXTA since mid 2001 and strongly believes that it has the potential to make a significant impact in the area of peer-to-peer computing. He spends his spare time writing articles, contributing to books, and exploring the endless possibilities created by emerging technologies.

Juan Carlos Soto is the Group Marketing Manager for Project JXTA at Sun Microsystems and the `jxta.org` Open Source Community Manager. On previous projects at Sun, Mr. Soto managed engineering groups implementing Java for small devices and managed business development for Java Software.

Prior to Sun, Mr. Soto was Director of Product Development at Diba, Inc., an early pioneer developing consumer information appliance. Diba was acquired by Sun in 1997. Prior to his work at Diba, Mr. Soto worked at Hewlett-Packard, where he held various positions in Engineering and Marketing management.

Mr. Soto has an MS in Engineering Management from Stanford, an MS in Computer Science from the University of Colorado, and a BS in Computer Engineering from the University of Florida.

Dedication

To my love, Mariann.

—Daniel Brookshier

Acknowledgments

First, I would like to thank Sams Publishing for recognizing the gold in JXTA and funding one of the first books on the subject. In addition, I'd like to thank the production staff and technical editors who helped produce a very professional book.

This book would not be possible without the input and encouragement of Sun Microsystems and the JXTA open-source community. The community is the key to JXTA, and this book is a result of the selfless contributions of the individuals and corporations involved.

The production of this book also owes thanks to the NetBeans open-source community and their NetBeans IDE, which was used to create and debug most of the examples (www.NetBeans.org). In addition, I would like to thank No Magic Inc. for their gracious granting of a free copy of MagicDraw (www.MagicDraw.com) used for the object analysis of JXTA and the creation of most of the UML diagrams.

Tell Us What You Think!

As the reader of this book, *you* are our most important critic and commentator. We value your opinion and want to know what we're doing right, what we could do better, what areas you'd like to see us publish in, and any other words of wisdom you're willing to pass our way.

As an Associate Publisher for Sams, I welcome your comments. You can email or write me directly to let me know what you did or didn't like about this book—as well as what we can do to make our books stronger.

Please note that I cannot help you with technical problems related to the topic of this book, and that due to the high volume of mail I receive, I might not be able to reply to every message.

When you write, please be sure to include this book's title and author as well as your name and phone or fax number. I will carefully review your comments and share them with the author and editors who worked on the book.

Email: feedback@samspublishing.com

Mail: Michael Stephens
            Sams
            800 East 96th Street
            Indianapolis, IN 46240 USA

Introduction

By Daniel Brookshier

When thinking about how to introduce this book, I thought I might start by welcoming you to a new concept in software. I have worked with many types of software, and I have programmed exclusively in Java since it was introduced in 1995. I've seen my share of new concepts and ideas that would change the world. Java has had the biggest impact in my life, and I believe the evidence shows that it has changed the computer world. What about JXTA? Why should you or I use a technology that is so new and a departure from Web Services and client server technology?

When I started looking around, I found that JXTA is not so much a new concept as it is a revolution. Not a revolution in the sense of new or groundbreaking—a revolution like the French Revolution.

As with most situations where things go wrong, you blame those in power. The French had some rather large grievances with their government. Under Louis XIV and Louis XV, there was extravagant spending, unpopular wars on foreign soil, state bankruptcy, and high taxes imposed mostly on the common man. The French revolutionaries decided that the monarchy and the elite class all had to go. And, as they say, heads would roll.

Peer-to-peer is a response to a sort of server-based tyranny. Client-server, multi-tier, and Web server technologies are like kings. Servers concentrate power and resources, limit access, and restrict an individual's ability to access and control his or her own data. This is not exactly an affront to our civil rights, but it can mean that a corporation has my data on their servers.

There is also a barrier to the entry. The rich and noble born and elite of France controlled resources, and only large organizations have the resources to buy and maintain large servers. With the rise of Linux, you can create a shoestring operation, but you still need to pay for bandwidth and other resources. Servers hold the applications and data we use, but we have no stake or control in them. As individuals and even large groups, we cannot muster the resources to create our own servers unless we were born rich like a noble or have the resources like a corporation.

Oust the king and suddenly you are looking for someone else to govern. The French, while architecting their revolution, had some of the same thoughts as today's JXTA developers. On August 26, 1789, the National Assembly of France approved a document, entitled *Declaration of the Rights of Man and of the Citizen*. They based it somewhat on the declaration of independence written in America. The French document seems to be more about individuals operating in a society and, thus, more like a peer-to-peer system. Let's look at a few of the articles of the declaration to see where the French revolutionaries and JXTA agree.

Men are born and remain free and equal in rights. Social distinctions may be founded only upon the general good (Article 1).

Peers also achieve social status via the information or unique processing they contribute. In a server world, the server has almost all resources, while clients have little or none.

The principle of all sovereignty resides essentially in the nation. No body nor individual may exercise any authority which does not proceed directly from the nation (Article 3).

JXTA creates a community where no individual computer has the ability to affect the entire network unless other member peers allow it. In a sense, this is like a democracy but on a more personal level, because you vote by participation in a group or application. Rights of individual computers are also granted by the protocols that every computer on the peer-to-peer network must follow.

In a server environment, the client must follow the rules of the server software and the owners of the server. When there are many servers, there are also many masters, causing the clients to follow too many different and conflicting rules.

Liberty consists in the freedom to do everything which injures no one else; hence the exercise of the natural rights of each man has no limits except those which assure to the other members of the society the enjoyment of the same rights. These limits can only be determined by law (Article 4).

Liberty in JXTA, like real liberty, is difficult to define. But the key difference from client/server technology is the ability to be an acting part of the application. The benefits are a bit ethereal, but imagine the ability to truly control your data. You can also process the data at any time. Is this freedom? Hard to say, but it is a start.

JXTA promotes freedom as well as the right to punish those that abuse it. Even a free society has laws. For a network to succeed, there needs to be some way to know when others are harmed and provide a consequence to those responsible. In a P2P network, the ability of one member to do harm is limited. The redundancy of the network reduces the impact on the society of peers but, like any society, there are criminals (or at least perceived to be). JXTA has the notion of a credential. If a peer fails to be a good citizen, its rights may be forfeited and the credential invalidated.

Server environments are a bit different. Beyond denial of service attacks, being a good or a bad client is a gray area, mainly because the applications are very constrained for normal users. The server is often cast as the villain, as a hoarder of data and even breaking the trust of clients by allowing the sale of a client's data.

All the citizens have a right to decide, either personally or by their representatives, as to the necessity of the public contribution; to grant this freely; to know to what uses it is put; and to fix the proportion, the mode of assessment and of collection and the duration of the taxes (Article 14).

Taxation should be compared to a service fee or cost to create a service. A JXTA peer determines the level of participation in the network and, thus, the cost of its hardware and other resources. Like a consumption tax, there is a tendency to pay more, the more you use the network. Due to redundancy and shared processing, all users benefit, rather than suffering because of poor hardware.

Users make their own decisions on how they configure and use their P2P software. Inappropriate and draconian controls instituted by a server's owners or chosen software are eliminated.

In another way, article 14 also shows the difference between server and P2P technology. With servers, an infrastructure must be maintained. Server software, because of its costs, looks like a government that requires a tax to operate that is usually flat rather than based on participation. With a peer network, peers share resources and each peer pays its share by its existence and level of participation.

> *A society in which the observance of the law is not assured, nor the separation of powers defined, has no constitution at all (Article 16).*

This is sort of an obvious statement for JXTA. If you don't use JXTA protocols (our Constitution and basic laws), you cannot be a member of the community. If you are using JXTA and do abuse its community, you are usually just hurting yourself.

> *Since property is an inviolable and sacred right, no one shall be deprived thereof except where public necessity, legally determined, shall clearly demand it, and then only on condition that the owner shall have been previously and equitably indemnified (Article 17).*

P2P started to become popular with the introduction of Napster. Sadly, the implication was that P2P was associated with piracy. Although Napster was originally formed with the idea that only valid owners of music would access digital versions, there was probably more piracy than legitimate use. Consequently, Napster has suffered in court with a severe reduction in the number of users.

P2P networks, such as Gnutella, are also devoid of rights management. These systems cannot be taken to court as Napster was because they are truly distributed. However, because of their uncontrolled nature, corporations and ISPs are restricting their traffic, and individual users are being charged with crimes or losing rights to services. It is highly probable that these systems will be disabled or at least inconvenienced.

The ultimate goal for JXTA is to be a good citizen and respect copyright and property laws. The reason is simple, without respectability, JXTA is seen as another Napster or Gnutella and will be filtered by ISPs and corporations. Respect others' rights to their property and you will be treated as a fellow citizen and allowed to use the Internet and corporate infrastructures.

Most of us live in a commercial society, and we deal with commercial entities. Where there is unfair trade or criminal activity, the system of government or those affected will tend to remove those who abuse the system. Although you may argue that entities like record companies are not acting fairly, the fact is that the laws are currently written to protect them—not those who dislike the law and protest it by circumvention. Napster and the newer incarnations have not changed any laws through their public protests and active breaking of laws. We still need to follow the rule of law to succeed.

JXTA Scale

Another revolutionary idea of JXTA is what it empowers you to build. Without a central server, with its costs and limits, much more is possible. This does not necessarily mean new types of applications, just a greater scale than was possible in a server environment.

A good example of the scalability of JXTA applications is simple catalog for e-commerce. Normally, you would need a large number of clustered servers to handle a large number of transactions. With JXTA, the catalog and its software are distributed automatically among peer computers. Instead of a server that must show the same catalog to millions of users, you just need one PC to distribute the first copy and any updates. All that needs to be centralized is the final order acceptance and credit card transaction, and even that is distributable to some extent.

There are many benefits of a P2P catalog from cost savings to the ability of a user to access the catalog offline. The application also runs faster because the user is not as limited to his or her connection speed or waiting in a queue of other users. Add to this 100 percent availability to most users, and you ensure that the verities of the Internet or of a server farm are no longer a part of the risk equation.

Another scale feature is raw computing power. In a server environment, each client has access only to limited resources that must be shared by all users. With JXTA, each peer has all the power of the machine it is running on, plus the shared power of all the other peers with which it is collaborating.

Is JXTA a New Concept?

Just by reading this far, you may have seen very familiar concepts. In the prior examples on scale, it is very easy to associate the same goals with distributed computing. The examples of P2P throughout the book are all possible using other methods. However, the point of JXTA is not necessarily to replace these methods. JXTA is a platform with specific protocols to talk to other JXTA platforms in a peer-to-peer network. It is not an application or a library created to build specific applications. The reason JXTA exists is to enable the refactoring of many different applications in a P2P environment. Like the catalog example, the idea is to move away from centralized infrastructures to gain the benefits of a distributed system.

RMI, CORBA, and Web Services are distant cousins of JXTA. They are either oriented toward a client/server or limited point-to-point communications. JXTA may seem to provide similar services, but the framework beneath is very different. For example, you can implement remote method invocation. The key difference between JXTA and others is that the delivery of the command to execute can span barriers like firewalls. The remote command can be sent to groups of computers or just a single computer, depending on the type of task.

JXTA Risks

I think we can safely agree that JXTA is not like anything else. Is JXTA something to bet your time as well as your fortune on? There are risks. Some are new and others are well known. Some are being fixed as you read this book, and others simply need to be implemented on the current JXTA platform.

The largest risk now is that JXTA will be in flux over the next couple of years. The good news is that the community of developers will try to keep the network stable for the purpose of keeping their products working. When you reach a certain point, developers learn to hate change, even when the project is open source.

It is not all a bed of roses in other areas. There are aspects to a P2P system that can be problematic. In our catalog example, it does take time to propagate the catalog to all users. The same time delay is true of updates and transactions.

We are at the start of the JXTA revolution. It is time to think revolutionarily thoughts. The reign of client server is about to fall. Read on and join the revolution. Viva la revolution!

Daniel Brookshier
turbogeek@cluck.com

JXTA Community Member, Java Consultant
January 2002, Dallas, Texas

What This Book Covers

This book will only cover the Java J2SE reference platform implementation of JXTA. We will not cover the C++, J2ME, Pearl, or other languages that are being used to create JXTA platforms. The J2SE version is the reference platform and best for experimentation or explanation of JXTA protocols. Java is also the most popular language for JXTA development at this time.

This book is intended to introduce new developers to the JXTA API and selected applications and services. Our goal is for the reader to understand P2P concepts and be able to build useful applications using JXTA.

We do not cover detailed aspects of how the JXTA platform is implemented unless it adds value to the explanation on how to use it.

Who Should Use This Book?

This book is written for readers who need an introduction to P2P and for those who want to learn JXTA. You should already be comfortable with Java. You do not need to know anything about JXTA or peer-to-peer programming.

By the end of the book, you should be able to create simple P2P applications using JXTA and the J2SE JXTA reference platform.

How This Book is Organized

This book is organized with two goals. The first goal is to explain P2P and JXTA in general terms. The second goal is to create applications that use JXTA. Finally, we cover specific applications with the aim of furthering an understanding of JXTA while showing how more complete applications are written. This arrangement was chosen so that the reader can get an overview of JXTA and then build an understanding of how to use its various parts.

Web Resources and Example Code

You can download the source code for examples presented in this book from www.samspublishing.com. When you reach that page, enter this book's ISBN number (0672323664) in the search box to access information about the book and a Source Code link.

The NetBeans IDE was used for much of the code that is found in the book. NetBeans is available at www.netbeans.org. Because Forte from Sun Microsystems is derived from NetBeans, it should work as well. You can also use your favorite editor or IDE, but the ANT scripts were created within NetBeans and Forte.

Also on the site are files that can be used with MagicDraw from NoMagic at www.MagicDraw.com. The tool is written in Java and runs on most Java-compatible platforms. The demo version will allow you to browse and print the JXTA diagrams used in the book, but it will not allow you to save changes. The MagicDraw files follow the XMI standard for UML representation in XML, so other UML tools that support the standard should work (drawings may look different).

1

What is P2P?

By Daniel Brookshier and Juan Carlos Soto

JXTA is a peer-to-peer networking platform, but what is peer-to-peer? How is it defined? What are the problems? What are the applications for the technology? Moreover, how does JXTA compare to other solutions? In this chapter, we cover these questions and more. Peer-to-peer networking is very different from server-based technologies, and understanding the differences is essential knowledge to have before creating your application.

Defining Peer-To-Peer

Peer-to-peer (P2P) computing is not a new concept. You can argue that when two computers were first connected, they formed a P2P network. Mail servers, network news servers (NNTP), and domain name servers (DNS) operate in peer-to-peer networks. For example, e-mail servers interact directly with each other to send, route, and receive e-mail messages and can be considered a P2P network.

A similar case can be made for DNS servers, although DNS relies on name registrars and authoritative name servers. The net effect is that the name resolution is done in a distributed manner by any of a number of cooperating machines, resulting in increased reliability and performance.

The term "P2P" is relatively new, despite the examples that have been in place since the birth of the Internet. Some people credit P2P to Gene Kan and the other early Gnutella pioneers. With all the hype and media attention around peer-to-peer computing in the late 90s, it became very handy to have a more compact way to describe the phenomenon when trying to explain it to the press and analysts.

Coming up with a concise definition of P2P, however, is not so simple. There are not only problems with what makes up a P2P application, many competitive P2P proto- cols and implementations that operate in very different ways. Let's now define P2P so that we can grasp the key concepts.

Defining P2P

P2P may be best described by what it's not rather than trying to pin down what it is. P2P is not about eliminating servers. It is not a single technology, application, or business model. Perhaps most controversial is that it should be not characterized strictly by degree of centralization versus decentralization.

Centralization in a P2P network can consist of a central catalog, such as Napster. Napster acted as a traditional client server when users were looking for music, and it acted as a P2P network when users transferred files. This means the system took advantage of the fact that it was easy to create a centralized database of music files and their locations, but very difficult and costly to host the music.

Gnutella is a completely decentralized P2P network. No one peer is different than another except in the content that it shares. The directory service of Napster is shared among the peers in Gnutella.

JXTA mixes centralization with decentralization, looking for a happy medium. JXTA takes the stand that some services in the P2P network are best done by a limited set of peers. Although not a complete analogy, e-mail servers and e-mail clients are a comparable idea. E-mail servers handle the temporary storage of e-mail messages and route messages between other e-mail servers to reach their destinations. JXTA could perform the same function, except that the e-mail could be routed all the way from peer to peer using a combination of dedicated and distributed peers.

In General, P2P is more a style of computing that makes the network interactions more symmetrical. Even though there may be centralized services, the end user peer is a significant focus of the application. If the centralized services are distributed, such as e-mail, the system is less susceptible to problems with the network. Napster is the ultimate example of a monolithic centralization that causes all the peer-to- peer functionality to fail if the main server fails or is disconnected. Gnutella is the opposite because no single peer, if removed, will significantly affect the quality of the network.

While P2P is not a new concept, many factors today make P2P practical for a wide number of applications. These factors include the explosion of connected devices, the rapid increase of affordable bandwidth, acceleration of computing power, larger storage capacities, and the proliferation of information at the edges of the network.

The Personal Computer

It's hard to find a PC with less than an 800MHz CPU, 128MB DRAM, and 20GB hard disk. Computers continually get faster, have more disk space, and become cheaper. Computers are not constrained by resources—only by technology. Even if reaching the minimum size of a transistor eventually repeals Moore's Law (the doubling of CPU speed every two years), companies will just make bigger chips and increase parallelism.

Today's PCs are sometimes more powerful than server machines of just a couple of years ago. About the only difference between a PC and a server is the greater I/O bandwidth that a server can effectively process. Other qualities separate the PC from the server, but they have more to do with management, reliability, and the ability to scale. When it comes to the CPU, and in general storage and memory, they are nearly identical.

Applications and their demands for greater speeds and storage drive the demand for these faster PCs. Most applications do not use 100 percent of the PC's resources, so there is a lot of excess capacity. P2P applications and protocols use the excess computing power and storage to create systems where all of the computing is done with peers and not servers.

The Server

The real problems are at the server side of the equation. Despite economic downturns, the number of people on the Internet is still increasing. The promises of every computer connected to a broadband connection is not yet a reality, so many of the planned services are too big for the miniscule dialup speeds.

Despite the reduction in costs of computers, Internet servers are still very expensive. The reason is that as the Internet grows, the capacity of the server needs to increase. Because CPU capacity can only double every couple years, servers must use multiple CPUs or clusters of servers to have the capacity to serve hundreds of thousands of users. Because of all this hardware, servers are costly to run and require very expensive software. Because of the large number of users, great leaps of technology have been made in the past few years to cluster Web servers and application servers. Databases have entered the terabyte range as well.

P2P gives users (peers) control to use and access their data as they see fit. In many instances, it is more efficient than replicating data on servers while providing the same type of access. P2P applications are flexible and tolerant of errors. They can replicate data as needed and broadcast data to multiple computers. With a server system, there are many points of failure, and many installations have several failure points as a tradeoff between cost and reliability.

The time is ripe for compelling P2P applications that take advantage of the readily available computing resources and data on the user's desktop. The desktop is currently at the edge of the network, but this is where the network should begin. The desktop is an untapped workhorse and is where users need to interact with applications—not half-way across the world with a browser technology originally just meant to share scientific papers. It is time for a revolution in how we think and how we use our resources. To give you an idea of the difference between server technologies, look to AOL and Morpheus. (Morpheus is a music-sharing application using the FastTrac P2P protocol.) Although AOL has more than 30 million customers, only 2 million can be online simultaneously because of hardware constraints. By comparison, Morpheus can sustain 1.8 million users and more without any new hardware. Perhaps this is an unfair comparison of apples to oranges, but consider the applications specific to AOL. AOL must support the connectivity of clients plus serve applications. To do so takes millions of dollars of equipment. On the other hand, Morpheus uses the user's computer and the user's bandwidth. The only cost of Morpheus's Web pages is included in the cost of operations.

Characteristics of P2P Systems

For the purposes of discussion, we'll describe the common characteristics of systems and applications typically considered to be P2P today. Example applications include the following:

- *Consumer file sharing*—Gnutella, FastTrack, and Napster.

- *Distributed resources sharing*—SETI@Home, Avaki, Entropia, and Grid projects.

- *Content distribution networks*—OpenCola, Blue Falcon Networks, Konitiki.

- *P2P communications*—AOL Instant Messenger, Yahoo!Messenger, ICQ, Jabber, and others.

- *Collaboration applications*—Such as Hive, Groove, and myJXTA. File sharing and P2P communications together are often the foundation capabilities used to build a workgroup.

The number of users of P2P communications and file sharing today is in the hundreds of millions and can be expected to grow as more users and new devices come online.

The common characteristics of today's typical P2P systems include most of the following:

- Peer nodes have awareness of other peer nodes.

- Peers create a virtual network that abstracts the complexity of interconnecting peers despite firewalls, subnets, and lack of specific network services.

- Each node can act as both a client and a server.
- Peers form working communities of data and application that can be described as peer groups.

The overall performance of the P2P application tends to increase as more nodes are brought online as opposed to typical client-server environments where more clients degrade performance.

The performance is also dependent on the application, the P2P protocol, and the network topology. The network topology is the arrangement of peers, their bandwidth, and the peer's computing capacity. The protocols pass messages and data on the network, which, will pass its messages. The applications combined with the overhead of the protocol and the speeds capable by sections of the network make up a system with a specific performance profile. Compared to server-based systems, even a small P2P network can be very complex. There is still a great advantage because despite the complexity, the P2P network is really a network of islands of PCs in different corporate, ISP, and home networks.

There are cases where the protocol or application can saturate a network with messages. Not all of the total P2P network may be affected, but large parts can be. A simple example of how this would happen is an application for searching. If a search message propagates (copied from peer to peer), the search message may be sent to peers multiple times. If most of the peers are forwarding search messages and propagating, and contributing search messages of their own, the available bandwidth could be quickly exhausted.

To prevent bandwidth saturation, the protocols should include message throttling, and the topology should be augmented by an ability to reduce duplicate messages and even store information that is commonly requested.

The following are some of the techniques used by JXTA:

- Some types of messages are only forwarded a set number of times. This prevents messages from reaching all peers. Most P2P applications work without needing all peers to participate.
- Data that the peer discovers is cached locally to eliminate the need to re-query information every time it is required.
- Data in the network, depending on its type, has a time-to-live property that prevents the network from accumulating stale data. When the time-to-live of a message expires, the message is deleted.
- High capacity peers are used to reduce the load on peers that have low bandwidth or inadequate processing power. This prevents low power peers with insignificant bandwidth from being saturated with messages.

- Message routing is intelligently planned by each node to ensure that the best routes are taken to reach a destination.

- The base protocol is selected based on the efficiency in the part of the network that is used. IP broadcasting is used in a local network to send messages to all peers with the bandwidth of a single peer, while TCP or HTTP is used between LAN networks and for direct peer communication.

Project JXTA provides similar services on an open platform. Additional techniques, plus those listed, can be added to the base parts of the platform's architecture. We'll look into some of these examples and characteristics in more detail later.

P2P Concepts

One of the common misconceptions is that P2P networking is a single protocol. The assumption is easy to make because some P2P networks only use one protocol. You can use many models alone or in combination for various applications.

Point-to-Point Communication

Point-to-point is the most obvious way to communicate between peers. This is nothing more than opening a communication port between peers. There are still a few ways to communicate including HTTP and with encryption.

Point-to-point communication is useful for messages that need to be directly addressed to a peer. Point-to-point is also used as a part of other models discussed in the following paragraphs.

Cross-Linked Peer Networks

Cross-linking is where each of the other peers is, in turn, connected to other peers. The effect is an explosion of interconnected peers. This allows you to access peers via a few hops to other peers. Because of cross-linking, no single peer is very far from any other peer in the network. This is often referred to as the *Six Degrees of Separation from Kevin Bacon Effect*. The theory, developed by Mike Ginelli, Craig Fass, and Brian Turtle, was invented originally as a game. The concept of the Kevin Bacon effect is that you can connect Kevin Bacon and any other actor through the films or television shows the two have worked on in no more than six steps. The concept is also used to show that you can pick any one person in the world and you should be able to connect yourself to that person via a chain of acquaintances.

The Kevin Bacon effect is directly applicable to peer-to-peer networking with a collection of interconnected peers, where no peer is connected to more than a few other peers but is able to see all other peers via a chain of peer connections.

In effect, one peer is never more than a few peers away from another. The beneficial result is that queries are quickly distributed to most or all peers on the Gnutella network.

The concepts can also be found in the *small-world effect*. The small-world effect results from interconnections that seem to make the world smaller. The world is smaller because most parts of the world are easily reached through associations or through technology or replications, such as how franchises and other businesses replicate around the world. The effective distance is reduced and, thus, creates a smaller world because the true distance between you and a person, a restaurant, or product is no longer part of the equation. The same effect can be seen in P2P when data and services become replicated and localized.

Broadcast Communication

Broadcasting is normally done within a subnet; there is a broadcaster and one or more listeners. The message is sent out on the network and other peers listen to a specific port. Broadcast messaging is very economical because there is only one message sent per subnet. Unfortunately, broadcast messages are sometimes filtered or blocked.

Broadcasting is very useful for discovery. For example, a new peer comes online and broadcasts its presence including an address that can be used to directly communicate with the peer. You could also use broadcasts to deliver identical messages to a group of peers at a very low cost. For this reason, broadcast is often used to deliver video, because only one copy is sent but all peers can watch the video.

Another useful application is to broadcast queries. This is useful when there are many peers that could answer a query, but you don't know which one has the answer. Similarly, this works just as well when you expect an answer from each of the other peers.

Multipoint Communication

Multipoint is also often associated with broadcasting. However, the difference is that multiple connections are made of multiple transmissions of identical data. In most situations where broadcasting is desirable, using the protocol for IP broadcasting is often impossible or at least cannot reach all of the peers you would like. The alternative is to open multiple point-to-point connections. In addition, bridge peers that will need to relay messages to other networks can only reach some areas.

The application for multipoint communications are identical to those that would use broadcasting, except that it used where the peers are unable to support IP broadcasting.

Multipoint can also be used in various ways to create transport messages. Some peers can specialize as routers, gateways, or even caches of messages.

There are problems with multipoint. First, messages have no guarantee they will be received simultaneously. It is possible that the delay between transmission and reception could be quite long because of relay peers. There may be additional problems because peers are generally just other PCs with dialup or other undependable networking, so messages may be lost. Finally, there are simply more bandwidth and computing resources required.

Despite the problems, multipoint networking is very useful and reasonably dependable as well as efficient. When the network is made up of cross-linked peers and redundant services for routing, gateways, and caching, the system is self-healing. In addition, the resources required, though more than broadcast, are still more efficient than brute force methods.

Network Graph Functions

Network graphs are the descriptions of interconnection of nodes, so network graph functions are tasks related to the arrangement or topology of the network. Included in this is the information or functionality at each node and the type, quality, and capabilities of the connections between the nodes. Network graphing functions include routing, loading, searching, and other functions.

Distributed Data Storage and File Sharing

Distributed data storage is another of the obvious parts of a P2P network. In essence, each peer represents either generic storage space or is a container for a specific list of items. Important issues with distributed storage are primarily concerned with searching for content.

Bandwidth Reduction

Bandwidth reduction as a P2P concept needs to be looked at two ways. First, think about traditional server applications like Web sites or file repositories on a server. You can significantly reduce the bandwidth of the server to that of a single peer. The peer can then transfer files to other peers that in turn share the files with more peers until ultimately all the peers on the network have the new file. Instead of one server, all of the peers share their bandwidth to distribute the files. This is an important model because it reduces the cost of creating applications that require client to transfer a large amount of data.

Distributed Computing

Distributed computing is a type of application that uses the processing resources of a group of peers to perform a task in less time by using more machines. Problems that can be solved with distributed computing are actually small. The problem is that many problems are easy, hard, or impossible to solve regardless of computing power. The other problem with distributed computing is breaking apart the task into units small enough for each computer to complete in a reasonable time.

Problems that have had the best success are those that process large amounts of information looking for small features. For example, SETI@HOME looks for signals in small sections. Because each computer in the network can effectively look for and find a signal, the application can be successful.

Another application that can take advantage of distributed computing is simulation of problems with large numbers of outcomes. FOLDING@HOME uses a distributed network, just like SETI@HOME, but instead of a processing sequence of radio data, each peer simulates and then tests a different sequence for folding a protean. Because there is currently no way to predict the folding sequence, simulation is the only solution.

Distributed searching is a little different than either of the previous methods. In distributed searching, different data is stored on different computers. The client to the search propagates a message to peers on the network. Each peer receives the search message checks to see if it has the answer and, if it does, returns it directly to the client of the search. If the peer does not have the answer, the peer forwards the request to other peers. The economy of the distributed search arises from not needing to store all the data in one location. The searches also can occur faster because there is less to search through on each peer.

Internet Barriers: NAT, Firewall, and Proxy Servers

One of the most significant problems prevalent on the Internet is that barriers prevent simple and direct communication between peers. The most obvious barrier is the firewall. Firewalls filter specific communication ports, limit access to specific computers, and can filter specific patterns of messages.

These barriers have been circumnavigated by using the HTTP protocol. HTTP is the most unregulated protocol in use today on the Internet. The HTTP protocol only allows a Web browser to initiate requests. This means that HTTP does not represent a threat, because an outside application cannot initiate activity from the outside. Because of this, most corporations allow HTTP to be unregulated.

By using HTTP for an application, known as *HTTP tunneling*, you can increase your chance of getting around firewalls that block almost all other protocols. The additional benefit is that proxy servers and NAT devices are also not barriers. We will cover these devices in more detail in Chapter 2, "Overview of JXTA."

The problem with HTTP tunneling is that the communication is stateless. A response can be linked with its request, but the context between each cycle of request/response does not have context with those that came before or after. Because of the stateless nature, some type of identifier must be passed from the client to the server side to maintain context. We often refer to these as cookies or its other form, URL encoding.

The other problem with tunneling is attempting to initiate a response or pass data to a client. As stated, the outside world cannot initiate a response. The only alternative is to wait for the client to contact the server and collect a waiting message. Not too difficult a problem, but it does introduce extra messages and increases the latency of the response. Another problem is that messages are not always waiting, so there could be a lot more traffic that is like the empty calories in a sugar coated doughnut.

In a peer-to-peer network, the analogy of the sugar on the doughnut increases until the network is overweight and has diabetes. If thousands or millions of peers are polling each other via HTTP tunneling, the number of poll messages will begin to flood the network. Another problem here is that some peers can only act as clients, because some networks may allow outbound requests, but not inbound as if there were a server.

The solution is to have relay peers that are allowed to be HTTP servers. If these servers have a reasonably high capacity, the polling of groups of peers is isolated to a single machine. With groups of relays scattered around the Internet and even strategically placed in corporate networks and ISPs, the tunneling technique becomes more efficient. JXTA employs this technique, but not all P2P solutions do.

A relay may not seem to be a very P2P concept. However, any peer, if capable, can be a relay. The relay is not really a server as much as a middleman in a random transaction. The relay is more of an appliance, such as a router, than a true server or true peer.

Applications for P2P

Many popular applications considered P2P today involve some degree of centralization. They range from fully centralized to completely decentralized, as demonstrated by Gnutella at one end and AOL Instant Messenger at the other. They all have distributed network computing in common.

Many of these solutions, if not all, can be implemented with client/server architecture. However, the characteristics of P2P can bring important improvements to traditional applications.

Chat

Chat applications are broadly considered P2P because of the characteristic that peer nodes directly interact with each other. Chat implementations vary widely, as do their associated business models. The most popular examples include AOL Instant Messenger, Yahoo!Messenger, MSN Messenger, and ICQ. Today, chats are also widely used by consumers and professionals alike, both at home and in the office. It provides a real-time communications medium that is often more appropriate than memos, e-mail, phone calls, and meetings.

The most popular commercial chat solutions use a centralized implementation. In short, all interactions go through one or more central servers that provide an accurate directory of connected members and route all messages. These implementations do not scale well and require very large data centers with large systems to support a large number of users. On the other hand, a centralized solution tends to be deterministic in its operation for a given number of users and in its ability to track use. Chat operators use their service as a tool to capture new members for their services, and most use this as a means to sell advertisements displayed on their chat applications.

The Project JXTA technology is ideally suited for chat implementations. It has been demonstrated on a range of chat implementations, including fully centralized, brokered, and fully decentralized. An interesting discovery is that using JXTA, the centralized implementation is most difficult (requires maintaining state and message queues on the server for all sessions), and the fully-decentralized solution was the simplest because the JXTA platform takes care of all the underlying issues to discover and communicate with other peer nodes.

Numerous other chat examples exist on JXTA. They include the myJXTA application (formerly known as InstantP2P), the Talk command in the JXTA Shell, the HotWire application, and several programming tutorials. These are described in more detail later.

Collaboration and White boarding

Collaboration comprises a broad category of applications that are P2P in nature. In the workgroup, collaboration involves sharing of ideas and resources through interactive communications. For example, to collaborate on a project, the team members are likely to need to exchange messages and documents with each other. The exchange of messages can be done by e-mail, phone, and chat applications.

During meetings, it may be helpful to have a shared virtual whiteboard to facilitate communications among distant collaborators. Documents are both developed individually and shared, or they are developed jointly. In both cases, P2P enables the documents to be shared in real-time without reliance on a central server.

The Project JXTA technology has been demonstrated in collaboration applications. It has been used to implement collaborative IDEs where more than one developer at a time can work on the same software files. One collaborative JXTA application was developed that allowed several people to edit the same spreadsheet simultaneously. Other JXTA projects have built collaboration toolkits that use JXTA for conferencing, shared browsing, and file sharing.

As with chat implementations, one of the advantages to using the JXTA technology for collaborations is that an application can be fully deployed with no reliance on servers or other centrally administered systems. JXTA handles the discovery of other nodes and the secure routing and exchange of user and inter-application messages among them.

Games

Gaming promises to be an attractive area for P2P. The advantages include the following:

- The mindset of the gamer is such that they are more likely to be open to new technologies, such as P2P.

- Message traffic generated by games is usually manageable and capable of operating on a P2P network.

- P2P allows for better community control as apposed to a central server that must support all gamers.

- Game designers are unlikely to have the resources to purchase and maintain reliable servers with the capacity for large numbers of gamers.

The Project JXTA technology has been demonstrated in several game applications. An interactive Chess tournament uses JXTA to exchange game moves among the two opponents and any number of observers. The chess game (see Chapter 10) and a similar tic-tac-toe game have also been demonstrated using JXTA for small devices.

A gamer can create a new JXTA peer group and invite other players from all over the world to join in his or her game, or he or she can restrict access to his or her game group.

File Share

File sharing applications remain the most controversial application of P2P technology. Applications, such as Napster and now Morpheus and KaZaA, are widely used to share media files, which in some instances violates existing copyrights. Whatever one's view of the current copyright laws, the power of P2P for file sharing cannot be overlooked. This power has direct benefits in the enterprise as well, where it has yet to be fully exploited.

One characteristic of P2P is that information tends to be distributed in an organic manner, making control very difficult. In the case of copyrighted material, this exacerbates the problem because content can be replicated very quickly. On the other hand, this phenomenon has the advantage that content becomes more readily available and less likely to become extinct. Several projects, such as OceanStore (UCB) and LOCKSS (Lots of Copies Keeps Stuff Safe—Stanford), take advantage of precisely those characteristics to create a network of highly-available, persistent data store.

The controversy around certain consumer file sharing implementations, such as Napster, runs the risk of overshadowing the real contribution. Consider the alternatives to P2P for content publishing (file sharing) in a way that the content is readily accessible to you and your peers; there are two. First is saving information to a group server and the other is creating a Web site. Saving your documents to a server has the advantage of being at a known location that is probably backed up and maintained by professionals. However, in practice, these servers tend to not be used as religiously as necessary to make the shared files reliably available to others in your group. In addition, the server is often completely inaccessible or not easily accessed outside the corporate firewall. Consequently, users often resort to mailing documents as attachments to deal with both issues that then introduce versioning problems.

Another solution is to create your own Web server. This is a major hurdle for most users. Typically, it requires getting a static IP address, reserving a domain name, establishing a DNS entry (assuming you have access to a DNS server), installing and maintaining a Web server, and administering access control to the system. Compare this to Napster, where all you had to do was copy a file to publish into a shared directory and that's it. Some Napster users resorted to renaming non-music files they wanted to publish and share (`<old file name.old file extension>.mp3`).

The popular file sharing applications today vary in their implementations. At one end of the spectrum are Gnutella and Freenet. Both of these are completely decentralized.

Solutions such as those based on FastTrack and Project JXTA technology are also decentralized. However, FastTrack has the concept of super nodes or rendezvous peers that facilitate the routing of messages and discovery of content.

Napster is considered the most centralized because it relies on a centralized server to index the content of the peer nodes. In Napster, all searches are done against the centralized indexes on the servers, although the actual file sharing is done with direct P2P.

Content Distribution

Content distribution is different from file sharing in that the files are replicated among peers. The content is distributed from an entity, such as a newspaper or other content company, to the peer. The key benefit to a P2P solution is that only the first copy of an article needs to be fetched by a peer. After that, the peers replicate the article among the peers. A newspaper that distributes data this way does not need a high volume, high-cost Web server, just a reasonably capable personal computer.

There is an additional level of savings within corporations. After an article is sent to a peer within a corporate network, IP broadcasting can be used to send the article to all of the peers at once. This means both that the link between the corporation and the Internet does not need the capacity for all the peers to fetch the article via a Web browser. In addition, internal traffic is greatly reduced.

Synchronization

Synchronization between peers is similar to content distribution except at a more granular level. All sorts of files can be synchronized from configuration files to calendars and address books. The synchronization would also be in a much smaller scope, perhaps just between your work and home computers.

Key P2P Issues

The following sections briefly explain possible problems of P2P. These problems are general and can occur in many situations. The JXTA community has tried to overcome many of the problems with the core JXTA protocols, but these problems are still possible, depending on your application and network topology.

Symmetric Bandwidth

Many P2P applications, because they represent both client and server parts of an application, probably utilize as much bandwidth going in as going out. On the other hand, traditional web applications use very little bandwidth outbound from the client and more inbound. For example, Web page requests are small, but the data for the page is large. P2P applications are more symmetrical because if they served Web pages, they would both read pages from other peers as well as serve pages to other peers. This is not how most ISPs are configured to work. For example, some cable modem and DSL ISPs have 1.5Mbps inbound and 128Kbps outbound. It would be better for the performance if inbound speed equaled the outbound speed. Even if there were more wideband ISPs providing symmetric access, the infrastructure of the ISP may still only support asymmetric loads tilted toward inbound and not outbound traffic.

There are no easy solutions to this problem. However, ISPs and corporations can benefit greatly from P2P if they support it directly. For example, by providing specialized P2P relays and rendezvous that are akin to network routers, the system is able to handle much more traffic and is able to even promote peers to cooperate within the ISP or corporate network.

The implication of this is that there is also an opportunity for hardware and software manufacturers to create specially designed P2P relays and rendezvous. Such P2P appliances would do for P2P what routers and firewalls have done for the corporate environment.

SOP Verses P2P

Networking infrastructures, techniques, and protocols for Web-based servers and applications are well understood. There are standard operating procedures (SOP) in place both at ISPs and corporations. Both entities are expecting users with Web browsers accessing services. However, P2P networking is not exactly like Web services. For example, P2P subverts port 80 to communicate to other peers. This is very much like what would be done in a normal Web service, but the amount of traffic on port 80 might be greater than expected. In general, the type of traffic within the networks will be different.

A P2P appliance may alleviate some of these problems. If the corporation supports P2P and is able to properly control traffic, there is no need to circumvent port 80 via tunneling or other technique. With standardized relays that have the capability of being controlled by corporations, such as corporate firewalls and routers, they can optimize their traffic and filter content.

Filtering content is probably the most significant use of P2P relays in corporations that are either trying to control users or prevent non-corporate applications from being used. An ISP may want to do this to provide filtered content to families with young children.

Many in the P2P world may find control and filtering to be at odds with the principals of P2P. The reality is that the Web was originally open and free. Corporations cannot live in a world that they do not control and will find ways to eliminate what they do not want. Add in security concerns and you can see that there is no way to create a P2P network that does not include control within corporate intranets and the boundary between the intranet and the wider Internet. By understanding corporate behavior, a P2P infrastructure that is friendly to corporate needs will succeed over those that do not.

Another aspect of modeling the current world is in value-added services. An ISP with specialized P2P equipment can provide its customers with enhanced connectivity to P2P applications. This would be similar to providing Web, e-mail, and Web hosting services.

Naming Space

Addressing Web servers is currently done with DNS. In the P2P world, there is no equivalent. Computers with DNS names are also static, while P2P peers are more dynamic as well as less persistent. No universal naming space has yet to be created that fits the need of a P2P network. Research is ongoing, but nothing is ready for primetime. Without a proper and unique way of creating names that can be related to hard objects, parts of the JXTA network can be problematic, with each developer choosing a different method for naming the bits that travel between the peers.

What about Ipv6, the extended IP addressing to any device? True, this does allow for unique addressing, but it is hardly likely to cause the disappearance of firewalls, NAT devices, and proxy servers. These still help manage local area networks and provide adequate security. Ipv6 will also not be generally available for several years. Because ISPs charge for unique IP addressing, it will still cost a user to have an IP address assigned and maintained with Ipv6. Virtual addressing is still the name of the game.

Intellectual Property Concerns

Intellectual property is more of an issue in a P2P network because there is less built-in control. In a server environment, the authentication and authorization of users to access data is simple. The data, authentication services, and rights management are centralized at the server. P2P decentralizes content distribution and is thus seen as uncontrolled.

The idea that control is lost is not a certainty. In fact, the only reason that control is lost is because most developers do not implement rights management. Very often, it is easy enough to trust the user. There are several different ways to track documents and who uses them. Not all of these techniques are foolproof, but many have a reasonable cost to benefit ratio.

For the most part, people are honest. You need to weigh ease of use and cost against the probability of loss by abuse.

Access rights and copyrights are important in the corporate environment too. In a P2P network, the corporation actually has the ability to enforce more control.

P2P systems can use the same authentication, digital signature, and LDAP mechanisms as Intranet applications.

Users Verses Abusers

Not everything is perfect in P2P. One of the harder things to do is to control what users do. The problem is that the peer network does not have a centralized point to store information about user behavior. A simple example is a file sharing system. Without a central authority, it is difficult to ensure that all users are behaving appropriately. The following are a few inappropriate things a user may do:

- Not share any files
- Shares invalid files
- Shares files infected with a virus
- Does not stay online to provide a fair share of file searches for other peers
- Does not allow others peers to complete file uploads
- Shares content of no interest to other users

In the server model, it is simple to control users. Resources and information about users is in one place. So, for example, access to data is easily matched and metered to the user's rights or his or her participation.

In a P2P network, it is difficult to tell if a peer has rights to data or services. The problem is that there is no central authority. The solution to part of this problem usually consists of digital signatures. The signature can be used to validate the peer or user, but there is still a problem with recording the behavior. Behavior can obviously be recorded at each peer interacted with, but only by collaboration can the group see if a member is breaking the rules.

Of course, applications can regulate users at the peer. Many applications do this now. The key is to ensure that the application really covers all types of bad behavior and is resistant to hacking.

In some cases, there is no need to protect from a bad peer. Most P2P networks are large enough that a rouge peer is barely noticed. A paper entitled "Free Riding on Gnutella," by Eytan Adar and Bernardo A. Huberman, exposed the fact that 70 percent of Gnutella users provided no files or resources to the system, and that 1 percent provided half of the total content available on the network. In other words, sometimes you need to expect the worst and plan to prevent it or decide if you can live with the worst-case scenario.

LEARN FROM NAPSTER

Napster seems to be in the news all the time. In the beginning, it was because of its popularity, and then because of its involvement with the courts. At the time of writing this book, there are still news reports from time to time. The most amazing thing about Napster was its popularity.

Napster's initial success had several features. First, Napster was like a pirate attack of the music industry. This attack appealed to many people who did not see any legal retribution in their futures. Like many hardened criminals, being caught and tried for their crime was far from their minds. Because there were hundreds of thousands using Napster at the time, there were literally not enough people to serve the warrants. In fact, the only one that actually went to court was Napster itself.

Secondly, like pirate booty, music was shared freely among the users and created a sense of community with a share-and-share-alike attitude. In the 1980s, when software piracy was rampant, the same attitude was common. It seemed normal to anticipate the cracking of the latest games and to then share them with friends. Here, it was hundreds of users with decades of music that they were more than happy to share with the world, and there were just as many looking for gaps in their collections.

Nevertheless, what caused Napster to take off was that the bigger the community got, the better the supply of quality music. This growth was a little selfish too. The system became explosive with just word of mouth that got friends to try it, which meant their friends music and their friend's computers would be added to the available music collection. As a subliminal afterthought, this added another user as fodder if the law started to affect users.

Another feature of Napster's success were the low bandwidth users. Very often, a low bandwidth user would set up the files he or she wanted to download and then go to bed to sleep through the download. This meant that the client was online and sharing his or her current collection plus what he or she have just downloaded. This meant there were many peers running through the night. Add to this the large number of users at work and at home with cable-modems, and you have a lot of content.

Because most bandwidth is fixed cost, the users did not worry too much about their time online. As we discuss in the "Bandwidth Sharing" section in this chapter, Napster is doing this for a very low cost, and most users don't see a large impact of running a Napster client. Because the client also played the MP3 files, the user is yet again given incentives to be a participant in the Napster network.

To summarize the reason Napster was a success: Free, Free, Free, and no extra cost to user.

Napster's death, however, is more than a story of the courts. The first thing that happened is that the law was seen on the horizon by many of the loyal Napster users. After a few days of above normal use (taking what they could before the door gets broken down) the users stopped using the system. The clear killer in this case was one band that got a hold of a bunch of usernames and got them kicked off Napster for violating copyrights.

But without the pirate users, Napster was devoid of content. All that was left was a few rare copyrighted albums and fringe music. Fringe music, by its very nature, is only listened to by a minority. Napster was essentially gutted of all of its users except for people that had been trading their non-mainstream music before Napster was ever invented.

But the real lesson here is in the following statements:

- More content causes more users that causes more content.
- More content causes more time online that causes more nodes.
- More nodes causes better performance.

We also have the equation for the death of a P2P application:

- Less content causes less time online that causes less content.
- Less content causes lower performance that causes fewer participating peer nodes.

Users=Success

For many applications of P2P, the number is a minimum number of users that is critical to success. Look at the Napster sidebar as a true story that proves this affect. In Napster's case, the number of users was related to the number of computers that had data to share.

JXTA is a little different from other P2P networks. The reason is that the JXTA is first a platform. The peer in effect becomes a general-purpose part of the network. The effect is that there could be a dozen different popular JXTA applications, but the JXTA network is populated with the total number of peers. The network should have a population of enough routers, gateways, and rendezvous to ensure that most general operations will be efficient.

The JXTA applications themselves may still suffer if they are small. For example, the JPDA application discussed in Chapter 9 would suffer if your friends and coworkers were not a part of the system because you could not share your address book and book calendar events with them. However, if your softball league all participated, it would still be very viable, at least for scheduling your games. The number of users will always have some impact. With JXTA, at least this does not impact the ability of P2P applications to operate with a very small community as long as JXTA itself is popular.

Seeding the Network

Building a P2P network is also important. How you add users is just as important as what the application does. With Napster, usage grew quickly because of the curiosity caused by news reports plus word of mouth of friends and coworkers. Napster was a revolution and it grew quickly because of its notoriety and even its daring in the face to the music industry and copyrights. Nevertheless, many P2P applications are far more pedestrian and do not have an aspect of novelty that would attract users. The odds of your application becoming overwhelmingly popular are very slim.

There is hope. There are other ways to create a P2P application with a large number of users. The first is to package JXTA as a part of another application. For example, in Chapter 9, we create an application with a calendar, a To Do list, and an address book. The idea is not to sell the idea of a collaborative system as much as it is to sell the idea of keeping your work and home computers synchronized with the same information.

Another application currently under development is called ResumeX$^{(SM)}$. ResumeX is an application that shares resumes on the JXTA network. There are two types of users—workers and employment agents. The resume creator must have his or her client up to help ensure that his or her resume is available. Next up is the agent. When you give your resume to an agent, it is in the form of a viewer that runs in the JXTA network. The application ensures that the resume is up to date and ensures that the agent knows the current job status of the resume holder. In addition, the application also makes it possible for the agent to see other resumes. So, people actively looking for jobs are keeping their client up to ensure that they get a job, and agents use the application in their daily searches, so they are online for long periods. Agents are also likely to add new resumes to the system that, in turn, allows the new users to pass their resumes to other agents. The application has the benefit of working with a small group of users that recruit users to form a larger network.

Creating a Community

Creating a community is another way to cause a P2P application to be a success. The best communities are those that need to communicate or share data on a regular basis. Examples of communities are tournament games, regularly updated news or stories, commonly-used resources, such as development references, chat areas, or even video monitoring, such as for a daycare or playground. All of these examples promote a community of similarly interested users to stay online.

Keeping Users Online

As discussed, the user needs to be kept online as long as possible to cause the network to have resources that are more available to all peers. There are some very sneaky ways to do this. The easiest is to just cause the application to be started as a service. This means that the application will be able to connect to the network from the moment the computer boots. If the computer is directly connected to the network, this is a great advantage.

Another way to keep the application up is by the nature to the application. If you are monitoring a camera at a daycare from work, first the images are available to other coworkers that use the same day care. Second, your peer is available for general use by other P2P applications.

A third way to create a P2P application that stays online is to add it to another application that users usually have on their desktops. This can include their e-mail client, personal organizer, word processor, instant messenger, news browser, music player, or streaming radio player. All of these may use P2P but may not rely on it. However, the P2P network is up and able to share networking resources and data.

Finally, you can use the same technique used by SETI@home. SETI@home simply asks the user to keep the application running as a curiosity or for a higher purpose of finding life in the universe, or even that one chance in millions for the fame of being the one person to have decoded the important signal from outer space. The SETI software allows two modes—a background and mode those only runs when the computer is inactive. With this method, by creating a creative screen saver, you can cause people to use your P2P application and use their resources. You could also create an atmosphere like SETI by offering a reward for the most participation or by a random drawing from all users. The key is that people will do certain things for altruistic reasons or simple fame and to play the odds. Take advantage of human nature.

Pay/Barter for Membership Privileges

Cheating is one of the bigger problems with P2P applications—take Gnutella, for example. Gnutella is a file-sharing program. Ideally, a user would share all his or her data. The reality is that many users avoid sharing too much data for many reasons. The system tries to promote sharing by forcing users to share a certain amount of data. To cheat the system, some users share very small and uninteresting files.

Users on Gnutella also only stay online long enough to search for files. After the user shuts down their Gnutella client, its resources are unavailable to other users. Worse, any client that was transferring files from this peer can lose the connection and the file loads are aborted.

There are ways of stopping such behavior. To stop the sharing of bad content, other users can rate the content they receive. If the peer gets a bad rating, it loses privileges to access services. This is a barter system that uses proper participation as the value of exchange (Mojo Nation and Free Haven are two P2P projects that are attempting to create such systems).

To stop the user from terminating his or her session after a short time, the system could throttle itself to require the user to be online a specific interval of time. To make a ten-minute transfer, the peer must have been available to other peers for at least ten minutes. If shutting down the client terminates other connections, the peer could also be penalized by an appropriate amount.

Any system that promotes that a peer pulls its weight, as long as it is not too intrusive, is probably worth participating in.

Network Trusted by Users

Not only should there be trusted data and users, the application and its network should be trusted by the users. The key to success also requires protection against the abuse of user's data, network bandwidth, and CPU resources. If your application allows your users to receive viruses or takes over their machine, users will go elsewhere.

Technologies Related to P2P

There are many other technologies that are P2P, related to P2P, or can be used as if they were P2P. We will cover the following:

- JINI
- Software Agents
- JXTA competitors (Gnutella, Freenet, and others)
- Web Services
- Others

This is not an exhaustive list. We just need to look at a few to understand different ways that P2P can be approached.

JINI

JINI network technology provides a simple infrastructure for delivering services in a network and for creating spontaneous interaction between programs that use these services, regardless of their hardware and software implementation.

One of the common questions asked when JXTA was introduced was how were JINI and JXTA related? At first, JXTA and JINI may appear to be so similar that they may seem redundant. However, this first impression is far from the truth. JINI and JXTA are meant for very different purposes.

First, JINI is a standard for services and devices to talk to each other. A common example is a laptop with bluetooth entering a building. As the laptop enters, it begins discovering the local network. One device the laptop finds is a printer. The printer, because it is JINI enabled, does one of two things, it either points to a configuration tool somewhere on the network that can be used to let the laptop print, or the printer sends an application to the laptop to talk to the printer. The key benefit is that the laptop did not need to have any specific printer drivers. The connection to the printer is also self-configuring, so there is no manual install process.

Another example of a JINI application is corporate chat. In this scenario, a laptop entering a building will have available, via a download from a local server or even another laptop, a chat application that can talk within the local area of the building.

In the prior examples, the key points are that the discovery of devices and services occurred in a local area, and the code for both applications was automatically loaded and configured (it would also be uninstalled if you entered a new network with new services). Most of the communications and software were Java-based, but there are implementations that can work with other languages.

The first key difference between JXTA and JINI is that JINI operates locally while JXTA works locally and across the Web. JINI is primarily for a local area network (LAN), and JXTA is for the Internet. There are bridges in JINI to allow communication to a local network from another, but the path is usually to a specific service in the network. With JXTA, applications are less concerned with network boundaries and are less likely to target a specific device or computer.

JINI also has a centralized service location broker. The broker, usually one peer on a subnet, is used to allow JINI peers to locate and discover each other and the available services. JXTA has a similar mechanism, except that the functionality is distributed among many peers. The JXTA service may be in the local network or provided by a peer that is not in the local subnet. The mechanism is also not location based. With JINI, the services usually known by the broker are within the local network. With JXTA, the discovery scope is as large as the Internet.

Both JINI and JXTA can be used for distributed and peer-to-peer computing. JXTA is probably a better choice for heterogeneous networks of computers, because it is easier to create a network of diverse platforms and languages because JXTA's primary means of communication is XML. Most JINI peers are Java based, and the communications are via RMI. JINI does have bridges to other languages, but these are exceptions rather than the rule. JXTA uses Java for the reference platform because of its popularity, rather than being a core part of the platform. JXTA is first a specification that uses XML as a data format that can be decoded and used by other languages, such as C, C++, Perl, and others. Therefore, the language of JXTA is the protocol, not a language or an operating system on which it is dependent. JXTA is also transport agnostic and can use HTTP, TCIP, or others available, such as IP broadcasting.

There are JINI projects underway at www.jini.org for peer-to-peer networking. The Space Bus project at http://developer.jini.org/exchange/projects/spacebus/ is one such project that was written as a message bus used to send and receive messages. The concept is very similar to JXTA's resolver service that is used to transmit and receive messages based on a broadcast or message propagation model.

Software Agents

An *agent* is an entity that does work for you. In our particular definition, an agent is a piece of code that is on another machine that does work. The key to agents is that data or data and code move through a network of peers.

There are two types of agent. The first is a package of code and data that travels from computer to computer. An analogy for this type of agent is a person that goes from store to store to buy things for you. The agent knows all about your preferences that can include your likes, dislikes, and other information you would have considered if you were there yourself. The agent knows how to buy things in each store it visits to fulfill your shopping list and preferences for brands and prices. This type of agent is often called a mobile agent.

The second type of agent is resident on many computers, but the data that represents how the agent should behave is sent to the agent. An analogy for this type of agent is a clerk in each store. The clerk is given a list of your preferences and is able to buy products in the store based on these preferences. The store provides the clerk and you provide the data. This is not a pure agent but is often included in the literature. Another way to classify this behavior is as a type of distributed computing.

Both types of agent are identical in their results when used in a P2P network. The only difference between the two is the overhead of moving code and efficiency.

JXTA, as it behaves for most applications, is of the second variety, where multiple copies of software are spread around the network. Data is sent to each peer or propagated to many peers to be used by identical processes. Each peer may have different data, such as different goods and pricing. A simple example is JXTA Search, where each peer acts as an agent to search for a specified string from within its local index.

Only a few applications behave like the first example where code and data move among peers. The reason is that there is usually too much processing that would be unique to a single user. Usually, software is constrained to a set of functions. Data is used to change the behavior, sequence, and number of functions executed. Another barrier to mobile agents is that security and control are difficult. It is very hard to determine if code is malicious or could cause problems when interacting with the host system.

Another problem with mobile agents is the belief that users customize code to change the behavior of their agents. This is a great leap of logic, because the number of people is probably quite small compared to programmers who could take full advantage. If we assume that only corporations could write such agents, it is probably better to work directly with corporations to expand the types of agent-like software installed rather than use mobile agents that can be abused by unscrupulous corporations or just bad programming caused by budget cuts.

With JXTA, you could build either resident or mobile agents. JXTA has all the utilities necessary for contacting multiple agents resident on machines. The moving of a mobile agent, though not implemented in the earlier versions of JXTA, could also be used to move code and data to other machines to process information on a specific machine.

Another aspect of agent computing is reduction of bandwidth. The key savings of an agent is that instructions move from machine to machine and only the results are returned to the initiating user. In other words, the agents do not have a permanent connection from where they are to their source. The drawback is that the agent must have enough information and decision making ability to survive and complete the job without constantly talking to the originating host.

A third way to look at agents, especially in the P2P world is to assume that each peer is an agent. Instead of a buyer going from peer to peer looking for goods, a seller goes from peer to peer looking for a buyer. Although this sounds like the same thing as the second example of an agent, this version probably has less connectivity to any single buyer peer and more work done by the selling peer. The key difference is that the buyer peer is not waiting its turn at the seller; rather, the seller is visiting its buyers one at a time. In other words, this is like a door-to-door salesman rather than a supermarket. The sales peer is also likely to arrive at random times at the peer. In the first two examples, the buyer peer is likely to arrive near the time that the buyer needs a product.

There are many frameworks for agent programming and many can be used with JXTA. In time, many will be integrated to work with JXTA, so refer to JXTA.org for any projects using them.

Gnutella, Freenet, and Others

There are a large number of ways to create a peer-to-peer network. Many companies and groups are creating platforms for P2P networking. This section discusses a few of these, including Freenet and Gnutella.

Gnutella

Gnutella was developed by AOL's Nullsoft division and was released as an open-source alternative to Napster. The project was quickly canceled and AOL removed all support of the project. AOL, as a commercial concern, could not support a system that allowed un-metered moving of copyrighted material. However, a community of developers outside of AOL already had the source code and the project continued to grow, even spawning several commercial companies.

Napster, at the time, was beginning to feel the pressure of lawsuits from record companies. Many predicted Napster's demise and were looking for an alternative that would be immune to legal action. Napster relied on a central server to arbitrate searches, and that was thought to be its downfall because the central server could be shut down via court actions. The creators of Gnutella created a system that performed similarly to Napster, except that there was no central search mechanism. By not having a central server, the network was immune to an attack because there was no easy target. Shut down Napster's server and Napster would be dead.

Gnutella is made up of a network of peers. Each peer is connected to a group of other peers. No single peer holds a resource that would cause the P2P network to stop functioning. The only threats to Gnutella come by falsifying information, filtering its protocol at the firewall, or prosecuting individuals. As can be seen by the history so far, sending out false data, such as songs that are random data, is annoying to users, but there are too many other copies of the song, so the attack is rather random. Filtering has been rumored to happen at several corporations, and a few individuals have had their ISP connection shut down because copyrighted files were logged as being copied via Gnutella. Gnutella continues to exist, while Napster has had months of continuous attacks in the courts that have shut down their servers and forced them to work with record companies.

Gnutella and JXTA are similar, but Gnutella was originally created as a tool to search for and transfer information. Gnutella is more of a collaboration application than it is a platform for P2P applications. Gnutella is being used to create P2P applications, but these are secondary to its original and more popular purpose of sharing files.

JXTA, unlike Gnutella, was created from the start to be a multi-purpose P2P platform. Like Gnutella, JXTA is able to gain the same advantage of interconnected peers. JXTA is far more complex than Gnutella, because it describes many different types of connections and XML-based protocols. Gnutella has limited messaging and, as has been pointed out, mostly slewed toward optimizing file sharing.

One other difference between JXTA and Gnutella is the compartmentalization of P2P services. In Gnutella, each node is essentially identical. In JXTA, a peer can be a relay, a rendezvous, and/or provide a variety of network available services. This means that super nodes can be created that can optimize the bandwidth of the network. Gnutella suffers from the fact that the interconnected network causes all the peers to participate equally, even though peers vary in capacity and bandwidth. Gnutella's community is debating whether the network can scale because of these issues. On the other hand, JXTA, though still maturing, will probably be able to scale because peers are so configurable and specialized peers can be created. In addition, JXTA supports protocols other than HTTP, such as TCP and IP broadcasting (Gnutella uses only HTTP), so it is able to choose the most efficient protocols for each situation.

Freenet

Freenet is a variation on file sharing using a peer-to-peer model. Freenet was created to implement the protocol described in Ian Clarke's paper "A Distributed Decentralised Information Storage and Retrieval System." Freenet's main claim is that content can be published and read without fear of censorship because individual documents cannot be traced to their source. In addition, because of the distribution, it is also difficult to determine who is reading information.

Freenet is P2P, but it is definitely not a generalized platform for P2P applications. The design is dedicated to content and the idea that publishers and readers are anonymous.

Many P2P applications require knowledge of participating peers. JXTA is oriented toward this type of network. In fact, it may be difficult for a JXTA peer to be an anonymous participant. Some JXTA applications may treat peers as anonymous, but you cannot remove the context from the underlying protocols used to move information in the JXTA network. Such functionality may be added, but it is not the central purpose of the JXTA protocols.

Agrocast

Another way to do peer-to-peer communications is via a distributed server system. Agrocast, developed by David Wallace Croft (`http://croftsoft.com/library/code/`), uses Internet news group NNTP servers to relay data. NNTP servers have long been used as discussion areas to allow users to collaborate. The system uses distributed NNTP servers to relay messages between each other to maintain an up-to-date list of messages. Users connect to their local NNTP, usually provided by their ISP, to read and submit messages. Agrocast takes advantage of the distributed nature of the NNTP servers to replicate its data to other NNTP servers to be read by other Agrocast clients.

Strictly speaking, Agrocast is a parasitic P2P application because the NNTP servers are unaware of its co-opting of the network. Agrocast is also never a true P2P application because there is always a third entity. However, the idea is similar to JXTA in that JXTA uses gateways to relay messages. The difference is that gateways are just other peers and are not necessarily dedicated to that single task.

SETI@Home

SETIT@Home is a distributed computing system. It is not strictly a peer-to-peer application unless you consider that the main SETIT@Home server is the equivalent of a very large peer. SETIT@Home is the world's largest distributed environment with a capacity of 26 TeraFLOPs/sec. That is nearly 100 hundred years of computer time per day.

The protocol is simplistic. The client peers contact the main server peer to report results and to request new data for processing. Because the average time for processing a segment of data is about 14 hours, there is no need to keep connected.

SETIT@Home, because of its popularity, is a target for both malicious and well-intentioned hacking. Malicious hacking is aimed at corrupting data or co-opting the network. The well-intentioned hacking is often done in the name of improving efficiency or porting the software to another platform. Any change to the processing can cause errors if not properly tested, so the managers needed to avoid tampering of the software to avoid corruption of the data. The SETIT@Home developers have mechanisms to verify that a valid client processed the data, and the SETIT@Home server performs additional post processing to ensure that data is consistent.

As a model for P2P distributed computing, SETIT@Home is the most successful so far. There are other features of SETIT@Home, including its behavior and its compelling nature. A P2P application, if not useful, should at least be entertaining or even appeal to our vanity and curiosity.

Web Services

Web Services is the name of a concept that includes technologies such as XML, SOAP, and UDDI to create services that are available via HTTP to any computer on the Internet. Web Services come in two types—those used by servers and those used by clients (usually Web browsers). Both another server and a client can use some Web services.

A good example of a Web Service is a credit card billing service. Let's imagine a company that sells novelty items on its Web site, `www.cluck.com`. The company has a catalog of very "fowl" novelties, but they need to be able to process credit card orders. Because some customers need a monthly supply of consumable products, such as itching powder, they also need to process monthly orders without customer intervention.

To use the Web Service in a Web page, the developers at `www.cluck.com` would place code on their Web server and Web pages that link the credit card Web service provider's Web service server. The service is operated by various methods, but consists mostly of exchanging XML as data or messages. The Web page in the online catalog uses an applet or JavaScript in the browser to convert user input to XML. Alternatively, it could do the processing in the servlet engine or a CGI. Though slightly complicated, there are usually scripts and layouts that just need to be configured by the developer. There is very little coding required.

The same process can be repeated for the monthly orders of itching powder. All the developer needs to do is create the XML requests and process the responses that are also XML. By using standards, such as SOAP, the Web Services are compatible, and it is easy for developers to choose from whom they get their Web services. They could even write their own Web Services. For example, www.cluck.com could provide a novelty catalog service.

At first, Web Services may seem similar to P2P. There does seem to be computer-to-computer interaction. Nevertheless, it is not P2P because there is no dynamic network of peers. The truth is that Web Services are, at least for the moment, almost exclusively server based.

Web services are also not cheap. A Web Service is still a server-hosted service. The provider of the service must maintain large servers, an infrastructure including routers and firewalls, and bandwidth. All of this costs money that is passed onto consumers. The cost savings comes from the offloading of support to the service provider that is shared by its customers. This is also known as an application service provider or ASP. A true P2P application uses the P2P network to share the load so costs are reduced.

The good thing about Web Services is that they can be used by JXTA. Because Web Services are usually HTTP based, they can breach firewalls and other barriers. You will probably find some service, such as a credit card processing service, to be quite useful—at least until JXTA has standardized such a system.

Others

There are many different incarnations of P2P networking. We have touched on some of the more successful examples. In addition, other P2P protocols are appearing as well as self-contained P2P applications, such as Morpheus. It is possible that there will be others. Some use instant messaging platforms as a backbone for P2P communications. In fact, Microsoft's Hailstorm can use instant messenger. In the future, you may see more applications that use an instant messenger infrastructure because instant messaging platforms provide a platform that gets around firewalls.

As can be seen from just a short selection, there are many different types of P2P platforms. Each of those that we have discussed was created with a specific goal in mind. JXTA may become the primary choice only because it was not intended to solve a specific problem but to make possible a host of possible applications. JXTA is definitely a larger code base that is, at times, less efficient than a purpose-built network like Gnutella, but it is easier to use for a variety of applications. JXTA is definitely not for the minimalist but for those who can use a general solution.

There are some things missing from JXTA, like Freenet's anonymity, but JXTA was designed with commerce in mind—not free speech, as was Freenet.

Summary

We have discussed many of the features as well as challenges of P2P networks. The challenges have been part of the design of JXTA from the start. Not all are solved, but some are, and work is in progress to solve the rest.

P2P is not a new concept. Many of the core protocols of the Internet itself were P2P applications.

While not easily defined, P2P may be characterized by the following properties:

- Peer nodes know about other peer nodes.

- Peers operate in a virtual network.

- Nodes have qualities of clients and servers.

- Peers are grouped into peer groups.

The time is ripe for new applications of P2P that either complement or replace existing more centralized solutions. The tremendous success of file sharing and chat applications has done more to attract new users more quickly than any Web site or Web Service.

P2P faces certain challenges with security, control, and network use, each of which is being addressed by the evolution of technology and the deployment of more sophisticated systems. Still, P2P's advantages outweigh today's challenges for many applications. P2P systems can provide the following capabilities:

- *Individual control by peers*—Users become very powerful. They create their own group—in effect, their own virtual firewall, and have lower barriers for publishing their resources.

- *Reliability*—It can be thought of as a poor man's high-availability system.

- *Scalability*—P2P has been demonstrated to support as many simultaneous users as the largest centralized systems.

- *Performance*—Resources are able to work together to tackle bigger problems more efficiently.

JXTA provides a P2P platform technology and a community of resources necessary to develop new P2P applications. JXTA's design supports the following:

- P2P applications that span from fully-centralized to fully decentralized.

- Any connected device running any OS on any network protocol.

- Highly secure applications.

- Interoperable components from different developers.

JXTA also provides the hooks, via peer monitoring, to allow the IT department to monitor and control peers. Without such control, IT departments would probably ignore JXTA. JXTA is being purposely designed to work within the constraints of corporate IT departments and ISPs.

As we discuss in more detail in the next chapter, JXTA is an open-source project with a vibrant community of developers. Complete access to the technology enables developers to extend and shape it as needed to support their applications. The community of developers provides an excellent resource ready to provide help or collaborate on new solutions.

Overview of JXTA

By Daniel Brookshier

Now we look at key JXTA concepts and the protocols used. In this chapter, we will reiterate aspects of that protocol from the author's point of view and in less formal language to ease you slowly into JXTA concepts. The JXTA protocol specification is a formal document that describes a standard for JXTA peers and their behavior. The goal of this chapter is to acquaint you with the concepts in preparation for Chapter 3, "JXTA Protocols," where we will begin covering Java API.

JXTA Defined

The following a quote is from the introduction of the JXTA protocol specification:

> The JXTA protocols are a set of six protocols that have been specifically designed for ad hoc, pervasive, and multi-hop peer-to-peer (P2P) network computing. Using the JXTA protocols, peers can cooperate to form self-organized and self-configured peer groups independently of their positions in the network (edges, firewalls), and without the need of a centralized management infrastructure.

What this all means is that JXTA is a framework with a set of standards that support peer-to-peer applications. JXTA is not an application, and it does not define the type of applications you write. The protocols defined in the standard are also not rigidly defined, so their functionality can be extended to meet specific needs.

JXTA is made up of three distinct layers. The first is the platform. The platform contains core functionality used by services, which are the second layer. Services provide access to the JXTA protocols. Finally, there are applications that use services to access the JXTA network and utilities.

This arrangement should be familiar because it is identical to a standard operating system, where there are three layers consisting of the core operating system, services, and applications.

JXTA adds several new concepts, such as the peer, peer group, pipe, and endpoints. JXTA uses a new concept in peer-to-peer communication and discovery with advertisements, which are XML documents that describe services and information available on the JXTA network. Finally, we have various types of identifiers used to distinguish one item or service from another.

Goals of JXTA

To begin, let's start with the goals of JXTA. The goals of JXTA are very simple:

- Operating system independence
- Language independence
- Providing services and infrastructure for P2P applications

In essence, the goals of JXTA are to support peer-to-peer programming on any device from a desktop computer to a PDA to a car or washing machine.

NOTE

JXTA is not a competitor to JINI. Although JXTA can run on devices, such as refrigerators, but that is not the ultimate goal—just something possible given the goals. Many new to JXTA confuse JXTA with JINI because of the many references to devices. JXTA and JINI have similar, but different, goals. JINI is aimed more at discovering and using devices. JINI is also more Java-centric where JXTA specifically uses XML instead of RMI, as does JINI. JINI was also designed to work within the bounds of a local area network, not to interoperate on the Web and across firewalls, as does JXTA. JINI is also more concerned with services located on a particular network, such as a printer, for example. JXTA would more likely be used to communicate with a software service that is not location specific.

There are also conceptual goals. These goals include the following:

- Use groups to organize peers and to give context to services and applications.
- Groups use authentication and credentials to control access and/or enable security at the group level.
- Distribute information about peers and network resources throughout the network.
- Queries are distributed throughout the system.

- Provide an infrastructure for routing and communications between peers. Communication with peers behind firewalls and other barriers is a key part of this goal.

- Provide mechanisms to allow peers to monitor each other and resources.

In addition to these goals, there are several other goals, such as encryption, support for various communications protocols, ease of use, stability, and performance. All of these goals were considered when creating the JXTA protocols and the initial Java API.

Additionally, there were other goals considered by the developers and the Sun Microsystem's managers:

- Create a system that would enable any device to be added to the JXTA network (similar to JINI).

- Create a system that would enable centralized management of peers within ISPs and corporate Internets.

- Create a system that can support digital rights management. This would foster JXTA's use in purchasing digital products, such as software, music, movies, and other digital media. File sharing P2P applications that do not account for digital rights will be seen as a legal liability and will be blocked by businesses and ISPs. By respecting intellectual property and copyrights, JXTA managers hope that JXTA will be allowed access.

- Encapsulate and abstract specific core functionality so that commercial applications can be created. In other words, enable manufactures to create appliances or hardware to perform functions similar to traditional networking products, such as routers, firewalls, and hubs. This enables hardware and appliance manufacturers to profit, as well as adds industry and corporate respectability.

The prior list has two key concepts. First, companies need to be able to feel like they have control. Most P2P systems do not have centralized management and are not welcome in most corporate situations. Secondly, the JXTA system needs to produce income for more than just application developers. This means that there needs to be hardware or hardware/software combinations that are sold by vendors. Because Sun Microsystems is in the hardware business as well as software, this is a very important goal.

Given all of the goals, JXTA is designed for industry acceptance, maintainability, robustness, and can be used to fulfill almost any P2P application concept. Because of the many goals, there is resulting complexity. Because the system is complex and there are many methods to implement a P2P platform, the specification is bound to change in the beginning. This chapter was rewritten several times as the specification changed in the early months of development of the JXTA platform.

In general, most of the following will be reasonably stable, but be aware that some name changes or structures may occur. Based on current experience, the differences will be minor and the following should remain mostly current for quite some time.

XML and JXTA

XML is the basis for most of the protocol in JXTA. The key reasons are its ability to be read by many languages and its ability to be validated. XML is also an easy choice just because of its popularity.

Overall, XML is a good choice because it is easy to sell as a protocol. To create a protocol that used a binary format would be more difficult to understand, and parsers would need to be built from scratch. With XML, there are many parsers that can be used, both commercial and free. XML is also becoming a standard for many different industries for representing data, so mixing data with the protocol is as simple as merging two XML documents.

There is a downside to using XML. XML is simply not a compact way to express data. Messages written in XML will be much larger than a binary equivalent. There are techniques that can be used, such as replacing tags with binary tokens or compacting data, but none of these are currently employed in JXTA because there are no widely accepted standards at this time. Consequently, the core JXTA developers have created a simple binary message transport and have used terse language and acronyms for tag names. Unfortunately, this means that the XML used in JXTA is devilishly hard to learn and read.

Because some developers are not familiar with XML, Appendix B, "XML Primer," has a short primer on XML concepts.

JXTA Concepts

Peer-to-peer networking, such as server-based networking, requires a lexicon of concepts that need to be understood. The concepts are similar to others you are familiar with, except that there are a few twists caused by the needs of a P2P network. Let's look at the important definitions and concepts that will be critical to understanding JXTA. We'll return to each of these concepts and discuss them in more detail later in the chapter.

Peer

A *peer* is a virtual communications point. You can have multiple peers on a computer or device. A peer is not the same as a user because a user may have peers on their phone, office/home computer, or other devices. It is also possible to have multiple peers on a single device, not necessarily an ideal situation but good for debugging.

Because a peer is not the same as a user, applications need to abstract the idea of user separately from peers. Any abstraction of users should be viable when a user has access to multiple peers.

Peers are also associated with special network services that they provide. In the reference implementation, peers can share basic services with the rest of the network, such as rendezvous, router, gateway, or a combination. These basic services provide search and communication services. In general, not all peers need to enable these services, but a percentage of them are required to ensure that other peers have access to these services. We will cover the concepts of these services a little later in this chapter.

ONE PEER ON ONE COMPUTER

Usually only one peer resides on a single platform. We assume a communications model where there is only one peer per device. When P2P is accomplished by a distributed network of computers acting as peers, we get the most value from collaboration, distributed searching, content sharing, bandwidth sharing, distributed processing, and other P2P applications. Nevertheless, there is nothing to preclude multiple peers from residing on a single platform or multi-CPU device. As long as the peers can be viewed as separate entities, there should be no problem, except for consuming extra resources. As a minimum, multiple peers can be launched on a single computer to simulate a network for debugging.

One reason for multiple peers on a single computer is to provide a proxy service for peers that are too small to be a JXTA client. This is true for cell phones or other portable devices. However, with advancements in portable devices, there is less of a need for this type of arrangement. There are cases where you need to do this, but they should be special cases. You should also realize that the same functionality could be created by a group of individual peers, each peer acting as a proxy for the telephone peer.

- *Context switching*—The number of peers you need to run are greater than the capacity of the server. As each peer is communicated to, you need to switch its state into active memory.
- *Size*—How much of a peer do you allow in the server? How big of an application? How do you constrain and manage it?
- *Application*—What is the application? Will all customers use it? Is there a value worth charging for?

Another possible solution that could have multiple peers is to interface to an existing server. The peers would act as a proxy view of the server so that the resources would be available over the P2P network. Nevertheless, this again can be solved with a distributed system of external peers that proxy the server. Resources can be added at will by adding more peers. A peer could also optionally use the server directly or use a proxy peer.

The whole idea of P2P computing is to distribute resources. By creating servers with multiple peers, you are going against JXTA and P2P philosophy. You are also burdening yourself with all the server problems that true P2P avoids.

Imagine true P2P solutions when faced with legacy servers or attitudes. Refactor your old server applications using JXTA when faced with costly or inadequate server technology.

Peer Group

A *peer group* is a way to group peers and to advertise specific services that are available to group members. You can create groups, join them, and of course resign from a group. There is also the ability to renew a membership in a group.

A group may need to limit membership for various reasons, such as secure communications between members, privacy, or there may need to be certain information that a user must supply before joining a group. There is an authentication protocol specifically designed to collect information and allow the group to determine if the information meets the requirements for membership.

The peer group provides context to use applications and to use the applications with other peers in the same group. For example, a peer group of jugglers would use a chat service in the juggling group. The effect would be to limit the chat to just those that joined the juggling group.

To further the juggling example, the group could authenticate users by validating a membership ID from a national juggling organization. Those without an ID would not be allowed to chat with the rest of the group, because they could not join the group.

Another way to look at groups is as a virtual private network (VPN). A VPN allows several computers to talk to each other without allowing the rest of the Internet to participate. VPNs include encryption so that the group conversation is not understandable to anyone who might eavesdrop. Peer groups also limit access to peers, and they can also use encrypted messages.

Membership to a peer group can take several forms. The two key models are local and remote membership services. A *local* membership service runs entirely on the peer that is applying for membership. All resources and ability to validate a user reside also on the same peer. So local membership services allow you to join without connecting to any other peer.

Remote membership requires accessing one or more peers in the group that you are joining. The idea is that peers that already belong to the group either have access to resources for validating a new member. Similarly, the set of peers in the group could query their users with the new member's application to see if the members are willing to accept the new member.

Endpoint

The *endpoint* is the basic addressing method used by JXTA applications to communicate with each other. An endpoint is an address of a peer that implements a specific protocol of communication. A peer can have multiple endpoints and thus can be communicated with via different protocols.

NOTE

Address as defined here is not necessarily a physical address. Endpoints allow the physical address to change. For example, in a DHCP-enabled ISP, the IP address of a computer that dials in, is going to be a random address each time.

A simple example of an endpoint is an IP address and port. By using these values, a stream could be opened to communicate to the target peer. However, JXTA places a layer on top of streams called *pipes* (discussed in the next section). Instead of connecting a stream to an address (represented by the endpoint), you connect a pipe to the endpoint. The beauty of endpoints and pipes is that you don't care what the real address is or what the best protocol to use for a particular peer. In addition, there are other services used to route and even forward messages. Using the pipe and endpoint abstraction provides a lot of power and reduces the complexity of building a P2P application.

Because pipes connect via a communications protocol, the endpoint describes the protocol and the specific information used to connect to it. Therefore, the endpoint can describe an HTTP, TCP, BEEP, or other supported base communications protocol.

A peer can support one or more endpoints. By supporting more than one protocol, the peer can use the most effective method. In other words, if two peers are behind a firewall, they can communicate through their TCP endpoints. When these peers communicate to peers across the firewall, which traditionally filters everything but HTTP, they would use the HTTP protocol.

Pipe

A *pipe* is a virtual connection between peers. Normally, we think of peer-to-peer communications as a single connection, but this is not always possible. The problem is that many peers cannot connect directly because of firewalls or other barriers. Pipes are intended as a layer over multiple communication protocols and to support relayed communications via gateway peers.

Pipes are a basic and important feature of JXTA. They create a very useful paradigm that allows peers to communicate in most network situation, despite firewalls or other barriers. Even if you do not know anything about a peer or where it is, you will to have a mechanism to communicate with the peer via a pipe.

Pipes are used as an abstraction to hide the fact that there may be other peers involved along with multiple connections. Pipes can also be implemented to be *self-healing* and reroute around an original peer. Self healing in important because a peer, unlike a server, is not meant to be available 24 hours a day and can be removed from the network at any time. The Java JXTA implementation has several flavors of pipe.

As discussed, the JXTA protocols support and encourage different types of pipe. The following is a list of a few possible (currently not implemented) pipes that are either part of the Java implementation or possible additions:

- *Uni-directional asynchronous*—This is a pipe that is only used for communications that are in one direction. The pipe is asynchronous and messages may arrive out of order. This is the most basic type of pipe and should be implemented on most JXTA platforms.

- *Synchronous request/response*—All messages sent will receive a return message of acknowledgment. Messages arrive in the order that they were sent.

- *Bulk transfer*—Used to move large amounts of data.

- *Streaming*—Used to efficiently move data in a stream similar to that of audio, video, and other data streams, such as a stock market data feed.

- *Bidirectional*—A combination of two asynchronous pipes.

- *Uni-directional synchronous*—All messages sent will receive a return message of acknowledgment. Messages arrive in the order that they were sent.

- *Unicast reliable secure pipe*—All messages sent will receive a return message of acknowledgment and the data will be encrypted.

There are two different types of addressing for pipes:

- *Point-to-point*—Point-to-point pipes connect two different peers. Multiple other gateway peers can be used to create the connection.

- *Propagate*—Connects one peer to multiple destination peers. Propagate pipes are also called *wire pipes* because of the project that originally developed them. Propagate pipes can also have multiple peers involved in the connection, including those that are endpoints in the communication.

In the current platform, the uni-directional asynchronous, unicast reliable secure pipe, and bidirectional pipes are implemented. In addition, there is a secure version of a unicast and reliable secure pipe.

Endpoints and Pipes

JXTA is very different from a traditional network. Most network protocols have either no address (HTTP clients) or they have a fixed address where a URL or IP address is used to pinpoint the clients. JXTA abstracts the idea of a client address and calls it an endpoint.

A peer can have more than one endpoint. Peers can communicate over one or more protocols, such as TCP and HTTP, so there are usually multiple endpoints. This sounds strange at first because we usually deal with only one protocol in most applications. The reason JXTA uses multiple transport protocols is to allow a service to communicate with peers over the best method possible.

If you were behind a corporate firewall, you would use HTTP to communicate outside the firewall and TCP to talk to peers on the local LAN behind the firewall.

With multiple transport flexibility, you can use a specific protocol for a specific peer and thus the best speed and response. Behind the firewall, the speed and response is very good. Crossing the firewall, the response is poor. Overall, you are better off than if you <u>only</u> used HTTP that would have sacrificed efficiency behind the firewall.

Advertisement

An *advertisement* is an XML document that describes a JXTA message, peer, peer group, or service. Advertisements follow standards for encoding, tags, and content. The advertisement is used to exchange information about what is available in the JXTA network.

For an example of how this would work, imagine a peer that creates a peer group with the name Trekker Chat. The peer would publish the advertisement to the local JXTA network. This is done with an IP multicast. In other words, any peer in the sub-net will receive a copy of the advertisement. In addition the advertisement is sent to the rendezvous.

Peers use a special class of peers called *rendezvous* peers to discover advertisements from the rest of the network. Rendezvous peers (discussed in the next section), store advertisements and support searches. A peer can now request the peer group advertisement by searching for its name or other property. With the peer group advertisement, these client peers can then instantiate and join the Trekker Chat peer group by using the information contained in the XML. When they're members, they can use the group context of services or locate peers that belong to the group.

NOTE

Most of JXTA's advertisements are encoded with UTF-8, which is an ASCII-preserving encoding method for Unicode (ISO 10646). Unicode could be used, but the advertisements do not use special language characters and foreign punctuation. Because UTF-8 is 8 bits and Unicode is 16 bits, the halving of the size of advertisements makes a lot of sense.

The only place you should find it necessary to use full Unicode is in the body of messages. Within messages, the encoding of the contents can be specified as Unicode or any other character set, including UTF-8.

Messages

Messaging in JXTA is done in two different ways. First is the standard way that would be expected with XML. The messages are packets that contain a payload of data formatted to follow XML standards.

The second type of message is a very economical binary message. Despite the desire to use XML for all JXTA messages, the reality is that there are many messages sent and received. The bulk of XML messages send in large volumes is very inefficient. Also, because messages are usually sent from application to application, it is simple to standardize on the contents of the message. The remainders of the protocols are still XML.

The use of binary messages in an XML protocol may seem counterintuitive. The truth is that there are more advantages than just compactness. The first is that data can be compressed using standard techniques. Compression of data, such as text, can create a huge savings in time to transmit.

Another reason for binary data is that many messages are already binary. For example, a document-sharing program will most likely share binary documents. If you were transferring messages via XML, the data would need to be converted to XML.

Another reason for binary messages is encryption. Because the data needs to be converted to binary for encryption, moving straight to and from binary instead of XML makes sense.

Identifiers

JXTA has a wide selection of different identifiers. Identifiers range from large, unique identifiers to names and URLs. Identifiers are used like pointers of references. In the reference platform, identifiers are used for indexing, filenames, and searching.

Rendezvous Peer

A *rendezvous* is a peer that processes queries from other peers. The rendezvous can also delegate queries to other peers, which must also be a rendezvous. A key purpose of rendezvous is to facilitate searching of advertisements beyond a peer's local network. Rendezvous usually have more resources than other peers and can store large amounts of information about the peers around it. In a peer network, information is scattered among peers and not stored entirely on any single machine, such as a server. Instead, there are rendezvous that distribute the storage of the advertisements.

Rendezvous peers can also act as relays of searches. The rendezvous peer can forward discovery requests to other rendezvous peers that receive their information from peers with whom they have exchanged advertisements. Each rendezvous will forward on a request if it does not have the information requested.

A typical search is illustrated in Figure 2.1. The remote search starts from Peer 1 which firsts queries local Peers 2 and 3 via IP Multicast. These Peers (2 and 3) are most likely on the local LAN and are quickly accessed. Next, if these Peers do not have the specified resource, a rendezvous peer is searched. If the rendezvous peer does not have the advertisement, successive rendezvous peers are searched. Note that besides the peers local to the query peer, only rendezvous peers are searched.

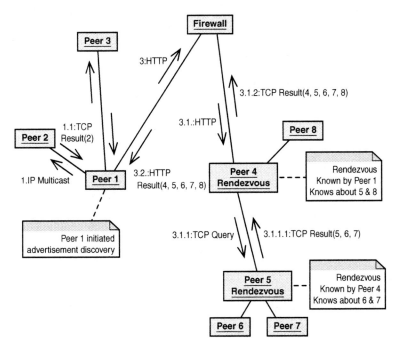

FIGURE 2.1   Rendezvous query routing.

IP MULTICAST

IP Multicast is a one-to-many messaging protocol. IP Multicast is used to send one copy of data to a group address, reaching all recipients who are configured to receive it.

IP Multicast has two benefits over P2P applications. First, because multicast uses a group address instead of IP addresses, a peer sending a message can do so without knowledge of the listening peer's address. The result is that all peers within the multicast network can now respond to the caller with information to the query and even their IP address for direct communication.

IP Multicast's second benefit is the reduction of bandwidth. Because all peers can see a single message, there is no need to send a copy of the message to each peer. This is very important when sending large amounts of data to a group of peers.

A drawback to using multicasting is that some firewalls and routers block multicast messages. There is some support for sending multicast messages via Internet backbones between Internet providers, but it is often a service for which you must pay extra. There are other barriers to IP-Multicast. These can include personal firewalls and subnet routers. This is why JXTA supports more than just IP-Multicast.

In general, the multicast support available behind a firewall is sufficient for most P2P needs. You can take advantage of localized multicast support by sending duplicate messages for each network to a specific peer within the network for rebroadcast via multicasting to the local peers.

Only a rendezvous allows searching beyond a local network. A peer has the option of being a rendezvous, but it is not required. There is a side benefit of being a rendezvous—the peer will retain a cached copy of the results from other rendezvous of the result of cached answers to requests.

On the negative side of being a rendezvous, the peer will use more memory and higher bandwidth. Because of the possibly high number of requests and the resources consumed by a large database of advertisements, the case can be made for a dedicated rendezvous peer. In corporate installations, the rendezvous could also perform the duties of gateway and router for the corporate intranet. The effect would be similar to the use of a traditional router. Additional scaling could use a rendezvous in each of the corporation's subnets.

The need for dedicated rendezvous peers depends on security and the scale of P2P applications used. The P2P network topology should be examined on a case-by-case basis and monitored regularly.

It is important to mention here that a P2P network becomes more efficient as services are duplicated among a large number of peers. However, there may be a point where additional rendezvous do not add to efficiency.

Rendezvous are used when a peer is searching for an advertisement or when other services use the rendezvous mechanism to route messages, so the need by a peer is not constant. A rendezvous connected to the Internet will be exposed to possibly thousands of peers. Within the bounds of a firewall-isolated network, having all peers configured as a rendezvous will probably not have a large affect caused by rendezvous tasks. Note that this observation may prove incorrect if there are many requests that have large search scopes.

Rendezvous are also used for application specific queries. In Chapter 9, "Synchronizing Data Between Peers," peers use peers acting as rendezvous to propagate information about new appointments in a calendar as well as synchronizing an address book.

> **NOTE**
>
> When considering any network topology or deciding if your peers should be a gateway, router, or rendezvous, be sure to check the current implementation for its efficiency and capabilities. Remember also that some applications may specifically use these services in unique ways. The JXTA platform will continue to evolve and should eventually cover most topologies or be configurable for many situations. But each environment is unique, so experimentation and monitoring of actual use may be the best way to configure your peers—especially in a large corporate environment.

Router Peer

A *router* in JXTA is any peer that supports the peer endpoint protocol. Not all peers need to implement the protocol because, like traditional network routers, you only need a few to support a large network. JXTA routers are very similar to a traditional router. The primary difference is that a P2P network is less stable and includes many addresses that are not static.

Figure 2.2 is an example of how a route is created. The request for a route starts at Peer 1 with the request for a route passed to available routers until the complete path to Peer 8 is built. Note that because a peer can be a gateway as well as a router, Peer 2 includes itself as a node in the route. Please understand that this is just conceptually how routers work, not how they are actually implemented. Routers can support caching or complex algorithms. For example, instead of the first router forwarding a request for the rest of the route, this router may already have a cached version of the route available.

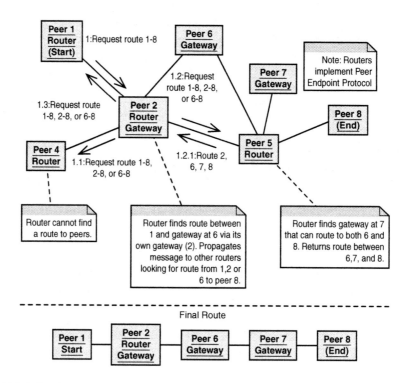

FIGURE 2.2   Conceptual example of peer endpoint routers creating a route between Peer 1 and Peer 8.

Gateway Peer

A *gateway* is a peer that acts as a communications relay. Don't confuse gateways with rendezvous. A gateway is used to relay messages between peers, not requests.

Gateways are like radio repeaters or a middleman between peers used to relay messages. Gateways are critical to connectivity because of firewalls, NAT devices, and network proxies. Gateways can store messages and wait for their intended recipient to collect the messages.

Gateways exist because the Internet is very messy. The mess is caused by the fact that we have all sorts of security and barriers that prevent a common way to communicate between peers. Another bit of this mess is the difference between protocols supported by peers. Some peers may use TCP, others may use HTTP. With wireless, we would need Wireless Application Protocol (WAP) as well. The gateway supports as many of these protocols as is possible so that it can act as a middleman between different types of protocols. JXTA started with support for TCP and HTTP, but other gateways are in development.

Gateways are key to getting around most of the security on the Internet. Firewalls, proxy servers, and NAT devices are the common security barriers. Figure 2.3 shows how the gateway Peer 2 is used to interface between Peer 1 and Peer 3. The gateway translates HTTP messages from peer 1 to TCP for delivery to Peer 3. When messages are sent from Peer 3, they are sent via TCP to Peer 2, which holds the message until Peer 1 makes an HTTP request to retrieve the data.

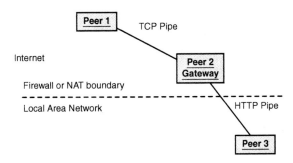

FIGURE 2.3   Example of gateway participation in a single pipe.

NOTE

JXTA has started using the term *relay* to merge the terms *rendezvous, router* and *gateway*. *Relay* will also be used to include concepts like proxy, transcoding, and related "JXTA network helpers," rather than proliferating a bunch of overlapping terms. It is also expected that there will be specialized peers or even commercial appliances that have just these functions, so a single name is more marketable. We will use the terms interchangeably for now, depending on the focus of discussion.

Why We Need Relays (Routers and Gateways)?

Although we have touched on the subjects, we need to specifically cover why relays are required for a P2P network. The following sections discuss each of the barriers to a P2P network. Each of these creates a need for us to abstract the network and create a virtual network where the P2P system provides routing and messaging via HTTP tunneling or to switch transport protocols.

Firewalls

Firewalls, which filter almost everything except HTTP, are most often found at larger companies, but they are also now found in homes that use special firewall routers. There are also personal firewalls, so called because they run on the user's personal computer. Firewalls are often configured to filter almost everything except HTTP. HTTP only allows communications that are initiated by the client.

For example, when you are requesting a Web page, connecting to a Web server, sending the request, receiving the requested page, and then disconnecting. At no time does the Web server initiate a connection to the Web browser.

Because there is only one direction of communication that can be initiated, the gateway acts as a virtual agent that accepts messages for later delivery. Therefore, if a peer attempts to talk to a peer that can only initiate HTTP communications, the gateway holds the message until the HTTP peer contacts the gateway and asks for messages addressed to it.

NAT (Network Address Translator)

A Network Address Translator (NAT) device is just as disruptive as a firewall. Most wideband routers for cable and DSL use NAT.

NAT lets you use a single IP address for a whole network of computers. Because Internet providers charge by the unique IP address, many use a NAT to save money. The NAT sits between the public Internet and the a local area network (LAN) where it rewrites IP addresses and port numbers in IP headers on-the-fly so that the packets all appear to be with the public IP address of the NAT device instead of the actual source or destination. This causes multiple problems with applications that pass addresses and ports back and forth across the NAT. The NAT simply cannot detect and correct the message to reflect the mapped address. Essentially, this means that if you are behind a NAT, you will have trouble telling anyone what your address really is.

Many NATs, for security reasons, only allow incoming traffic from an outside address only if an outgoing packet has already been sent to that outside address. This is like a poor man's firewall, because it prevents anyone from directly connecting to your computer without you first initiating communications. This is like a phone that cannot receive calls but will still let you call anyone.

A socket connection may be assigned to the same external address/port on subsequent connections. This means that you cannot be sure of a return path for messages. This makes it very difficult to create a two-way conversation.

The gateway gets around the NAT the same way it gets around a firewall. By using the HTTP protocol, the gateway on the other side of the NAT ensures that peers can communicate with the peer behind the NAT.

Proxy Server

A proxy server is a device that sits between the Internet and a LAN. The proxy servers provide services like filtering, caching, and monitoring of traffic.

The result of having a network proxy is similar to a NAT. The proxy device can limit addresses as well as map them to others, such as NAT. Proxy devices can be as sophisticated as a firewall and limit certain types of communication. For example, a proxy service can prevent you from accessing a forbidden Web site. Some proxy servers can even detect viruses embedded in incoming e-mail before they ever reach your e-mail's in-box.

The gateway can usually get around a proxy server by bridging the gap with HTTP. Some very sophisticated systems can be programmed to detect and prevent such traffic. Some companies only allow pure HTML to pass and discard all other types of data. In some cases, you may not be able to use JXTA applications without specific configuration and permission of the network administrator.

DHCP

Many companies, and especially Internet service providers utilize Dynamic Host Configuration Protocol (DHCP). DHCP allocates IP addresses dynamically. The effect is that each time the DHCP server re-boots or a user's computer re-boots, the IP address is changed. The address can also change if the IP address lease expires. The effect is that even a known address is a temporary address. Because of DHCP, even when you are behind a firewall, peers may still not have addresses on which you can depend. This makes it difficult when communicating across the firewall to peers on the other side.

The possibility of changing addresses is greatly improved by router peers. Router peers are able to create new routes between peers when addresses change.

Volatile Network

Peers may also seem to disappear and reappear. This is a very common occurrence. Many computers are not connected to the Internet 24 hours a day. Many computers are still connected via dialup and are only on-line part of the day. We also have to consider wireless devices that are usually only on-line for very short periods. A laptop or a PDA can both appear and disappear as they are docked in and out of the network. In these cases, the peer may even seem to pop up in a different city in a completely different network topology! Because of the possibility of such changes, it is very important to be able to invalidate a route and reroute connections.

Gateway Issues

One of the problems with gateways is that they could significantly increase the time it takes for a message to be sent between two peers. If there are too many gateways, the total time for transmitting a message could be several minutes.

With the possibility of messages taking a very long time to transmit, there is a huge problem with managing a user's expectation. An important number to think about here is 200 milliseconds, which is the amount of time between clicking a button and something happening that seems to be associated with the button. In other words, if an action occurs 200 milliseconds or less after you click a button, the action and its response appears to be simultaneous. If the application's reaction to the button click takes longer than 200 milliseconds, your user is waiting. The longer a user waits, the more likely that the user is going to think that something has gone wrong. When the user believes that the application is not working, he or she could hit the button again, terminate the program to try again, or perform another action that you would like to avoid.

Any JXTA processing that is a result of a user's input to the user interface should immediately display some kind of wait symbol or pop-up dialog as feedback. Any area of your software that has some type of JXTA network communications will most likely need to be in a thread separating it from the user interface. In addition, while waiting on the JXTA network, some type of user feedback, such as a wait dialog or a status display, is a necessity. Applications will be more complex, and you will need much more code to make them thread safe, but the effort is required to make your application acceptable.

JXTA Protocols

JXTA protocols are used to help peers discover each other, interact, and manage P2P applications. The protocols are not applications in themselves and require much more code to create something useful. The protocols hide a lot of detail, which makes writing JXTA applications much easier than developing a P2P applications from scratch.

JXTA defines its protocols in the *JXTA Protocols Specification*. The specification describes how peers communicate and interact; it does not attempt to describe the specifics of implementation or how to write a peer-to-peer application. In this section, we are going just give you an overview of the protocols and discuss related issues.

The following is a list of the JXTA protocols. We have included their acronyms, but we use acronyms rarely in the rest of this chapter:

- *Peer Discovery Protocol (PDP)*—Allows a peer to discover other peer advertisements (peer, group, service, or pipe). The discovery protocol is the searching mechanism used to locate information. The protocol can find peers, peer groups, and all other published advertisements. The advertisements are mapped to peers, groups, and other objects, such as pipes.

Queries are made by specifying an advertisement type (peer, group, or advertisement), an XML tag name within the advertisement, and the string to match against the data represented by the XML tag.

- *Peer Resolver Protocol (PRP)*—Allows a peer to send a search query to another peer. The resolver protocol is a basic communications protocol that follows a request/response format. To use the protocol, you supply a peer to query and a request message containing XML that would be understood by the targeted peer. The result is a response message.

The resolver is used to support communications in the JXTA protocols like the router and the discovery protocols. For example, the protocol is used by the discovery protocol to send queries that represent searches for advertisements.

The resolver also allows for the propagation of queries. For example, if a peer receives a query and does not know the answer, the resolver sends the query to other peers. This is an interesting feature, especially because the originating peer does not need to have any knowledge of a peer that may actually have the result to the query.

- *Peer Information Protocol (PIP)*—Allows a peer to learn about the status of another peer. The information protocol is used partially like ping and partially to obtain basic information about a peer's status. The body of a PIP message is free-formed, allowing for querying of peer-specific information. In addition, this capability can be extended to provide a control capability.

- *Peer Membership Protocol (PMP)*—Allows a peer to join or leave a peer group. The protocol also supports the authentication and authorization of peers into peer groups. The protocol has three key advertisements for authorization, and the credential. The credential created in this protocol will used as proof that the peer is a valid member of the group.

- *Pipe Binding Protocol (PBP)*—Is used to create the physical pipe endpoint to a physical peer. It is used to create a communications path between one or more peers. The protocol is primarily concerned with connecting peers via the route(s) supplied by the peer endpoint protocol.

- Rendezvous Protocol (RVP)—The Rendezvous Protocol is responsible for propagating messages within JXTA groups. The Rendezvous Protocol defines a base protocol for peers to send and receive messages within the group of peers and to control how messages are propagated.

- *Peer Endpoint Protocol (PEP)*—Is used to create routes to route messages to another peer. The protocol uses gateways between peers to create a path that consists of one or more of the pipe protocols suitable for creating a pipe. The pipe binding protocol uses the list of peers to create the routes between peers.

One of the more significant problems is that traditional routers and DNS servers fail because of firewalls, proxy servers, and NAT devices. This protocol searches for gateways that allow the barriers, such as firewalls and others, to be traversed.

This protocol also helps when the communicating peers don't support each other's protocols. For example, if you are connecting peer-A that supports TCP and peer-B that only supports HTTP, the endpoint protocol would choose either one gateway that could make the translation or multiple gateways with multiple but compatible protocols.

We can also describe these protocols in terms of what they provide to a JXTA application. The next list is very basic, but probably is the best way to look at what the protocols really do.

- *Peer Discovery*—Resource search
- *Peer Resolver*—Generic query service
- *Peer Information*—Monitoring
- *Peer Membership*—Security
- *Pipe Binding*—Addressable messaging
- *Rendezvous*—Propagation messaging
- *Peer Endpoint*—Routing

In the remainder of this chapter, we will describe these concepts further. In the following, we relate the concepts of peers, groups, and how the protocols are associated. In Chapter 3, we will cover the concepts again, but in terms of the Java implementation and the API.

Peers and Groups

The two primary concepts to understand about JXTA are peers and groups. Because peers and groups are a little complicated, we will discuss each one in detail.

Peers

As discussed earlier in the chapter, peers are individual nodes on the JXTA network. The peer is similar to a computer on a network, except that you can run multiple peers on a single machine. Peers can be a standard PC, a PDA, an appliance, or even a super computer.

A Peer Is Not a User

The concept of the peer should not be confused with the concept of a user. A peer is a node on the network. Think of a normal computer on the Internet; you should not assume that a single person uses the computer. The computer could be shared by a family or be a publicly used device, such as an Internet kiosk. You also should not assume that a peer node is the only place a user will access the P2P network. The user can access the network from home, work, or through various devices.

In your design of services and applications, be very careful to avoid linking the user to a peer, either permanently or for long periods. Sometimes, you can link a user to a peer, but always be able to log the user off and log in another.

One of the many things you need to manage in a P2P application is identity. The peer is associated with the user in many respects, so for now we will discuss this in terms of a peer. You should create an authentication system where multiple peers could be aggregated as a single user.

The types of things you should manage are authenticating the peer's rights to use services. The identity of the peer in JXTA is a *credential*. The credential is used throughout the system to ensure that certain operations have the correct permissions. The credential is officially created when a peer joins a group. The credential can also simply be some type of token created ahead of time and presented as part of the joining process. The group recognizes the credential during the authentication process when joining the group.

Why Use Groups?

P2P networks have several key differences from traditional networks, the most important being the ability to control what peers can do. The following are some of the problems:

- Too many peers connecting to one peer for a resource.

- Peers that use resources but do not contribute to resources.

- Certain resources should only be accessible to a set group of individuals.

- Hackers of the general network who are seeking to damage or take over the network.

In P2P networks, it's very difficult to control behavior of rogue peers. There are many different types of mischief, including abuse of other peer's resources. There is also the obvious need to limit access to applications or resources for security or privacy reasons.

To begin to understand how these problems can be overcome, let's look at a use case diagram of a simplistic P2P system. In Figure 2.4, users interact with different instances of a service-A, which collaborates with other services to access specific resources attached to specific instances. In this sort of P2P network, the services are left with the responsibility of security. Each service on each peer must act as a gate-keeper to the data controlled by the peer.

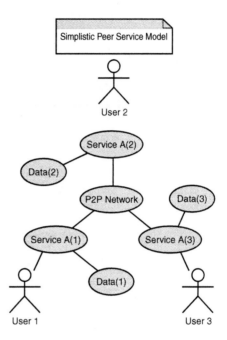

FIGURE 2.4   Functional view of the peer service use case.

The drawing in Figure 2.5 is representative of how JXTA works. In JXTA, the peer group is a virtual gatekeeper. The service, and thus the service data, resides in the context of the group. The group code is replicated on each platform, but we are showing it as a single entity accessed by all of the group members. The services are accessed through the group, and the services have a context of the group.

The key difference here is that the group contains the security features while the services are only concerned with verifying that other peers are valid members. Credentials created by the group and given to the peers (not shown) will be validated by the group context. Figure 2.5 shows how groups are seen programmatically in JXTA. As can be seen, users interact with a service controlled by the group. The group is ensuring a single point of control, despite the fact that the service and data is distributed.

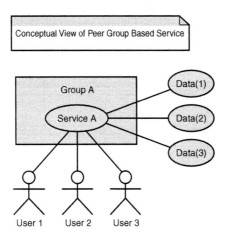

FIGURE 2.5   Conceptual view of group-based service.

By using groups, you have at least a chance of controlling peers with a common authentication scheme. You also have a platform to disseminate information to a limited set of group members. For example, you could send a message to other peers that a rogue peer should be ignored.

JXTA Applications

Given the discussion so far, you may be confused as to what a JXTA application is. We have talked a great deal about how an application would do its work, but not where the code for the application resides.

To begin with, the general notion of an application has not changed. The key difference is that your JXTA application begins with starting the JXTA platform by accessing the world group. The *world group* is a group that is accessible to all peers. The world group is used to locate any peer or information that is available to all peers.

After the platform is started, your peer is a member of the default world group. From this point, you could begin your application with the world group and use all of the default services in the world group.

Group Membership

Group membership is probably one of the more important service protocols. Membership has two key features—authentication and credentialing. Authentication is the gatekeeper for the group, while credentialing is a token that ensures that authentication occurred. Both authentication and credentialing could be complex or simple, depending on how rigorous you need to be in your group.

Authentication is a multi-step process where the group requests that the peer supply information to join the group. The information supplied is then validated against the group's requirements for membership. The most obvious validation would be a user ID and password. Less restrictive systems may not ask for information or may be just a simple questionnaire. In the most restrictive systems, the authenticator may ask for an encrypted digital signature.

Credentials can also have various contents. Because credentials are passed around, they are usually fairly small to reduce overhead. In the least restrictive groups, the credential will just be a simple token. In groups that are paranoid about user identity, the credential would be a wrapper for encrypted digital signatures.

Peer Group Services

Peer groups are a context for services that interoperate in the group's domain of users. The peer group provides a set of services called *peer group services* that implement the JXTA protocols to supply the group with the necessary functionality. These services are not required, but most groups will probably have these services available for use by other services and applications. Groups can contain any set of services, and different groups can contain the same services of other groups.

Services are always associated with a group. You cannot have access to a service unless you are a member of the group. The services that a group supports are listed in the group advertisement.

The importance of the associating services to a group is to limit their scope. As a rule, services should not interact with peers not in their group. One reason is a matter of respect for peers that are not a part of the same group. There is also the practicality that there may be no reason to interact with peers outside of the group because they will not have the resources the service requires.

It is possible to write a service that will operate across groups. Such a service is unlikely because of the access service. The access will forbid any messages that are not properly marked as belonging to the group. Any service that goes across groups would need to have the cooperating access services.

If you need to interact with multiple groups, it is simpler to have an application that joins each group. There is no limit on how many groups a peer may join.

Core Services

Not all groups have the same advertisements, but it is expected that all groups support a set of standardized services that represent the core protocols. It is possible that none of these services are included or a completely different set of services would be provided. Without these core services, it would be difficult to interact with other peers. However, you could imagine a peer that uses a custom gateway that provides the functionality without requiring it on the peer itself. In addition to these core services, the creator of the group can add additional services. There are no specific requirements for these services. However, the services are expected to only work within the bounds of the group. If you use the core services for discovery and communication, limiting the scope to the group is automatic. The core services are described in the following sections.

Discovery Service

The discovery service provides access to Peer Discovery Protocol in the context of the group. It searches for peer group resources (peers, peer groups, pipes, and services). The search usually only searches within the group that contains this discovery service reference, so if a group is created and you use its discovery service, only advertisements published in that group will be found. Note, however, that this also depends on the implementation of the group that may expand the search scope to parent, sibling, or sister groups.

Some groups may inherit the search scope of the parent group. By default, the world group has access to all Peer advertisements and others created in its context. The default behavior of other groups is to search only in their scope.

Membership Service

The membership service provides access to a group-specific version of the Peer Membership Protocol. It is used as a gatekeeper to membership in the group. Peers wanting to join the group must fulfill the requirements of this service. The model is that of a membership application form where a document is submitted to the peer to be filled in and submitted for approval. If the peer is approved, the peer is considered a member of the group and is issued a credential that is used as proof of membership during communications. The membership service can extend the model from an application to external validation (such as a server that validates the user's initial credential) or by querying other peers or a manager peer for final approval (voting). We will cover group membership in more detail in Chapter 6, "Working with Groups."

Access Service

The access service is part of the membership service and is used to ensure that the peers are actually valid members of the group. This service uses the credential created when the peer joined the group. A peer receiving a request provides the requesting peer's credentials and information about the request being made to the access service, and the service determines if the context and credentials are correct; if so, access is permitted.

Peer Authentication Service

The authentication service uses credentials created by the membership protocol to verify that that messages are from a valid member of the group. The concept is that the application examines a credential for certain operations as needed to ensure that communications are with valid peers.

Authentication uses the credential as a standalone packet of information that is either self-authenticating or can be verified with other information the current peer obtained from another source.

NOTE

The peer authentication service is not currently implemented in the Java JXTA platform.

Pipe Service

The pipe service implements Pipe Binding Protocol. The pipe service is used to manage and create pipe connections between the different peer group members.

Resolver Service

The resolver service implements the resolver protocol. The resolver service distributes queries to other resolver services running on peers within the group. The resolver also listens for the answers to these requests. We discuss this subject in more detail later in the chapter, in the "Resolver" section. We also use the resolver directly in Chapter 9, "Synchronizing Data Between Peers."

Monitoring Service

The monitoring service is used to allow a peer to monitor other group members of the peer group. The specification of what is monitored is left to the implementer. Monitoring can be used to collect data on peers to ensure they are following the group's rules for behavior or just to gather simple statistics.

Monitoring of peers is mentioned in the specification, but few people have implemented the concept. There also appears to be no API harness to use as a base. The implementation would need to be a service that you create and make a part of your group.

The reasons for having a monitoring service are many. The following are a few:

- Keep a log of peer activities (downloads, contributions, and so on) that are sent to other peers. This relates to the next item.

- You could manage a peer's ability to use the group. This is similar to Gnutella that prevents a peer from downloading unless they also share a minimum of their content. This can be expanded to include other information, such as uptime and other statistics that trigger certain rights. The opposite is that other peers receive these statistics before they interact with the peer, so that they can decide if they want to interact with the peer. This can be automated or just presented to the wizard behind the curtain.

- Management of the user access is also important. In the specification, there is no mention of a revocation of a group membership. There is the idea of expiration and renewal. The problem is that you may not want to wait for expiration and want to remove a user early. This relates back to using a credential, which is a part of the specification and can be used to notice when a user is no longer valid.

- Managing issues like those that cause problems in JXTA, including abuse of resources, falsification of identity, hacking/hijacking of the group for other purposes, and denial of service attacks against the group or some of its peers.

Note that some of these core services, such as discovery and membership, implement JXTA protocols. Others, such as the monitoring service, are not associated with a protocol, but are useful in a group context.

Customized Services
Core services are not necessarily specific implementations. Core services for the group can provide specific behavior for the group. For example, the membership service is likely a specific implementation.

Core Services Are Optional
Core services, besides being customizable, may not even be supplied. For example, the monitoring service may not be provided if there is no reason for monitoring. Also, the discovery service may not be required if the peer is already populated with all the advertisements it needs.

The only service that is most likely to be supplied is the membership service. The reason is that when a peer joins the group, the membership service is used. If a group does not need membership, you should use the Null membership implementation that allows the join functionality to operate but does not impose membership requirements.

Groups as Applications
One aspect of groups that may seem odd at first is thinking of groups as applications. A group application is not a real stretch of imagination and actually provides a lot of utility. The simple fact is that an object needs to exist to represent the group. Because there is an object, it would need methods to create, destroy, and manage resources. As mentioned, a group also has other services that need to be started and stopped. For all of these reasons, associating groups with applications is reasonable.

However, groups do not need to be associated with applications in a programmatic way. Groups can simply be used as a context to manage the groups of peers or groups of information. You do not need to add services to your groups and simply use the default services. For example, you could have an application such as SETI@Home implemented as a JXTA group with services for membership, communication, and reporting results. These would begin operation as soon as the group was joined and the default application in the group started. We will cover more of this in Chapter 3, when we discuss the Java implementation of groups.

Finding Information about the JXTA Network

When using the peer discovery protocol, there are three scoping parameters. These include the advertisement type (peer, peer group, or advertisement), a tag name to search with the contents to match, and a limit on how many advertisements for which to search. Only the first two are important to us here. The first scoping parameter specifying the type is useful to limit what you are looking for to just one of three different types of advertisements. The second, which allows you to specify a name and value, is then used to search each advertisement for matching XML tag and value.

The important qualifier is the name of the XML tag. This lets you choose a specific element of an advertisement, such as the name tag or an ID tag. This allows you to look up, for example, a named peer, a named group, or any other advertisement based on some tag name and its contents. Because the * wildcard is supported in the Java implementation, you can do more creative searches.

Passing Extra Data in Advertisements

It should be noted that many of the advertisements in JXTA can be expanded with additional XML tags. In some cases, these areas are clearly marked, such as the param section of the peer group advertisement. Be careful where you do put data and what type of tags you are using, because the messages may fail a syntax check. This version on JXTA does not support XML syntax checking but does have various places where unexpected XML could cause problems. You should only add data where allowed or use queries or pipes to pass information.

Adding data to advertisements that are outside of the protocol specification should only be done when you are implementing a variation on a protocol. For example, you could create a new transport type and add it to the group membership advertisement's TransportAdvertisement tag.

Caching and Aging of Advertisements

Advertisements are usually cached. Caching is not required by JXTA, but it is very useful and efficient to do so. Aging is a way to set an expiration time when an advertisement should be considered too old to be useful. Some advertisements can last a very long time, like peers, and others that are more volatile, like pipes.

There are two different ages—one local set by default to 365 days and one remote age set to 2 hours. The assumption would be that if the peer created the advertisement, it has value and should have a long lifetime. Advertisements coming from remote systems are suspect and should expire much sooner. Because advertisements are renewed, the shorter lifetime is moot unless the advertisement was really temporary or its peer unstable.

Advertisements

Advertisements are the language of JXTA. All of the information about peers, groups, services, and other JXTA constructs are defined by an advertisement. The following is a quick list of the main advertisement types:

- *Module Class Advertisement (MCA)*—Defines the specific version of a module.

- *Module Specification Advertisement (MSA)*—Defines the module with a cross platform definition that includes behavior.

- *Module Implementation Advertisement (MIA)*—Specific instance of a module on a platform.

- PipeAdvertisement—Defines. See PipeAdvertisement; a pipe available in a group or at a peer.

- PeerGroupAdvertisement (PGA)—Defines the peer group. The group also defines the services, endpoints and other information.

- PeerAdvertisement (PA)—The peer advertisement defines the peer.

- EndpointAdvertisement—The endpoint advertisement defines a communications protocol and the termination.

We'll discuss these in more detail in the next section, "Details of the Advertisement Types."

There are really only three classifications of advertisements. These are peers, peer groups, and everything else. It is difficult to say why these are the highest level, but the cache management system in the Java implementation uses these types to separate the advertisements into three separate directories.

Details of the Advertisement Types

Now we will look at each of the advertisements that JXTA uses in detail and talk about what they mean. We will also show some XML so that you will know how to recognize advertisements when debugging.

Peer Group Advertisement

The peer group advertisement is used to define both an identification of a group and the services of that group. Peer group advertisements have the following information:

- *Name*—Name of the group.

- *Description (Desc)*—Description of the group.

- *PeerGroup ID (GID)*—An ID that is associated with this instance of this group.

- *PeerGroup Specification ID (MSID)*—A Module Spec ID that this group uses. The ID is used to locate a module that references the services this group uses.

- *Service (Svc)*—Optional list of elements that associate a group service, denoted by its Class ID (the value of an MCID element), and parameters via Parm elements.

The following is an example of an XML PeerGroupAdvertisement for a peer group created in Chapter 9:

```
<?xml version="1.0"?>
<!DOCTYPE jxta:PGA>
<jxta:PGA xmlns:jxta="http://jxta.org">
    <GID>
        urn:jxta:uuid-AAA122616461AAAAAA124615032503302
    </GID>
    <MSID>
        urn:jxta:uuid-DEADBEEFDEAFBABAFEEDBABE000000010306
    </MSID>
    <Name>
        JPDA_ROOT_GROUP
    </Name>
    <Desc>
```

```
      Root application group
    </Desc>
</jxta:PGA>
```

Peer Advertisement

A peer advertisement is almost identical to a peer group advertisement. The key difference, of course, is its type.

- *Name*—Name of the peer.

- *Description (Desc)*—Description of the peer.

- *PeerGroup ID (PID)*—An ID that is associated with this peer instance.

- *Debug Flag (Dbg)*—Optional tag used for debugging.

- *Service (Svc)*—Optional list of elements that associate a group service, denoted by its Class ID (the value of an MCID element), and parameters via Parm elements. In most implementations, this will hold data that details information used to converse with the peer.

The following is an example of XML PeerAdvertisement. The service defined in this example defines the parameters for the MCID that references the default implementation for a peer. The data includes the endpoints for TCP, the group, and an HTTP ID used by an HTTP gateway. The second MCID refers to the implementation of secure pipes and defines a certificate:

```
<?xml version="1.0"?>
<!DOCTYPE jxta:PA>
<jxta:PA xmlns:jxta="http://jxta.org">
    <PID>
        urn:jxta:uuid-59616261646162614A7874615032503356➥
                        CFE39F036E4038ABE1801D40772DC803
    </PID>
    <GID>
        urn:jxta:jxta-NetGroup
    </GID>
    <Name>
        Super Chicken
    </Name>
    <Svc>
        <MCID>
            urn:jxta:uuid-DEADBEEFDEAFBABAFEEDBABE0000000805
        </MCID>
```

```
    <Parm>
      <Addr>
        tcp://198.1.0.70:9701/
      </Addr>
      <Addr>
        jxtatls://uuid-59616261646162614A7874615032503356CFE39F036E4038A
                  BE1801D40772DC803/TlsTransport/jxta-WorldGroup
      </Addr>
      <Addr>
        jxta://uuid-59616261646162614A787461503250
              ➥3356CFE39F036E4038ABE1801D40772DC803/
      </Addr>
      <Addr>
        http://JxtaHttpClientuuid-5961626164616261
              ➥4A7874615032503356CFE39F036E4038ABE1801D40772DC803/
      </Addr>
    </Parm>
  </Svc>
  <Svc>
    <MCID>
      urn:jxta:uuid-DEADBEEFDEAFBABAFEEDBABE0000000105
    </MCID>
    <Parm>
      <RootCert>
```

MIICODCCAaGgAwIBAgIBATANBgkqhkiG9w0BAQUFADBkMRUwEwYDVQQKEwx3d3cu
anh0YS5vcmcxCzAJBgNVBAcTAlNGMQswCQYDVQQGEwJVUzESMBAGA1UEAxMJU2th
bmRhLUNBMR0wGwYDVQQLExRDMkEwND1GMDBBRjc4NkEyOUI0RTAeFw0wMTEyMjEw
NDIzNT1aFw0xMTEyMjEwNDIzNT1aMGQxFTATBgNVBAoTDHd3dy5qeHRhLm9yZZEL
MAkGA1UEBxMCU0YxCzAJBgNaBAYTAlVTMRIwEAYDVQQDEwlTa2FuZGEtQ0ExHTAb
BgNVBAsTFEMyQTA0OUYwMEFGNzg2QTI5QjRFMIGbMAsGCSqGSIb3DQEBAQOBiwAw
gYcCgYEArRbPEHoij/J0PYaI/b7xPmj1MsVX5BmrJqNUjsaEroJewTJ3ffDAyNOl
WWC/lTGD8maUhlK7vycVozboaaelOJSDjkZ/gDBYglwDrciFsMsKTcwdYdp6x3/s
PmUwAHDu8AvPvpyq/2UNNCMxPL9G+OfVnBAxG5TdNvnpSVZXX8MCAREwDQYJKoZI
hvcNAQEFBQADgYEAGRmbIRoq0EQQEfg3jIdc/WIChIpYCIZq06VLkESntqBCCnfN
z/YWFMeJRwXGZmZqG321wMVpQytRMUr2ewnVXJjvsVZiH1erd1bgUzKoIpcJy6Bd
X+/cuiFUWxkQu+GTNcjt1ytjGbpNy/kUxg7bPTOXU55c1XDzN/+ASMLqxo8=

```
      </RootCert>
    </Parm>
  </Svc>
</jxta:PA>
```

Modules

Modules are definitions of services and applications available on a peer or in a peer group. Modules are used to define the code to be executed. To ensure that different peers written with different languages, versions, and operating systems, modules are defined with three different XML advertisements:

- *Module Class*—Defines the specific version of a module.

- *Module Specification*—Defines the module with a cross platform definition that includes behavior.

- *Module Implementation*—Specific instance of a module on a platform.

Each advertisement is used to narrow the final implementation used by the peer. However, only the respective IDs may be available and no true advertisement available on the general network. The reason is that some modules are not public or they do not have different versions or implementations. Instead, the advertisements are internal to the peer and only referenced by their identifiers as needed. The following three sections define the detail of the different module advertisement types.

Module Class Advertisement

A Module Class advertisement defines behavior. Peer groups, peer, and other advertisements reference a module class ID that is defined by the module class advertisement. The advertisement has the following parameters:

- *Module class ID (MCID)*—Unique identifier used to reference the module class.

- *Name*—Name of the module. Used for searching and identification. Not guaranteed to be unique.

- *Description (Desc)*—Description used for searching and identification.

The following is a sample advertisement. This is the module class advertisement for the EX1 advertisement:

```
<?xml version="1.0"?>

<!DOCTYPE jxta:MCA>

<jxta:MCA xmlns:jxta="http://jxta.org">
   <MCID>
      urn:jxta:uuid-2584FEB44D3B40E9A16A8419C9ABE09F05
   </MCID>
```

```
<Name>
   JXTAMOD:JXTA-EX1
</Name>
<Desc>
   Tutorial example to use JXTA module advertisement Framework
</Desc>
</jxta:MCA>
```

Module Specification Advertisement (Module)

A Module Specification Advertisement is the specification of a module. The advertisement contains information about the implementation referred to by a module specification ID. Because the code for a module is usually part of the peer application, there is no need to publish the advertisement for each ID, but it is a good practice to document the module via the advertisement. Each module has the following tags:

- *Module spec ID (MSID)*—An ID that specifically defines this module.

- *Compatibility statement*—An XML specification used to define the compatibility of the code to a language and version.

- *Name*—Name of the specification.

- *Description(Desc)*—Description of the specification used for searching and identification.

- *Creator (Crtr)*—Creator of the specification.

- *Specificaton URI document (SURI)*—URI of a specification document.

- *Version (Vers)*—Version of this specification.

- *Parameters (Parm)*—List of parameters to be used by the implementation.

- *Proxy*—ModuleSpecID of a proxy module if one exists.

- *Authenticator (Auth)*—ModuleSpecID of an authenticator module if required.

The following is an example of the XML for the module specification for the EX1 example. Note that in addition to its standard tags, there is a pipe advertisement used to communicate to the module. This is done as a convenience, so that the user of the code does not need to look for an extra pipe advertisement:

```
<?xml version="1.0"?>
<!DOCTYPE jxta:MSA>
<jxta:MSA xmlns:jxta="http://jxta.org">
   <MSID>
```

```
       urn:jxta:uuid-88A7B34E2B354A75A181B34E6058D3DA0F➡
                  230D7557A24F159F80ABA479BC0C3B06
    </MSID>
    <Name>
       JXTASPEC:JXTA-EX1
    </Name>
    <Crtr>
       sun.com
    </Crtr>
    <SURI>
       http://www.jxta.org/Ex1
    </SURI>
    <Vers>
       Version 1.0
    </Vers>
    <jxta:PipeAdvertisement>
       <Id>
          urn:jxta:uuid-9CCCDF5AD8154D3D87A391210404E59➡
                     BE4B888209A2241A4A162A10916074A9504
       </Id>
       <Type>
          JxtaUnicast
       </Type>
       <Name>
          JXTA-EX1
       </Name>
    </jxta:PipeAdvertisement>
 </jxta:MSA>
```

Module Implementation Advertisement

The Module Implementation advertisement is the final link in the chain to define a
module. The advertisement defines specific references to a specific language representation on a peer. This advertisement is used to launch the code.

- *Name*—Optional name associated with the module.

- *Description (Desc)*—Optional string used to describe and allow for searching of
  key words to locate a module.

- *ModuleSpecID (MSID)*—ID that uniquely identifies the specification being implemented.

- *Compatibility (Comp)*—An element that describes the execution environment.

For Java this would be the JVM version.

- *Package URI (PURI)*—Optional URI used to download the code of this implementation (not implemented in version 1.0).

- *Code*—Contains a reference used to load and execute the code of this implementation. For a Java module, this is a fully-qualified classname.

- *Parameter (Parm)*—Arbitrary parameters to be interpreted by the implementation's code.

- *Provider (Prov)*—Provider of the implementation.

The following is the module implementation for the standard peer group. Note that this implementation contains further implementation advertisements in the param tag. Also note that the last entry is the shell application. The shell is defined this way as the default application of the peer group. If the peer group is started after it is initialized, the code in the application tag is executed:

```xml
<?xml version="1.0"?>

<!DOCTYPE jxta:MIA>

<jxta:MIA xmlns:jxta="http://jxta.org">
  <MSID> urn:jxta:uuid-DEADBEEFDEAFBABAFEEDBABE000000010306 </MSID>
  <Comp> <Efmt> JDK1.4 </Efmt> <Bind> V1.0 Ref Impl </Bind> </Comp>
  <Code> net.jxta.impl.peergroup.StdPeerGroup </Code>
  <PURI> http://www.jxta.org/download/jxta.jar </PURI>
  <Prov> sun.com </Prov>
  <Desc> General Purpose Peer Group Implementation </Desc>
  <Parm>
    <Svc>
      <jxta:MIA>
        <MSID> urn:jxta:uuid-DEADBEEFDEAFBABAFEEDBABE000000060106</MSID>
        <Comp> <Efmt> JDK1.4 </Efmt> <Bind> V1.0 Ref Impl </Bind> </Comp>
        <Code> net.jxta.impl.rendezvous.RendezVousServiceImpl </Code>
        <PURI> http://www.jxta.org/download/jxta.jar </PURI>
        <Prov> sun.com </Prov>
        <Desc> Reference Implementation of the Rendezvous service </Desc>
      </jxta:MIA>
    </Svc>
    <Svc>
      <jxta:MIA>
        <MSID> urn:jxta:uuid-DEADBEEFDEAFBABAFEEDBABE000000030106 </MSID>
```

```
      <Comp> <Efmt> JDK1.4 </Efmt> <Bind> V1.0 Ref Impl </Bind> </Comp>
      <Code> net.jxta.impl.discovery.DiscoveryServiceImpl </Code>
      <PURI> http://www.jxta.org/download/jxta.jar </PURI>
      <Prov> sun.com </Prov>
      <Desc>
        Reference Implementation of the DiscoveryService service
      </Desc>
    </jxta:MIA>
  </Svc>
  <Svc>
    <jxta:MIA>
      <MSID>
        urn:jxta:uuid-DEADBEEFDEAFBABAFEEDBABE000000050106
      </MSID>
        <Comp> <Efmt> JDK1.4 </Efmt> <Bind> V1.0 Ref Impl </Bind> </Comp>
      <Code> net.jxta.impl.membership.NullMembershipService </Code>
      <PURI> http://www.jxta.org/download/jxta.jar </PURI>
      <Prov> sun.com </Prov>
      <Desc>
        Reference Implementation of the MembershipService service
      </Desc>
    </jxta:MIA>
  </Svc>
  <Svc>
    <jxta:MIA>
      <MSID>
        urn:jxta:uuid-DEADBEEFDEAFBABAFEEDBABE000000070106
      </MSID>
        <Comp> <Efmt> JDK1.4 </Efmt> <Bind> V1.0 Ref Impl </Bind> </Comp>
      <Code> net.jxta.impl.peer.PeerInfoServiceImpl </Code>
      <PURI> http://www.jxta.org/download/jxta.jar  </PURI>
      <Prov> sun.com </Prov>
      <Desc> Reference Implementation of the Peerinfo service </Desc>
    </jxta:MIA>
  </Svc>
  <Svc>
    <jxta:MIA>
      <MSID> urn:jxta:uuid-DEADBEEFDEAFBABAFEEDBABE000000020106 </MSID>
      <Comp> <Efmt> JDK1.4 </Efmt> <Bind> V1.0 Ref Impl </Bind> </Comp>
      <Code> net.jxta.impl.resolver.ResolverServiceImpl  </Code>
      <PURI> http://www.jxta.org/download/jxta.jar </PURI>
      <Prov> sun.com </Prov>
```

```
              <Desc>
                Reference Implementation of the ResolverService service
              </Desc>
            </jxta:MIA>
          </Svc>
          <Svc>
            <jxta:MIA>
              <MSID> urn:jxta:uuid-DEADBEEFDEAFBABAFEEDBABE000000040106 </MSID>
              <Comp> <Efmt> JDK1.4 </Efmt> <Bind> V1.0 Ref Impl </Bind> </Comp>
              <Code> net.jxta.impl.pipe.PipeServiceImpl </Code>
              <PURI> http://www.jxta.org/download/jxta.jar </PURI>
              <Prov> sun.com </Prov>
              <Desc> Reference Implementation of the PipeService service </Desc>
            </jxta:MIA>
          </Svc>
          <App>
            <jxta:MIA>
              <MSID> urn:jxta:uuid-DEADBEEFDEAFBABAFEEDBABE0000000C0206 </MSID>
              <Comp> <Efmt> JDK1.4 </Efmt> <Bind> V1.0 Ref Impl </Bind> </Comp>
              <Code> net.jxta.impl.shell.bin.Shell.Shell </Code>
              <PURI> http://www.jxta.org/download/jxta.jar </PURI>
              <Prov> sun.com </Prov>
              <Desc> JXTA Shell reference implementation </Desc>
            </jxta:MIA>
          </App>
        </Parm>
      </jxta:MIA>
```

Pipe Advertisements

Pipe advertisements describe the type of pipe. Pipe advertisements are rather simplistic. They only have a name, ID, and type. As we have discussed, there are several different types of pipe. The specific pipe type is listed in the Type tag.

Pipes contain the following tags:

- Name—Name of the pipe.

- Id—The ID of the pipe.

- Type—The type of the pipe. Type is related to a protocol and therefore to endpoints on a peer. Types are UnicastType, UnicastSecureType, and PropagateType.

The following is an example of an XML pipe advertisement. This pipe is a unicast pipe:

```
<?xml version="1.0"?>
<!DOCTYPE jxta:PipeAdvertisement>
<jxta:PipeAdvertisement xmlns:jxta="http://jxta.org">
  <Id>
    urn:jxta:uuid-59616261646162614E50472050325033A10C➥
                     F46E7B7041B48C3EBF32A5DA2A4404
  </Id>
  <Type>
    JxtaUnicast
  </Type>
  <Name>
    frodo.replyTo
  </Name>
</jxta:PipeAdvertisement>
```

Endpoint Router Messages

The router protocol uses query and response messages to discover routes. The query message supplies the peer ID of the destination. The ID of the origin is assumed that of the source. This message is sent from a peer to a peer, which implements the peer endpoint protocol. The XML endpoint router query message schema is as follows:

```
<xs:element name="EndpointRouterQuery" type="jxta:EndpointRouterQuery"/>
<xs:complexType name="EndpointRouterQuery">
    <xs:element name="Credential" type="xs:anyType" minOccurs="0"/>
    <xs:element name="Dest" type="xs:anyURI"/>
    <xs:element name="cached" type="xs:string"/>
</xs:complexType>
```

The router answer message contains the information about the route that was located by the router or a router it collaborated with to create the answer.

The actual route is a list of peers that are all gateways, except the final destination that is not required to be a gateway:

```
<xs:element name="EndpointRouterAnswer" type="jxta:EndpointRouterAnswer"/>
<xs:complexType name="EndpointRouterAnswer">
    <xs:element name="Credential" type="xs:anyType" minOccurs="0"/>
    <xs:element name="Dest" type="xs:anyURI"/>
    <xs:element name="RoutingPeer" type="xs:anyURI"/>
    <xs:element name="RoutingPeerAdv" type="xs:string"/>
```

```
<xs:element name="Gateway" type="xs:complexType"/>
</xs:complexType>
```

Messages

Message advertisements are used for the various messaging protocols, as well as for user defined messages. There are two different types of messages—XML and binary.

XML Messages

XML messages are used for transport mechanisms that only support text or as a general way to send a message. Because messages are seen as the most used type of data that is transported between peers, the binary message is offered in most cases because it is much more efficient.

The XML message format consists of a message tag that encapsulate the data of the message. Each element has a name, a mime type, and an optional encoding parameter. By changing the mime type and the encoding, you can place any supported data type between the enclosing element tags that is valid XML. For data that is not XML, the < character is replaced with the string <, and & symbols are replaced with & as equivalent. The following is an example of an XML message:

```
<!DOCTYPE Message>
<Message version="0">
<Element name="jxta:SourceAddress" mime_type="text/plain">
tcp://123.456.205.212
</Element>
<Element name="stuff" encoding="base64" mime_type="application/octet-stream">
AAECAwQFBgcICQoLDA00DxAREhMUFRYXGBkaGxwdHh8gISIjJCUmJygpKissLS4vMDEyMzQ1Njc4
0To7PD0+P0BBQkNERUZHSElKS0xNTk9QUVJTVFVWV1hZWltcXV5fYGFiY2RlZmdoaWprbG1ub3Bx
cnN0dXZ3eHl6e3x9fn+AgYKDhIWGh4iJiouMjY6PkJGSk5SVlpeYmZqbnJ2en6ChoqOkpaanqKmq
q6ytrq+wsbKztLW2t7i5uru8vb6/wMHCw8TFxsc=
</Element>
</Message>
```

Binary Messages

Binary messages are compact packets used to send information with as compact a data stream as possible. Two-byte lengths are sent with the high-order byte first. All strings start with a two-byte length, followed by the UTF8 string value. The message format is specified by using ABNF (see IETF RFC 2234 at http://ietf.org/rfc/rfc2234.txt). The format of the binary message is defined by Tables 2.1 and 2.2.

TABLE 2.1   Binary Message Format

Section	Description
"jxmg"	Start of the message.
Version	One byte. Must be 0 for the 1.0 binary format.
Namespaces	See Namespaces.
element_count	Two bytes designating the number of elements to follow.

TABLE 2.2   Message Element

Section	Description
"jxel"	Element signature.
namespaceid	One byte that designates the name space.
Flags	Indicates which parts follow 0x00 if type is not present and 0x01 if type is present.
simple_name	Name of this element. If the namespace ID is 0, the simple name is the name. Otherwise concatenate the namespace name designated by the ID with a colon (:) and the simple name. The next byte is the flags byte.
[type]	Present if the flags byte has the least significant bit set (0x01).
len4	Four byte length of content.

Pipe Binding Protocol

The Pipe Binding Protocol is used to create virtual channels between peers. The protocol uses the Endpoint Protocol that it abstracts to allow pipes to be created that use supported transport protocols, such as the JXTA HTTP Transport, the JXTA TCP/IP Transport, or the secure JXTA TLS Transport.

To use a pipe, an advertisement must be published and then used by other peers. When a peer has a pipe advertisement, the peer makes a pipe bind request, which is responded to by a peer accepting the pipe.

To bind the pipe, there is a pipe bind request and a pipe bind response. The request for a pipe has the following data:

- MsgType—Defines this message as a query an answer. For the query, it will be Query.

- PipeId—Pipe ID being resolved.

- Type—The type of pipe resolution requested.

- Cached—False if the answer can not come from the cache.

- Peer—A peer ID of the only peer that is to answer that request. This tag is not required because, in many instances, you do not explicitly connect to a specific peer.

The reply to a pipe bind uses the same schema, but there are additional tags and a slightly different interpretation applied to their contents. With the data from both messages, the Pipe Binding Protocol can use the Endpoint Protocol to create a route between peers and select the appropriate protocol based on the peers involved. The following is the reply message that contains the other peer that can then be used to locate the other peer's endpoint:

- `MsgType`—Defines this message as a query an answer. For the answer, it will be `Answer`.

- `PipeId`—The Pipe ID being resolved.

- `Type`—The type of pipe resolution requested.

- *Found*—Response value showing success or failure that an Input Pipe was found on the specified peer.

- `PeerAdv`—Peer Advertisement of the peer that connects to the Input Pipe.

The following is the XML schema for the pipe-binding message:

```
<xs:element name="PipeResolver" type="jxta:PipeResolver"/>

<xs:complexType name="PipeResolver">
 <!-- should be an enumeration choice -->
 <xs:element name="MsgType" type="xs:string"/>
 <xs:element name="PipeId" type="xs:anyURI"/>
 <xs:element name="Type" type="xs:string"/>

 <!-- used in the query -->
 <xs:element name="Cached" type="xs:boolean" default="true" minOccurs="0"/>
 <xs:element name="Peer" type="xs:anyURI" minOccurs="0"/>

 <!-- used in the answer -->
 <xs:element name="Found" type="xs:boolean" minOccurs="0"/>
 <!-- This should refer to a peer adv, but is instead a whole doc -->
 <xs:element name="PeerAdv" type="xs:string" minOccurs="0"/>
</xs:complexType>
```

Resolver

The resolver is used to send queries throughout the P2P network. The resolver is used by base services, such as the discovery mechanism to search for advertisements. You can also use the resolver when you have a query response model of communication where answers come from a group of peers rather than a specific peer.

The following is the XML schema for the ResolverQuery message:

```
<xs:element name="ResolverQuery" type="jxta:ResolverQuery"/>
<xs:complexType name="ResolverQuery">
    <xs:element name="Credential" type="xs:anyType" minOccurs="0"/>
    <xs:element name="SrcPeerID" type="xs:anyURI"/>
    <!-- This could be extended with a pattern restriction -->
    <xs:element name="HandlerName" type="xs:string"/>
    <xs:element name="QueryID" type="xs:string"/>
    <xs:element name="Query" type="xs:anyType"/>
</xs:complexType>
```

The following is an explanation of the tags:

- Credential—This is the credential of the peer sending the query.

- HandlerName—The name associated with a resolver handler that listens for messages of this type.

- QueryID   An ID that is used to link to the response. This ID is important because the order of responses to queries is not guaranteed. It is also used in case there are duplicate responses to the query, which is also possible.

- Query—This is where you put application data for the other peers to examine. If you plan on an XML message, the message must be escaped.

The following is the XML schema for a ResolverResponse message:

```
<xs:element name="ResolverResponse" type="ResolverResponse"/>

<xs:complexType name="ResolverResponse">
    <xs:element name="Credential" type="xs:anyType" minOccurs="0"/>
    <xs:element name="HandlerName" type="xs:string"/>
    <xs:element name="QueryID" type="xs:string"/>
    <xs:element name="Response" type="xs:anyType"/>
</xs:complexType>
```

What follows is an explanation of the tags for the resolver response message:

- Credential—This is the credential of the peer sending the response.

- HandlerName—The name associated with a resolver handler that listens for messages of this type.

- QueryID—An ID that is used to link to the query. This ID is important because the order of responses to queries is not guaranteed. It is also used in case there are duplicate responses to the query, which is also possible.

- `Response`—This is where you put application data for the other peers to examine. If you plan on an XML message, the message must be escaped.

Rendezvous Protocol

The Rendezvous Protocol describes how messages are propagated peers in the member group. The Rendezvous Protocol uses the Peer Endpoint Protocol to locate the peers in the group and determine routes and transports. The Peer Resolver Protocol uses the Rendezvous Protocol to send messages, so you should not access the Rendezvous Protocol or its implementation directly.

Even though the Resolver Protocol should be used instead of the rendezvous, it is important to understand the messaging that occurs to get an idea of how messages flow in the system.

Rendezvous Advertisement (`RdvAdvertisement`)

The Rendezvous Advertisement (`RdvAdvertisement`) is very simple and only has the following three tags:

- `Name`—Name of the rendezvous peer

- `RdvGroupId`—PeerGroup UUID

- `RdvPeerId`—Peer ID of the rendezvous peer

Peer Connection

The connection between a peer and a rendezvous peer is achieved by a connection, associated with a lease. A *lease* is a concept that basically means that the connection is promised for a certain period of time. The lease must be requested before the connection is allowed. When the lease is granted by the rendezvous, the peer can begin using the connection until the lease expires or the lease is canceled by the peer or the rendezvous. The length of the lease is determined by the rendezvous and is not guaranteed to expire normally. When a peer is done with the connection, it can send a cancel request, which, if granted, the rendezvous will reply with a lease canceled message. A set of queries and responses are defined by the Rendezvous Protocol to establish connections:

- `LeaseRequest`—Message a peer uses to request a connection to a rendezvous. A rendezvous that grants a connection lease returns the `LeaseGranted` message.

- `LeaseGranted`—Message sent by a rendezvous to indicate the lease has been granted.

- LeaseCancelRequest—Message is sent by a client to its rendezvous to cancel an existing lease. The rendezvous should reply with LeaseCancelled, but this is not guaranteed.

Propagation Control

Determining three qualities about each message received controls propagation. First is its time to live (TTL) parameter. If the message has expired, the message is ignored. Second is the loop; if the message has been seen before, it is discarded. Third is the duplicate that tests to see if the message has been processed.

The reason for loop and duplicate tests is that a looped message is a message that has already been ignored or processed while the duplicate test checks to see if it was processed. A message may be handled differently if it is looped but not yet processed. This is because the rendezvous may discard a message, process it, or be interested but not at this instant. A message must be alive, not processed and not looped, before it can be processed completely. It may be optionally processed if it is still alive, has looped, but not processed.

Remember that a propagated message may be seen several times by the rendezvous. By using the path, the TTL, and the ID of the message, the rendezvous can avoid forwarding messages to peers that have already seen the message or that the rendezvous has already processed itself.

This control is accomplished by adding a RendezVousPropagateMessage message element within each propagated message. The XML schema for the element is as follows:

```
<xs:element name="RendezVousPropagateMessage"
            type="jxta:RendezVousPropagateMessage"/>


<xs:complexType name="RendezVousPropagateMessage">
    <xs:element name="MessageId" type="xs:string"/>
    <!-- This should be a constrained subtype -->
    <xs:element name="DestSName" type="xs:string"/>
    <xs:element name="DestSParam" type="xs:string"/>
    <xs:element name="TTL" type="xs:unsignedInt"/>
    <xs:element name="Path" type="xs:anyURI" maxOccurs="unbounded"/>
</xs:complexType>
```

The RendezVousPropagateMessage holds the information used by the rendezvous to determine specific information about the message and its routing.

JXTA Identifiers

JXTA has many identifiers. We have shown most of them earlier in the chapter as parts of the advertisements. They are used for identification, indexing, and searching. There are usually two specific identifiers in most advertisements. The first is the advertisement ID. This ID is generated when the advertisement is created. One way to look at the advertisement identifier is that it is like an object reference. The identifier has no real value other than to give each advertisement a unique number. The second identifier is one associated with the advertisement type.

The format of identifiers vary according to their intent and use. Identifiers vary from simple names to unique identifiers that can consist of rather long sequences of numbers and letters (please refer to the earlier section titled "Modules" for examples of the different identifiers).

Codat ID

Codat is an invented word that is short for "code and data." In the documentation of the Codat class, we find the following definition:

> The JXTA platform defines Codat as the unit of information shared and exchanged within a JXTA group. All instances of Codats reside within a peer group. The PeerGroup content caching service provides storage and retrieval methods for codats using codatId as index.

A codat, therefore, represents data and can contain code or a reference to code. In a group advertisement, the code is defined by the service definitions in the parms tag. These service advertisements have unique names that reference code implementations.

A Codat ID is defined in the JXTA spec as follows:

> Codat IDs refer to codats. A Codat ID should canonically, uniquely and unambiguously refer to a codat. ID Formats may OPTIONALLY support this ID Type. If a JXTA binding recognizes the ID Format, it should be able to extract a Peer Group ID from a Codat ID. This Peer Group ID identifies the peer group to which the codat belongs.

In the definition, *canonical* simply means unique. To say it more precisely, there is no more than one ID or official name for the same resource. On the Web, an HTTP URL is a canonical name for a Web page.

Peer ID

The peer ID is a reference to a specific peer. The peer ID is valid for the time that the peer exists. Because peers are persistent, the peer ID is reused each time the JXTA peer is started. The only time the peer ID is destroyed is when you delete the configuration manually or uninstall the peer platform. The next time the peer is started, a new peer ID will be created.

Group ID

Peer group IDs are used to locate and index groups. The lifetime of a group ID is variable. Public groups do not change. Groups that are temporary should have an expiration associated with them. It is up to the group creator to define the lifetime of the group.

Service/Module ID

The service ID is used to define a codat. The ID is associated with a unique piece of code.

Pipe ID

The pipe ID is used to advertise a communications channel within a group or service. The pipe is often only valid for the running time of an application. In at least the initial versions of JXTA, the pipe ID has a very good chance of being invalid. It is possible to reuse a pipe ID, but this is not of much use. The pipe ID also contains the ID of its parent group to help with indexing and verification of the group context.

Summary

This chapter has covered the top layer of the JXTA protocols. You should at least have a grasp of how JXTA works and its key systems. You should now also understand P2P networking and P2P applications a little better.

We have not gone too deeply into the protocol because this should be all you need to begin understanding how JXTA works. Remember, the JXTA protocol is really just a set of messages. So far, we are just brushing the surface of JXTA. The protocol is relatively useless without a platform that implements it. You also need to know how we can take advantage of the protocol.

3

JXTA Protocols

By Daniel Brookshier

In this chapter, you are going to read about the Java implementation of the JXTA protocols. We will highlight the important classes, interfaces, and functionality. The JXTA API is fairly large, not simple, and not always obvious. Consider this chapter an introduction to the API rather than a comprehensive treatment. We will cover important aspects of the JXTA API in more detail in later chapters. The Java version of JXTA is quite large, with almost three hundred Java files in the core platform. In the description here, we will use class diagrams that show relationships, the parent package, and sometimes the methods. Remember that JXTA is evolving, so there may be minor differences over time. With Sun Microsystems' acting stewardship, the changes at this level should be minor. Just in case, please check this book's Web page at www.samspublishing.com where we will track all the changes to JXTA from the time this book is published.

Protocol and API

The Java JXTA platform is a series of classes and methods for managing and transmitting application and control data between JXTA compatible peer platforms. These core services are used to create peer-to-peer applications.

One of the first concepts to cover is that JXTA was not initially defined as a Java API. JXTA was originally defined as a set of behaviors and messages. The messages were defined as XML documents with language and operating system independence. The Java version of JXTA is just one of many possible implementations of the JXTA protocols.

A *protocol* is a repeatable procedure for regulating data transmission between computers. There are implementations of the protocols written in Java, C, Perl, and others.

Each of these languages has a different API. The Java API covered in this book is the J2SE (Java 2 Standard Edition) version. There is also a J2ME (Java 2 Micro Edition) version for small devices like phones, PDAs, and other devices. Each API is written to be useful to its developers and does not need to match the Java reference platform in any way other than the JXTA protocol. Some versions, such as the JXTA for the J2ME platform, only implement certain part of the JXTA protocols.

The API can hide many of the details of a protocol. The differences between the Java JXTA API and the JXTA protocol are blurred in some areas and obvious in others. For example, the XML advertisements specified by the protocol are fairly well represented by Java classes and interfaces. Some actions, such as routing, are fairly well hidden from application programmers.

The key parts of the XJTA API are peer membership, pipes, discovery, and the resolver. Less used, but interesting, are the peer endpoint and peer information APIs. In addition, other APIs make up functionalities for rendezvous, gateways, and routers. Rendezvous, gateways, and routers are only of interest to the application developer because of the enhanced services they provide. This chapter covers some of their functionality because it does help to know where some of the mechanics reside.

JXTA Goals

The goal of JXTA is not to have Java everywhere, but peer-to-peer networking everywhere. The Java implementation of JXTA should be completely compatible with any other version, whether written in C, Pearl, or other popular language.

JXTA goals also include corporate and ISP acceptance. To that end, the platform can be configured to provide basic services that can be placed on a dedicated computer. The services can be controlled by the ISP or corporate network administrators, similar to how routers, firewalls, and proxy servers are used today.

Another goal of JXTA is to create a platform rather than an application. The JXTA platform aims to be application agnostic with services provided that can support a hopefully unlimited number of application types.

Finally, JXTA needs to be fast. Speed is a bit harder goal to master, especially for JXTA. Because JXTA is a platform, it is attempting to be all things to all applications. Because of this, the protocols are written with a general use in mind. Speed and efficiency can be measured via tests, but only use by applications will show how good the design is. P2P networking may seem simple, but the reality is that even the simplest system can have very complex behavior. JXTA has attempted to create a fast and efficient system by caching results, modularizing services, and allowing for specific helper services, such as routers.

Another goal that is related to the JXTA platform is to test the JXTA protocol. The platform is a test bed to refine the protocols and ensure that peers can interoperated both between peers based on the Java platform and other languages.

Finally, an important goal is to allow other developers to create applications on the platform. JXTA requires applications to succeed. Like Java, the platform is free to use as long as the open-source license is followed.

Now that we have a few goals, let's look at how the platform is designed. Note that you will not see everything we talked about in Chapter 2, "Overview of JXTA." We are at a higher level where applications can interact with JXTA services.

> **NOTE**
>
> Unlike the JXTA protocol specification, this chapter will focus on the Java implementation of the protocols. You should refer to the JXTA protocol specification and Chapter 2, "Overview of JXTA," for a more generic discussion.

JXTA Peer and Java

A *peer* is a node in the JXTA network. Each peer belongs to one or more groups and implements a set of services that allows other peers to interact with this peer, or to others of which the peer is aware. For most of the initial applications written, the peer is synonymous with the user, even though this is not ideal. Identity is left up to the implementer of the application. The peer is best thought of as a computer that does not care about identity. Keep this in mind when you write a JXTA application, and be sure to add some form of user identity.

A JXTA peer in the Java implementation is associated with one JVM. Having only one peer per device, such as a PC, is the normal scenario. You can start multiple JVMs to create multiple peers on a PC, but this is only really worth doing for debugging and experimentation. If you want to start multiple copies of JXTA applications, you need to do so in separate directories and use different communication ports to avoid the applications from conflicting. The key reason to use a separate directory is because of the cache management system.

The cm Directory

The cache management system is used to store information about the peer-to-peer (P2P) network. This information is primarily advertisements created by the peer or found on the network during discovery. The advertisements are stored as files with filenames that use the ID of the advertisement. Note that this is just the first version of the cache manager, and future versions may use a database instead of files.

The reason for such persistence is obvious when you consider there are hundreds of peers to interact with. Without local caching, you would need to contact a good portion of these peers to rebuild information required for your application.

The cache is required because it is very costly to accumulate advertisements. For example, to get a peer advertisement of a peer you would like to chat with, you may need to pass through several rendezvous peers just to locate the peer. If you had to perform this operation every time, you would significantly reduce the performance of your application over time. The network would also be clogged with discovery messages from peers constantly rediscovering the information each time they started.

Each JVM instance has one associated peer because information is stored in the directory from which JXTA is launched. There are files in this rooted directory, along with various other directories and files.

One root directory created when the peer is started for the first time is the cm (cache management) directory. The content that is being managed are the advertisements that are both created locally and fetched from the P2P network. The role of the cm directory is to act as a local cache of these advertisements. The cache acts as a form of persistence between sessions. Without the cache, the advertisements would have to be reloaded from other peers.

Below the cm directory are group directories. For each group you join, there is a corresponding directory. There are two directories , which are always created because all peers belong to the World and Net groups. These directories are named jxta-NetGroup and jxta-WorldGroup for the Net and World groups, respectively.

As the peer joins new groups, new directories are added. Using the group ID, JXTA creates the directories. Each group directory contains information about advertisements discovered in the group and any other information about the group, such as membership and credentials.

> **NOTE**
>
> You can use the cm directory for monitoring the health of your peer and for debugging. If you are having problems with your messaging, the cm directory is very useful for debugging.
>
> Looking at files in the group directories can help show that your application is connecting to the JXTA network. As you do remote discovery, peer and other advertisements will get written to these directories. Without writing code, you can examine the XML and learn about what is happening.

Another directory that can exist in the cm directory is the HttpTransport directory. This directory exists only if your peer is an HTTP gateway. The directory is used to manage messages from other peers that are using this peer as a middleman. Remember, from Chapter 2, that peers behind a firewall need a gateway that stores incoming messages.

Additional directories can also show under cm or other subdirectories (tmp, public, and private show up under group directories, but are not used). In future versions of JXTA, a database could be used instead of the file system. For now, using the file system is adequate for many applications.

PSE Directory

Another directory that appears where you run your peer is pse. The directory contains certificates, password files, and other information related to peer security.

Be careful not to modify any of these files. You can delete the pse directory if you want to start your peer security from scratch, but be careful about doing this. In the future, this directory may contain other data for the application that should not be deleted.

When the peer configuration tool cannot find the pse directory, it creates it. The system then asks for your login and password to create the appropriate files and initialize the security system.

The current implementation uses the pse information for secure pipes. In addition to pipes, there are additional uses for this information, such as logging into groups and signing messages.

Overview of the JXTA Protocols JAVA API

The JXTA protocols are based on XML messages. Each message is an XML document. The XML document defines its part in the communication and the data of the communication. These XML messages are passed between the peers to convey information or are exchanged as part of a longer communication with queries and responses. The sequencing of the XML messages, and the rules under which they are sent, completes the protocol.

JXTA for Java takes the obvious route to implement JXTA by mapping XML to classes and adding management, control, and the ability to extend a base advertisement to a more complex one by inheritance. This sounds like the system is well thought out, but there were and are a lot of growing pains.

Summary of the API

There are several base services that need to be performed in a peer-to-peer system. These services include discovery, membership, and communications. The JXTA protocols further break communications into pipe binding, endpoint, and resolver protocols. There is also a peer information protocol, which is similar to a network ping except that it can have more information about the peer.

Peer Group Modules, Services, and Applications

Each peer group has a set of services. There is a core set that is usually implemented that covers the JXTA protocols. Each service is a module, which is like a mini executable. Applications can also be a type of module. The UML diagram in Figure 3.1 shows these interfaces, their relationships, and the methods to implement them.

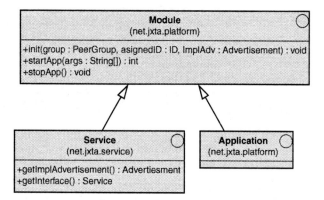

FIGURE 3.1   Module, Service, and Application interfaces.

The core services implemented by the reference platform are all derived from services. Each of these is displayed in Figure 3.2. Note that MembershipService is an abstract class and not an interface.

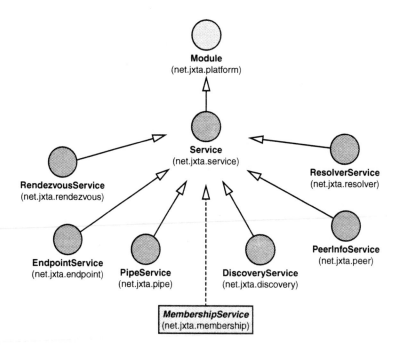

FIGURE 3.2   Core PeerGroup services and relationships to Service and Module interfaces.

Summary of Java API for JXTA Protocols

JXTA protocols are used to help peers discover, interact, and manage P2P applications. The protocols are not applications in themselves and require much more code to create something useful. The API hides a lot of detail about the P2P network, and its management that makes writing a JXTA application much easier than developing a P2P capable application from scratch. This section introduces the various APIs that we will discuss in detail later in the chapter.

Peer Discovery API

The peer discovery is an implementation of a searching mechanism with a local cache and the ability to forward requests.

The root of the discovery API is the `DiscoveryService` class. The `DiscoveryService` is obtained from the `PeerGroup` class, because discovery is always limited to its group.

Peer Resolver API

The resolver API is used by other APIs that need a request/response format. The resolver is accessed through the `ResolverService` interface.

The resolver should be thought of as a network-wide query. Instead of specifying a single peer, a group of peers is queried. An example of a use for this is the discovery service that passes a query to multiple rendezvous in search of answers.

Peer Information API

Peer information API is a way to request status information about a peer. The peer information API is accessed via the `PeerInfoService`.

Peer Membership Protocol

The peer membership API, like the discovery API, is only from the viewpoint and context of the peer group. The membership API is really in two parts—the membership authentication and credentialing. Credentialing is used in much of the messaging to prove that the peer is a valid member of the group, so the communications containing the credential are valid.

The membership protocol is accessed via the `MembershipService` abstract class. Note that this may be converted to an interface in a future version of the JXTA Java API.

Pipe Binding API

Pipe binding API is one of the more dynamic APIs. The reason is that the API is used for many different styles of pipe. The protocol is accessed via the `PipeService`.

It should be noted that the pipe service uses the resolver and the endpoint services. A module called EndpointRouter does the routing of pipes.

The PipeService interface does not define pipes, just the creation and management of pipes. Pipes are defined by implementing the InputPipe and OutputPipe interfaces.

Peer Endpoint API

The peer endpoint API is an API that is mostly invisible to JXTA application developers. The reason is that the endpoint API is really an implementation of a router. There are uncountable numbers of routers in use in corporations and the Internet that are just as invisible to the writers of browsers and other network software. However, this API can be used directly by applications that could be used to create applications that are more powerful. This API holds the key to accessing the transports available to other peer services, such as pipes and the resolver.

The key difference between a router and the endpoint router is that the routing is performed in the peer instead of a specialized piece of hardware and software. In the future, it is possible that there will be dedicated JXTA routers, but there is a great advantage to controlling your own destiny and routes. The API is probably less efficient than a dedicated router, but the endpoint router is built to route in some of the worst conditions caused by the mess of corporate LANs, firewalls, proxy servers, and NAT devices.

The router uses the resolver to query other peers for parts of the route. The endpoint protocols, such as TCP and HTTP, are defined and managed here too. The endpoint API is accessed with the EndpointService interface.

Where JXTA Applications Begin

JXTA applications need to be able to deal with the JXTA P2P network as the first thing they do. We call this *booting the peer platform*. This is very much like booting a computer on a network. The key difference here is that instead of a simple network, we are starting a peer in the JXTA network.

The JXTA platform is a group that implements the initial set of default behavior and protocols. The platform is also in the World peer group. The World group is the root of all other groups. Every peer is automatically added to the World group via the initialization of the platform.

Net Peer Group

The next thing that is done when starting a JXTA application is to load and join the Net peer group. The Net group is a specific group that is the default context for the peer. The World peer group has only limited capabilities and a very standard set of behavior. The Net peer group can be any group you desire.

The aim behind the separation of the root group is for supporting various devices. The JXTA's specification does not impose any kind of assumption about the peer capabilities, so they first join the basic world group (very easy to support) and then join other groups that may need to have more resources.

Most of the time, you will use the default Net group. The Net group is a placeholder to define a group if you need initial behavior that is different from the World group. The specific behavior includes different endpoints and knowledge of specific gateways or rendezvous. The Net group can also start monitoring services or even an initial application.

Another useful thing to do with a Net group is to specify a specific membership protocol. By placing the authentication in the Net group, you ensure that the peer is authenticated as soon as the platform boots. By becoming a valid member of the group, other peers can trust the peer. This trust can be used to prevent other peers from becoming a part of your P2P network. Normally this would only be done in a corporate network.

Starting peers in a group with secured membership is important for a P2P network that needs to be isolated. One reason for this is if all the cooperating peers are behind a firewall. Even though isolated, any other peer started behind the firewall could join. The new peer is free to interact with others on the corporate P2P. If the Net group does have a specific membership protocol, the peer booting into the network will be unable to interact with the other peers unless it joins with the specified membership.

Using a default membership may seem odd, but the simple fact is that all it takes is someone with a laptop and a JXTA peer running to compromise your P2P network.

The Peer

A peer is an identification of a specific instance of JXTA. The peer is associated with just about everything because it represents the identity of the platform. The concept of peer is similar to the way a computer is named on a LAN, except that the name is not guaranteed to be unique. As a way to make sure that peers are unique, there is a peer ID. The peer ID is generated like other IDs.

The concept of peer ID is used because there are multiple methods to reach a peer, so a fixed address or name is not that useful. Also, in the case of computers behind security barriers such as firewalls or NATs, the actual computer name or address is quite useless.

Peer ID

The peer ID is created during the initial configuration of the JXTA platform. The Configurator class creates a new PeerAdvertisement and calls the advertisement's setPeerID method with the ID built by the IDFactory. The following line shows how the factory is used. As you can see, the World group ID is used in the call. What this does is register the ID as a member of the World group:

```
IDFactory.newPeerID(PeerGroupID.worldPeerGroupID)
```

Remember that when a peer is a member of a group, the peer can be located via discovery by another peer in that group. All peers are members of the World group, so all peers can see each other from the World group discovery service. The reason that the world peer group is used is to associate the ID with the group to which it belongs.

Peer Classes

Peers are represented by a peer advertisement, which in the Java JXTA API is represented by the PeerAdvertisement class. In the Java implementation, the total implementation of a protocol is usually separated into two different packages. In this case, there is the PeerAdvertisement class that has methods that pretty much match the peer advertisement's XML specification. The PeerAdv class adds additional features used to complete the Java implementation. Figure 3.3 shows the PeerAdvertisement, its implementation, and associated ID classes.

NOTE

There are two different types of packages found in JXTA applications. These are an API and an implementation. The API is mostly abstract classes or interfaces. Some general functionality is provided in the API if the functionality is generic. Packages that are in the implementation have the platform specific code. Because the API is young, not all of the implementation is reflected by the API; so some parts of the implementation need to be accessed for some applications to work properly. In general, you should not need to use the implementation class explicitly unless it is a true extension of the API. This is true for the GenericPeerGroup class that adds the ability to look at child groups (discussed later in this chapter).

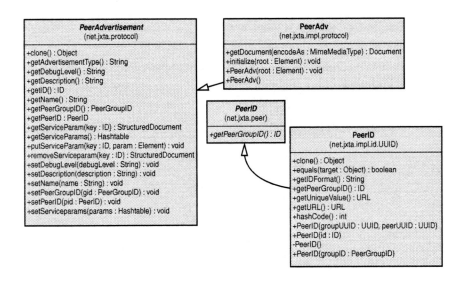

FIGURE 3.3   Peer classes used by JXTA applications.

Starting JXTA

Before we can start talking about any specific Java API for the JXTA protocols, you need to start JXTA. JXTA applications begin by joining the Net peer group. The Net group provides your default behavior and starts the JXTA services.

The following line of code is the usual way you start JXTA. The `PeerGroupFactory` is used to create a Net peer group. The Net group is a special group that is meant to be defaut or defined by a system administrator:

```
PeerGroup netPeerGroup = PeerGroupFactory.newNetPeerGroup();
```

The variable `netPeerGroup` in this line represents a layering of two groups, the World group and the Net group. The services available are in the Net group but are mostly passed on to the World group. For example, if you use discovery services, the World peer group is used and all peers will be available.

Peer Discovery Protocol API

Peer discovery is one of the more important tasks performed by a JXTA application. Most of the time, the peers, groups, and other information is not known until a peer uses the discovery service. An example of this is the shell application. The shell discovers all of its information and has no starting information about the network.

Applications may have some built-in knowledge, such as well-known peers, peer groups, and other information. However, most peers know very little about what is available. A peer may also not know the peers or the data they manage until they are discovered.

In the Java API, advertisements that are discovered are stored locally. Because of the local cache, there are two types of discovery—local and remote. The remote discovery uses the resolver to find advertisements, while the local discovery uses the cache.

Classes in the Peer Discovery API

The discovery API is implemented as a service to peer groups. The API consists of the following key parts:

- DiscoveryService—This is the base interface that is used to access core functionality of the peer discovery protocol.

- DiscoveryListener—Listener interface used to wait for remote discovery messages.

- DiscoveryEvent—The event passed to the listener that contains information about the discovered advertisements.

- DiscoveryResponseMsg—The actual data payload that contains information about the discovered advertisements.

- DiscoveryServiceImpl—Implementation of the DiscoveryService interface.

A high-level UML class diagram of these classes is shown in Figure 3.4.

The discovery API uses other classes like Cm, which is an implementation of a content manager. The Cm class is used to manage JXTA advertisements discovered. Cm persists messages to search and retrieve advertisements. In addition, the discovery API uses other APIs implementing other JXTA protocols, such as the peer resolver protocol used to send discovery queries to other peers in the JXTA network.

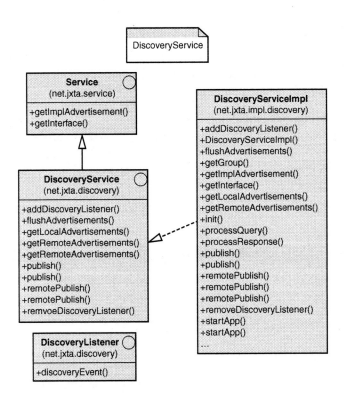

FIGURE 3.4   UML diagram of important classes in the Discovery Service API.

Accessing the Discovery Protocol

The discovery protocol takes place in the context of a peer group, so you need to have an instance of the PeerGroup interface. Peer groups are very important to discovery, because the group is a context that limits the scope of search. This means that if you are looking for peer advertisements, the only peers you should see are those that have joined your group. The same goes for subgroups, and all other advertisements created in the context of the group.

Now that you know that the group limits the discovery, you should understand that the World group is the first group you are given by the JXTA platform. The actual group you are in when you complete initialization of the platform it Net group, but World is the scope for discovery.

The Peer Group Interface

The peer group interface is a grab bag of methods that are associated with the information in the PeerGroupAdvertisement and other XML documents that describe features of the group. The interface is the primary access point to services. The services are either base services or services like the discovery service, which operate in the context of the group. In other words, if you access a service from a group, the service only works with peers in that group. This should be the preferred behavior of any service accessed from a specific group. The reason for isolation to the group is to limit the number of peers associated with actions enacted by peers that belong to the group.

The PeerGroup interface is a critical entry point to many of the services available in a peer group, so we will take a little more time to talk about the methods in the interface. Figure 3.5 shows the complete signature of the PeerGroup interface, and the following are summaries of the methods available in PeerGroup interface:

- getLoader—Returns the JxtaLoader object from which this peer group was created and launched. JxtaLoader is an extension of Java's ClassLoader class.

- isRendezvous—Returns a Boolean true if this instance of the group is a rendezvous peer.

- getPeerGroupAdvertisement—Returns the group's PeerGroupAdvertisement.

- getPeerAdvertisement—Returns the PeerAdvertisement for this peer as a member of the group.

- lookupService—Look up a service by its name ID. Returns the service registered by the name specified.

- compatible—Returns true if the given compatibility statement is loadable. This is required because a PeerGroupAdvertisement may be incompatible either by version or language that it supports.

- loadModule—Loads a given module. If the module is compatible and loadable, the object of the Module is created, initialized, and returned.

- publishGroup—Force publication of this group. Only useful if the group is being created from scratch and the PeerGroup advertisement has not been created beforehand. In such a case, the group must have been named and its description set before making the call.

- newGroup—Methods to create instantiate and initialize new groups.

- getRendezVousService—Returns the RendezvousService for the group.

- getEndpointService—Returns the EndpointService for this group.

- getResolverService—Returns the ResolverService for this group.

- getDiscoveryService—Returns the DiscoveryService object for this group.

- getPeerInfoService—Returns the PeerInfoService for this group.

- getMembershipService—Returns the MembershipService service for the group. Note that this is an instance of NullMembershipService or a customized implementation by default.

- getPipeService—Returns the PipeService for this group.

- getPeerGroupID—Gets the ID of this group.

- getPeerID—Gets the PeerID of this peer in the context of this group.

- getPeerGroupName—Gets the Name of this group.

- getPeerName—Gets the Name of this peer in this group.

- getConfigAdvertisement—Returns the configuration advertisement if any exist.

- getAllPurposePeerGroupImplAdvertisement—Gets an all-purpose peerGroup ModuleImplAdvertisement compatible with this group. The advertisement is initialized with all the data of a default peer group.

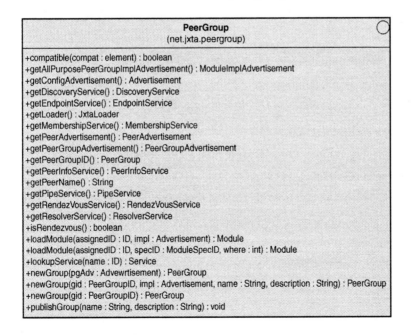

FIGURE 3.5 UML for PeerGroup interface.

Peer Group Inheritance

The classes and interfaces that make up the peer group API include several different layers used to isolate different aspects of the PeerGroup interface. Figure 3.6 shows the implementation and extensions of interface and classes to create the platform class.

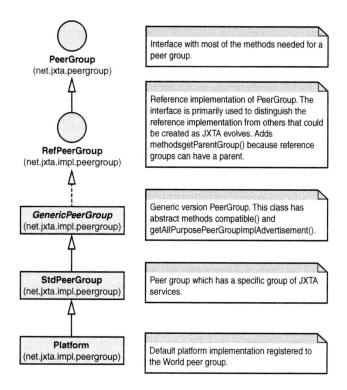

FIGURE 3.6   UML for PeerGroup interface.

When you first look at this stack, the reasons for so much abstraction is not immediately obvious. First, you have the PeerGroup interface, which gives you the core functionality as defined by the JXTA specification. The RefPeerGroup interface is primarily used to ensure that this implementation is isolated from any other. The primary reason you need this interface is to associate the reference implementation from any others that may be created. In addition, the interface adds the ability to discover a parent peer group if one exists.

The GenericPeerGroup is an abstract class that is used to further add to the reference platform for peer groups. In this class are additional methods used to ensure compatibility and add the ability to create a specific advertisement that is compatible with the reference group. This class also defines most of the static final constants used to access services.

The StdPeerGroup class is an abstraction with which you will most likely interact. The class implements most of the functionality required by a peer group.

The Platform class is the final concrete implementation of the PeerGroup and represents the World peer group. This class is instantiated as JXTA is started. The platform class is then used to for discovery and communications with other peers in the network. The platform group is also used as a parent to other groups.

Local Discovery

Local discovery is simply a method to search the locally cached advertisements in the cm directory. The following method of the DiscoveryService class does the work:

```
getLocalAdvertisements(int type, String attribute,String value)
```

The getLocalAdvertisements method will return an enumeration of base type Advertisement. The parameter type is an integer that corresponds to the constants in the DiscoveryService class shown in the following table.

Value	Name	Types of Document Returned
0	PEER	Peer advertisements
1	GROUP	Peer group advertisements
2	ADV	All other advertisements including peer and group

The document type constants are used for all of the following methods discussed for the DiscoveryService class.

The attribute parameter in getLocalAdvertisement is a string that matches a tag in the XML representing the Advertisement. Of course, the value parameter is the value of the contents between the tag, excluding leading and trailing spaces.

When the values for the attribute and the values are null, all of the specific type of advertisement will be retrieved.

The following is an example that searches for a peer named "Mariann":

```
getLocalAdvertisements(DiscoveryService.PEER, "Name","Mariann")
```

The next example returns all advertisements (excluding Peer and Peer Group):

```
getLocalAdvertisements(DiscoveryService.ADV, null,nul)
```

The final example returns all the groups already known by the peer:

```
getLocalAdvertisements(DiscoveryService.GROUP, null,null)
```

Note that if there are no matches in the cache, an empty enumerator is returned.

One of the most important things to understand about local discovery is that it is based on remote discovery locating the advertisement first. If you don't run a remote search, you won't find any advertisements unless they are hardcoded by your implementation.

Advertisement Types

There are various advertisements returned. Figure 3.7 shows the many different types of advertisements and the classes that implement them. To access specific elements of these advertisements, you will need to cast the advertisement to the appropriate type. Note that there are API and implementation versions.

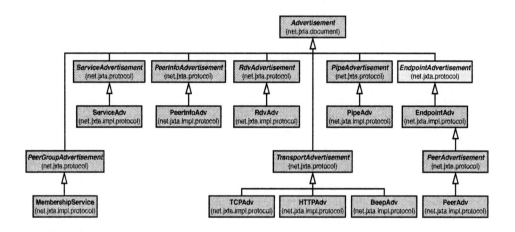

FIGURE 3.7   UML of Advertisements classes used in JXTA Java API.

Local Cache Created versus Remote Discovery

You should always run local discovery first. The reason is that remote discovery can take seconds to several minutes to locate advertisements specified by your search. By using the local cache, you make your applications run faster by avoiding network searches each time you need an advertisement.

Remote Discovery

Remote discovery is a process where one or more peers are queried for advertisements. Remote discovery is initiated by the getRemoteAdvertisements method found in DiscoveryService. The following method sends queries to rendezvous to search their local database for the advertisements that match the pattern specified:

```
int getRemoteAdvertisements( String peerid,
                             int type,
                             String attribute,
```

```
                        String value,
                        int threshold );
```

The parameters of this method are used as follows:

- peerid—A specific peer ID that created the advertisement. This parameter may be null to obtain advertisements from any peer.

- type—The type of advertisement (PEER, GROUP, ADV).

- attribute—An XML tag name that matches one in the advertisement. The attribute may be null, which selects all advertisements that match the type and the peerid parameters.

- value—The value of the contents of the tag enclosed by the tag specified by the attribute parameter. This value may be null if the attribute tag is null. If not null, the only advertisements returned are those that match the value.

- threshold—The upper limit of responses from one peer. This is an important variable, because the number of advertisements can be very large if the other parameters do not restrict the number of possible advertisements.

NOTE

The threshold parameter, in addition to limiting responses, is also a form of politeness in the P2P network. If the threshold is very high, you are utilizing a lot of resources from the rendezvous peer that is probably busy with other peers and its own operations. Remember that other peers share the discovery service.

This method is non-blocking. The method returns after threads begin the process of sending out queries to rendezvous. As answers are returned, the advertisements are stored in the local cache for later retrieval by the getLocalAdvertisements method.

This method is really only useful for populating the local cache periodically. The problem is that the peer really does not know when the advertisement has been found. The better method is the one described next that uses a listener to know exactly when an advertisement is found.

Remote Discovery with Listener

The next method is similar to the last, except that there is an additional parameter that passes in a listener. The DiscoveryListener interface is called each time a query response is returned from a rendezvous with an advertisement matching the other parameters in the method:

```
void getRemoteAdvertisements( String peerid,
                             int type,
                             String attribute,
                             String value,
                             int threshold,
                             DiscoveryListener listener );
```

The `DiscoveryListener` interface has only one method `DiscoveryEvent`. The method is used to pass an event parameter of type `DiscoveryEvent`. You can see the complete spec for these in the UML diagram in Figure 3.8.

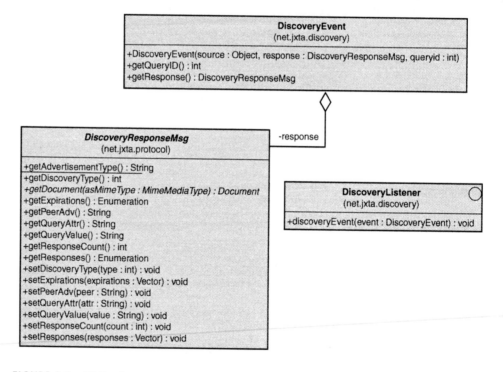

FIGURE 3.8   UML of `DiscoveryEvent`, `DiscoveryListener`, and `DiscoveryResponseMsg`.

The `DiscoveryEvent` object contains `DiscoveryResponseMsg`, which contains all of the advertisements returned from a specific rendezvous. Be careful not to call any of the set methods, because the methods are used for processing messages, not for manipulation by you. The only methods you should use in this class are the "get" methods. The getResponses method is the most important because it returns an enumeration of the advertisements found. You can also get the original query information via getQueryAttr, getQueryValue, and getDiscoveryType. The advertisement returned by the getPeerAdv is for the rendezvous from which peer the advertisements originated. The getDocument and getAdvertisementType methods are of little value because they are just the XML the XML document type of the response message.

CAUTION

Do not use the setter methods of the DiscoveryResponseMsg. They are only to be used by the DiscoveryService when building the DiscoveryResponseMsg object. Using these methods does not guarantee changes to the XML representation of the advertisements returned by the getResponses method.

Advertisement Expirations

Advertisements have an expiration that is managed by JXTA. There are default expiration times, and you can override the lifetimes of advertisements when you publish with the remotePublish method and should not be set or overridden by other means.

Do not cache advertisements in application variables or use some other form of persistence, such as a database, to store advertisements. Only use the discovery mechanism and its cache. If you request an advertisement from the discovery cache when it has expired, you will not receive the advertisement in the results, and the current expired advertisement will be deleted. You should then rediscover the advertisement via the getRemoteAdvertisement method.

The publisher of an advertisement will automatically publish advertisements on a regular schedule as long as the peer is running. If the peer is shutdown, on restarting, it may publish the advertisements if the interval has expired. The only way to stop this is to flush the local version of the advertisement.

If a peer is not running, any advertisements that have propagated to other peers will eventually expire. If your peer is down longer than the expiration, the time to locate its published advertisements may be unnaturally long. If your peer is off for long periods, you should use a reasonable timeout when you first publish the advertisement.

The default expirations for locally created advertisements is one year in most cases, but some have longer defaults or none at all in the case of a peer advertisement. When advertisements are remotely published, the default is 2 hours, but this can vary depending on the value set during publishing. Note that you should not change the expiration value of the advertisement. You should set the expiration only via the remotePublish method.

Managing Advertisements

One of the critical management problems is handling advertisements that may be invalid. Part of the problem is that we just don't know when an advertisement is truly invalid. Either the peer or the member of a group is not currently on the JXTA network, or the advertisement is truly transient and the need for it is gone. The other problem that can occur is that by the time an advertisement is propagated to another peer, the need for it has expired or the peer that published it is already disconnected from the network.

To alleviate problems with invalid advertisement, you will need to manage how you treat a certain types of advertisements. You should start by avoiding communication with specific peers. This simply means that you write your application to rely on random peers in a group rather than a specific peer.

If you do need to contact a specific peer, you should create a mechanism to retry if there is a failure. In the case of multiple peers that are transient, you may want to use a specific peer that is more persistent to exchange information. For example, a set of PDA peers would use a set of relay peers to hold information until the target PDA is connected to the network. There are other possibilities; you just need to use a little imagination and some experimentation.

A big problem is a peer that is not operating or is disconnected from the network. You should probably characterize specific peers as being transient to avoid deleting advertisements that are probably still good. For example, a peer advertisement from a laptop is probably still valid, even though it cannot be contacted. Instead, the laptop may simply be disconnected from the network while moving to a new location. Your application should attempt to contact the laptop later.

If you are developing, try to use a very short lifetime for advertisements. You should also make sure that old advertisements are purged to ensure that your test peers are not using old data.

Removing or Flushing Old Advertisements

One of the important things to do in a JXTA application is housekeeping. The number of advertisements can get quite large if the P2P network is large. There is also the problem of invalid advertisements caused by development and testing. To ensure that the system is working correctly, you will need to delete advertisements. The mechanism is the DiscoveryService class with the following signature:

```
void flushAdvertisements( String id, int type ) throws IOException;
```

To use flushAdvertisement, you need to have both the ID and the type of advertisement. It probably seems logical that all you would need is the ID, but there is a good reason this is not true. Please remember that the content management system, used to maintain advertisements, does so by the primary types of peer, peer group, and general advertisement. Consequently, you have to tell the system where to look for the advertisement by its type (PEER, GROUP, ADV), as well as the ID.

The best time to flush advertisements is when you have an advertisement that no longer works. You should be careful, because just because an advertisement fails does not mean that the advertisement is to blame. It is just as possible that the peers associated with the advertisement are not available. The good news, though, is that you can always search again for the advertisement. The bad news is that it may be the exact same one and the peer still not available. As a result, you may want to try an advertisement a few times over a set period before flushing the advertisement.

Remember also that advertisements have a built-in expiration. Expiration and the deletion is hidden, and there is no reason for you to flush advertisements if they are expired. Expiration and expected lifetime should still be considered when flushing advertisements. The reason is that those advertisements that are more volatile (shorter expirations) are more likely to be invalid. As a result, when dealing with pipes, you are more likely to get an invalid advertisement. Conversely, a peer group advertisement is less likely to be bad, because peer groups have a long lifetime.

Something else of note in this method is that the ID is a string and not a class. The reason for this is again related to the cache manager that stores advertisements by using the ID as a file name. In our example of this method, flushing the advertisement of a peer, we convert the peer ID to a string:

```
discovery.flushAdvertisements(padv.getPeerID().toString()
                    , Discovery.PEER);
```

Dealing with the Advertisements Discovered

One aspect about the way that JXTA was developed is that advertisements are not directly useable. To take advantage of an advertisement, you need to build another object that uses the advertisement as its initialization.

For each advertisement, you should find a class that accepts the ad in a constructor, init, or factory method. You will see many of these throughout this chapter and the rest of the book.

Also, not all of an advertisement is exposed by a get method. This is especially true for customized sections. To use the data, you need to call the getDocument method and retrieve the values of the tags that interest you.

Modifying Advertisements

Another slightly different aspect of advertisements is that they are not necessarily two-way. The fact that an advertisement has set methods does not guarantee that the getDocument method will return an advertisement that is equivalent to the object. This may become true in the future, but for now, be sure to use the AdvertisementFactory class.

Group Services and Discovery

An important aspect of discovery is that because of its scoping of searches to its group, the items used by services in the group are also constrained by the group. What this means is that you should be able to search for any type of advertisement and expect that advertisement to be compatible to your group context and, thus, your services.

Finding Other Group Members

Another nice feature of group scoping is finding other users. When looking for advertisements of type PEER, you should only receive advertisements of peers that belong to the group from which you are searching. Be careful to remember that not all peers are visible at all times, and that sometimes peers change their name, ID, or both.

Peer Resolver Protocol API

The peer resolver protocol API can be thought of as rather misnamed. A resolver is classically defined for TCP/IP as a protocol for formatting requests to be sent to a domain name server to convert hostnames to an Internet address. However, a resolver is also defined as resolving a question, which is much closer to what the peer resolver protocol is actually used for. Simply, the JXTA resolver protocol is used to send a query to another peer and receive a response.

Simple P2P Messages, No Guarantees

The messages of the resolver are quite simple. They are also not guaranteed to reach their destinations nor are the results, if they exist, guaranteed to arrive back at the source of the query. The rendezvous may refuse or fail to transmit either message, or the answer may not exist. There is also no guarantee of an answer or even a notification that there is no answer.

Query Message

The query message is a standard wrapper of XML around a payload of information defined by the implementation. The implementation is specified by the handler name.

The wrapper contains a credential, the handler name, the source peer ID, a query ID, and the query. The DTD for the query is as follows:

```
<!ELEMENT ResolverQuery  (Credential,
                          HandlerName,
                          SrcPeerID,
                          QueryID,
                          Query)>


<!ELEMENT Credential  #PCDATA>
<!ELEMENT HandlerName #PCDATA>
<!ELEMENT SrcPeerID   #PCDATA>
<!ELEMENT QueryID     #PCDATA>
<!ELEMENT Query       #PCDATA>
```

Response Message

The response message is very similar to the query. The differences are in the credential and the response. The credential is the credential of the responding peer. Like the query message, the credential is the one created when the response peer joined the group. The credential could be checked to verify that the peer that answered the message was a valid member of the group.

The query ID in the response is identical to the query. This allows you to quickly match a query to a response if you perform multiple queries. Also, because queries can arrive out of order and may be repeated, the query ID can be used to order responses and consume duplicate messages.

The resolver finds your query handler using the specified handler name. The handler name should be the same as the query handler name. The handler interface has both a process query and a process response. The duality of the interface, and a single name, help promote the idea that all peers participate in both queries and responses.

Like the query, the payload is in a tag, this time called Response. The DTD for the XML is as follows:

```
<!ELEMENT ResolverResponse (Credential,
                            HandlerName,
                            QueryID,
                            Response)>


<!ELEMENT Credential  #PCDATA>
<!ELEMENT HandlerName #PCDATA>
```

```
<!ELEMENT QueryID    #PCDATA>
<!ELEMENT Response   #PCDATA>
```

Message Security

The credential is not a guarantee that the response message is from a valid peer. It would be very easy to copy a credential and masquerade as the response peer. To ensure that the message is not counterfeit, the message should either be encrypted or signed in a way that the signature contains verification of the peer, the message ID, and that the data has not been modified.

Resolver API Classes

The UML for key resolver classes can be seen in Figure 3.9. The classes and interfaces are as follows:

- ResolverInterface—A class that implements the resolver management. This class is the focal point of functionality for sending queries and distributing responses. The class implements the ResolverService and the GenericResolver interfaces.

- ResolverService—Interface that defines the interface to register and unregister query handler classes. The interface also extends the GenericResolver interface, which completes the resolver service by defining the methods used for sending queries and sending responses.

- GenericResolver—Interface that defines the methods used for sending queries and sending responses.

- QueryHandler—This is the interface to implement to handle queries and responses to queries.

- ResolverQueryMsg—This is the message that is sent to other peers for processing. The ResolverQuery is the default implementation and extends ResolverQueryMsg.

- ResolverResponseMsg—This is the message that is sent to other peers for processing. The ResolverResponse is the default implementation and extends ResolverResponseMsg.

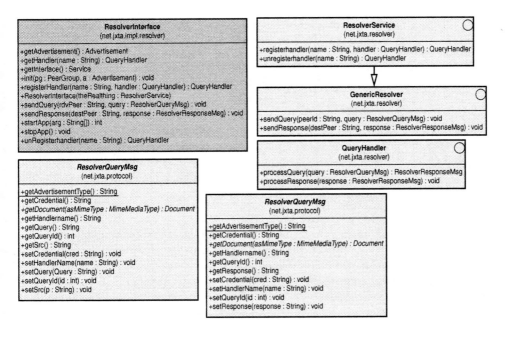

FIGURE 3.9   Key classes in the Peer Resolver API.

Coding and Starting the Handler

To create the handler, you simply implement the `QueryHandler` interface. The interface only has two methods—`processQuery` and `processResponse`. The `processQuery` method is called when a peer receives a query and `processResponse` is called when the query returns.

The `processQuery` Method

The `processQuery` method is, as we have just pointed out, used by a peer to process a query message. The method is called from within the resolver after the query is received. The query message is passed to this method for processing.

The `processQuery` method is used called on the responder peer. In other words, this method is only called if you receive a query message from another peer. The process response method of this interface is only called when a response is received from a peer you have queried.

The return from the method is the message to be sent back to the peer that asked the question. The signature of the call is as follows:

```
ResolverResponseMsg processQuery(ResolverQueryMsg query)
                         throws NoResponseException,
                                ResendQueryException,
                                DiscardQueryException;
```

The exceptions thrown are quite important, because they result in very specific behavior of the resolver. Depending on the error, processQuery method throws NoResponseException, ResendQueryException, or a DiscardQueryException. The following are the exceptions that you can throw from the method and what the resolver will do in response:

- NoResponseException—Throw when you do not have a response, but the response peer is interested in getting an answer for itself. The resolver system will propagate the query and resend it. Note that the query will only be propagated if the peer is a rendezvous.

- ResendQueryException—Causes the resolver to resend the query.

- DiscardQueryException—The query is discarded and not forwarded from the peer. Remember that the response peer is not required to return a response.

NOTE

Java veterans may notice that the processQuery exceptions are used as a form of logic control. Expect this to change because the cost of processing an exception is very high.

Traversing a try...catch block costs nothing in most JVM implementations. When an exception is thrown, there are several operations that involve manipulations and examination of the stack, lookups of catch locations, and catch types. Although simple to use, exception handling is very expensive. Exceptions, which should be rare errors, are rarely seen, so the cost is for a single exception is not noticeable. This is not the case for processQuery method.

Look for this method to change in a future version.

Processing Responses

The processResponse method in the QueryHandler interface is a little simpler than the processQuery method because this is a termination point of the query. There are no exceptions to throw to drive resolver behavior. However, because this is a handler, be careful about allowing an exception to be thrown here. By throwing an exception, you can cause the resolver to cease functioning:

```
void processResponse(ResolverResponseMsg response);
```

Example QueryHandler

The query handler has two methods to be implemented. In Listing 3.1, the
processQuery method adds a time stamp to the payload of the query message. The
processResponse method simply prints the message that was received. Because you
always have an answer (the time stamp) you never throw an exception.

LISTING 3.1   Sample implementation of a QueryHandler

```
class TestQueryHandler implements QueryHandler{
   protected String handlerName;
   protected String credential;
   protected SimpleDateFormat format    = new SimpleDateFormat (
                                      "MM, dd, yyyy hh:mm:ss.S");

   public TestQueryHandler(String handlerName, String credential){
      this.handlerName = handlerName;
      this.credential = credential;
   }// end of constructor TestQueryHandler()

   public void processResponse(ResolverResponseMsg response) {
      System.out.println("Received a response");
         String textDoc = response.getResponse();
         System.out.println(textDoc);
      }// end of processResponse()

   public ResolverResponseMsg processQuery(ResolverQueryMsg query)
                                  throws NoResponseException,
                                         ResendQueryException,
                                         DiscardQueryException,
                                         IOException {
      System.out.println("Received a query");
      System.out.println(((ResolverQuery)query).toString());
      StructuredTextDocument doc = null;
      String textDoc = query.getQuery();
      doc = (StructuredTextDocument)StructuredDocumentFactory
            .newStructuredDocument
            ( new MimeMediaType( "text/xml" )
            ,new ByteArrayInputStream(textDoc.getBytes()) );

      // Use the original payload and add the time
      Element e = null;
      long now = System.currentTimeMillis();
```

LISTING 3.1   Continued

```
        e = doc.createElement("timestamp 2",format.format( new Date(now)));
        doc.appendChild(e);
        // Return a generic response;
        ResolverResponseMsg message = null;
        String xml = serializeDoc(doc);
        message = new ResolverResponse( handlerName
                                     , credential
                                     , query.getQueryId()
                                     , xml);
        return (ResolverResponseMsg)message;
    }// end of processQuery()
}// end of class TestQueryHandler
```

Accessing and Setup of the Resolver

The resolver is found in your group. It is simple to just call the getResolverService method of the peer group you are using. The return type is a ResolverService, but actually you get an instance of ResolverServiceImpl. ResolverServiceImpl contains the actual methods used to submit the queries. The ResolverService interface specifies the adding and removal of query handlers.

The GenericResolver interface defines the methods for sending queries and responses. In GenericResolver, you really only use the method to initiate queries, while the method for sending responses is called by the internals of the resolver in response to the QueryHander.processQuery method:

```
ResolverServiceImpl resolver;
resolver = (ResolverServiceImpl)group.getResolverService();
TestQueryHandler handler = new  TestQueryHandler(handlerName,credential);
resolver.registerHandler(handlerName, handler);
```

Getting Ready—Finding a Rendezvous Peer

The resolver only operates in terms of rendezvous peers. Queries must begin at rendezvous. If your current peer is configured as a rendezvous, there is no problem. If your peer is not a rendezvous, you will need to know about a rendezvous.

Note that there is no guarantee that a specific peer will answer. The peer that answers is the peer that actually sends the response. If the specified rendezvous peer has the answer, it will reply and take no further action. If the peer does not have an answer and throws NoResponseException or ResendQueryException, the query is forwarded to another rendezvous for processing.

One way to look at this is to imagine a group of 100 people. Among the group are 10 areas that are rendezvous for each of 10 people. One person at the rendezvous is responsible for communicating with the other ten rendezvous. We will call these peers *rendezvous managers*. Peer 1 asks rendezvous manager 1 a question. If any of the other eight peers have communicated the answer or the manager knows the answer, it returns the response to peer 1. If manager 1 does not know the answer, it contacts all the rendezvous managers it knows about for an answer.

The manager does not need to know about all of the other managers, just enough that know of others, and so on. In other words, if there is a chain of relationships between the managers that connects all ten, all rendezvous are visible to the first peer. The topology here is that of the small world effect we talked about in Chapter 1, "What Is P2P."

Using the Resolver

Using the resolver is fairly simple, but there are several steps. Listing 3.2 covers just about everything you need to send a query.

NOTE

The code in Listing 3.2 is from a simple test of the resolver that can be found online at www.sampspublishing.com.

Create a document with the time, serialize that into an XML document, create a ResolverQuery object, and send it. As you can see, most of the effort is dedicated to building the message while the actual messaging is very simplistic.

LISTING 3.2   Example Used to Start a Query

```
// Create a document with the time
StructuredTextDocument doc = null;
doc = (StructuredTextDocument)
    StructuredDocumentFactory.newStructuredDocument(
        new MimeMediaType("text/xml"),"Pong");

Element e = null;

long now = System.currentTimeMillis();

e = doc.createElement("timestamp 1", format.format( new Date(now)) );
doc.appendChild(e);
String credential = "Sams";
// Create the message;
```

LISTING 3.2   Continued

```
ResolverQueryMsg message = null;
String xml = serializeDoc(doc);
message = new ResolverQuery( handlerName
                       , credential
                       , group.getPeerID().toString()
                       , xml
                       , 1);
System.out.println("Sending query");
// Note that the following may throw a RuntimeException
// if the peer is not found.
resolver.sendQuery(peerID, message);
```

Processing Responses

The rendezvous peer can operate in several different ways. First, the rendezvous can be given answers by other peers. This is what happens in the discovery process. When a peer does a remote publish of an advertisement, it publishes it to a rendezvous. Any remote query for advertisements in the discovery mechanism causes each rendezvous to look to see if it has that advertisement. If there is no copy of the advertisement, the query is forwarded to other peers.

The query could also cause the rendezvous to contact peers that are not rendezvous. This would occur in the handler. The peers that the rendezvous knows about could be contacted to get an answer. This rendezvous to peer mechanism takes place outside of the resolver mechanism. If none of these peers has an answer, the rendezvous can forward the query to another rendezvous that will repeat the process.

Remember that there is no direct addressing guaranteed in this process. You should use pipes if you want to get a response from a specific peer.

Removing a Handler

When you are no longer interested in receiving answers to queries, unregister your handler. This is very important to do as soon as possible because you could waste time on processing an answer multiple times. The following is the signature to unregister the handler. It simply takes the name of the handler you specified when you registered it:

```
QueryHandler unregisterHandler( String name )
```

Peer Information Protocol

The peer information protocol is a specific implementation of a peer resolver query. When a peer is first initialized, it publishes its PeerAdvertisement that is picked up by at least one rendezvous. When a request for a specific peer's information is requested, a query is made to locate the PeerAdvertisement. Recall that the PeerAdvertisement contains endpoint information for contacting the peer. Using the endpoint, the peer is contacted directly to obtain its peer information.

PeerInfoService

The PeerInfoService interface is very simple and very complete. To compare it to the ResolverService, the interface has more methods, but this is because the behavior is more constrained. The only actions are to locate peer information and manage information. You may recognize some of the functionality as being similar to the DiscoveryService. The two services are very similar and manage data in the same way using the content manager to store advertisements. In the PeerInfoService, the only advertisement that is cached is the PeerInfoAdvertisement. The UML for this advertisement is shown in Figure 3.10.

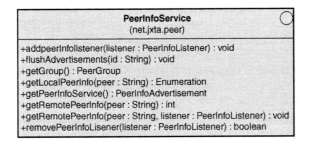

FIGURE 3.10   UML for PeerInfoService.

The PeerInfoAdvertisement

The PeerInfoAdvertisement is a bit different from the other advertisements in JXTA because it includes volatile data like uptime. The UML for the advertisement is shown in Figure 3.11.

```
┌──────────────────────────────────────────────────────────────┐
│                    PeerInfoAdvertisement                       │
│                      (net.jxta.protocol)                       │
├──────────────────────────────────────────────────────────────┤
│ +getAdvertisementType() : String                               │
│ +getIncomingTrafficChannels() : Enumeration                    │
│ +getIncomingTrafficOnChannel(channel : String) : long          │
│ +getLastIncomingMessageTime() : long                           │
│ +getLastOutgoingMessageTime() : long                           │
│ +getoutgoingTrafficChannels() : Enumeration                    │
│ +getoutgoingTrafficOnChannel(channel : String) : long          │
│ +getSourcePid() : String                                       │
│ +getTargetPic() : String                                       │
│ +getTimeStamp() : long                                         │
│ +getUptime() : long                                            │
│ +PeerInfoAdvertisement()                                       │
│ +setIncomingTrafficElement(channel : String, bytes : long) : void │
│ +setLastIncomingMessageTime(t : long) : void                   │
│ +setLastOutgoingMessageTime(t : long) : void                   │
│ +setOutgoingTrafficElement(channel : String, bytes : long) : void │
│ +setSourcePid(pid : String) : void                             │
│ +setTargetPic(pic : String) : void                             │
│ +setTimestamp(milliseconds : long) : void                      │
│ +setUptime(milliseconds : long) : void                         │
└──────────────────────────────────────────────────────────────┘
```

FIGURE 3.11   UML for `PeerInfoAdvertisement`.

The `PeerInfoListener`

The acquisition of a peer's info will vary according to how the information is finally accessed. Because you cannot predict the time it takes to get the peer info, the API uses a listener to notify the application when the information is available.

The interface of the listener is quite simple, with only one method. The `PeerInfoResponse` method passes a `PeerInfoEvent` to the listener. The `PeerInfoEvent` holds the peer info advertisement retrieved. The UML diagram in Figure 3.12 shows the specification for both the `PeerInfoListener` interface and the `PeerInfoEvent`.

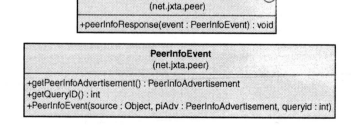

FIGURE 3.12   UML `PeerInfoListener` and `PeerInfoEvent`.

Flushing Advertisements

`PeerInfoAdvertisement`, like other advertisements, will automatically expire. However, you may want to remove peer info advertisements on a regular basis to ensure that the information is up to date. You should also remove the advertisements if your application accesses multiple peers because that may impact memory.

Why Use the Peer Info Protocol?

Of all the protocols, peer info probably seems the least useful in its current implentation. The protocol can help gauge the health of the network with uptime statistics and other information about messages. Overall, the protocol can provide interesting information, but not a lot.

You could write your own implementation of the protocol and use it in your custom groups. By implementing your own, the amount and richness of the data can be made to fit your requirements. The API may not lend its self to easy extension, so you are probably better off creating your own protocol.

Peer Membership Protocol

The peer membership protocol is a mechanism for joining peer groups. The protocol should not be confused with group creation and management except that when you create a group, you specify a specific implementation of this protocol.

What the membership protocol does is impose and verify specific requirements for a peer to join a group. In other words, the protocol makes sure you give the right answers to questions that identifies you as a valid group candidate before you are allowed to join a group. Alternatively, the implementation could look up other information or even ask other peers to vote. The possibilities are endless, and the protocol works as a framework to begin the process and allow the user to join once the requirements are met.

After you have successfully joined a group, you are issued a credential. The credential is an XML document that is used as a token of proof that you are a member of the group. The membership protocol does not keep track of users that have joined. In a peer environment, it is impractical to use a server for validating membership. The credential serves as a way to allow peers to recognize each other as valid members of the same peer group (see Chapter 6, "Working with Groups," for a complete example of peer membership).

Membership Service

The `MembershipService` class is an abstract class that defines generic methods used for a concrete membership service class. Figure 3.13 shows the UML for this abstract class. This class is described in detail in Chapter 6 but the following is a short description of the methods:

- getName—Returns the name of the service. The name is often used to match the membership service with its authenticator.

- getInterface—Returns this object as a service.

- apply—Request the necessary Authenticator object to join the group based on a given policy. An AuthenticationCredential is provided to help select what version of Authenticator should be used and/or to initialize an Authenticator object. Returns an Authenticator object associated with the join. The Authenticator object has setter methods that must be properly set so that the authenticator returns a valid state to allow the peer into the group.

- join—Join the group. A valid Authenticator object from the apply method is provided. The result is a Credential object that can be used when needed to prove the peer is valid.

- resign—Method called to resign a peer from the group.

- getCurrentCredentials—Returns an enumeration of current credentials that identify the peer.

- getAuthCredentials—Returns an enumeration of the current AuthenticationCredential objects.

- makeCredential—Helper method used to create a credential from an XML element. This can be used to recreate a credential that was stored as XML.

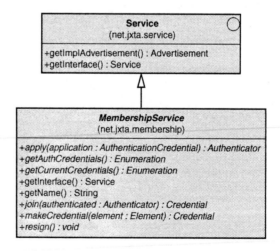

FIGURE 3.13   UML for MembershipService interface.

AuthenticationCredential

AuthenticationCredential provides the authentication method and an identity. In the UML diagram in Figure 3.14, the getMethod method of the Authentication class returns a string that is used to look up the authenticator. The identity information is derived by the implementation of the Credential interface methods.

One way to look at the AuthenticationCredential is as an initial introduction. Because of the object passed via a join, the membership service knows the peer, its current group, specific credential information, and the method with which the peer is attempting to join.

FIGURE 3.14   UML for AuthenticationCredential class.

Credential

After you have joined a group, you are issued a credential. The credential implements the credential interface that was shown in Figure 3.14. The credential is a custom implementation that can hold some type of data that is used to identify the peer to the group. Usually, the basic implementation is used because many groups are not concerned with security.

Null Membership Service

The UML in Figure 3.15 is an implementation of the Null membership service. The classes NullMembershipService, NullCredential, and NullAuthenticator are based on MembershipService, Credential, and AuthenticationCredential, respectively. The Null membership is the default membership for the world peer group and any sub-group unless specifically overridden by adding a custom membership service class.

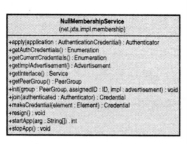

FIGURE 3.15   UML for `NullMembershipService`, `NullCredential`, and `NullAuthenticator` classes.

The Join Process

Joining a group via the membership protocol is a multi-step process. The steps are as follows:

1. Obtain or create an initial `AuthenticationCredential` object. The `AuthenticationCredential` constructor takes a credential document, the peer group, and the authentication method that the group uses.

2. Get the membership service from the group. Calling the `getMembershipService` method of the peer group you are going to join does this.

3. Call the apply method of the membership service with your authentication credential. This primes the membership service for step 5.

4. Fill in the appropriate data in the authenticator object.

5. Test the authenticator. You call the `isReadyForJoin` method of the authenticator and, if true, you can safely join the group.

6. Call the membership service method `join`.

The result of the join is a final credential that you can pass to other peers in messages. The group also contains this credential that will automatically be added to standard XML messages that require a credential.

Joining a Group

There are two different ways to join groups—via a null authenticator and with a custom group.

Null authentication is the default authenticator for the World group and the default for any new group. Null authentication does not care who you are and performs only token processing to start the peer group normally. The following is a very simple join:

```
MembershipService membership;
membership = (MembershipService) newGroup.getMembershipService();
credential= membership.join( null );
```

Joining with a custom group is a little more difficult. The first step is to obtain the actual membership service from your group:

```
MembershipService membership;
membership = (MembershipService) newGroup.getMembershipService();
```

Now you create an authentication credential. The following example uses the group you are joining, the authentication method name, and an initial credential:

```
AuthenticationCredential authCred;
authCred = new AuthenticationCredential( newGroup
                             , authenticationMethod
                             , credentials );
```

Note that the authentication method string needs to match an authentication method supported by the membership service. The reason for specifying by name is so that different authenticators can be used in diffeereent languages.

Next, you obtain an authenticator by applying to the group. What this does is create an authenticator that is based on your credentials, the group, and the type of authentication you are requesting. Note that you could have multiple authentication methods and credentials represented by authentication credentials. In other words, an insurance group could be made up of patients and doctors. Patients could use a different credential and authentication method than a doctor who may need a different level of identification and processing. Here is an example of the apply method:

```
Authenticator authenticator = (Authenticator)membership.apply( authCred );
```

At this point, you now have an object that implements the Authenticator interface. The object is going to have specific methods to configure the authenticator that are specific to the requirements of the group, the method of authentication, and the initial credentials. The settings may be as simple as the username to a series of questions to a name and password.

The Authenticator interface includes a method called isReadyForJoin. The method is implemented to return true if the state of the custom data represents the requirements for a valid join. The following lines check the authenticator to see if it is valid. If you pass, you go ahead and join the group. The isReadyForJoin is also called during join. Make sure you check prior to joining to ensure proper handling of an invalid authenticator object:

```
if( authenticator.isReadyForJoin() ) {
    finalCredential= membership.join( authenticator );
}
```

If the join method fails because the authenticator returns false for the isReadyForJoin method or for some other reason, the PeerGroupException is thrown.

Final Credential

Notice in the prior example that the return value from the join is a custom implementation of a Credential object. The credential is used for all communications with other peers to prove that you have joined the group. The credential is used by the authenticator service to ensure that only valid peer group members can use services.

Renewing Membership

The protocol specification states that the membership protocol includes the ability to renew a membership. The initial version of the Java API does not include the ability to renew a membership. However, you can write your custom authentication credential that specifies a renewal authentication method and accept the final credential that was created after you joined the group.

Resigning Membership

Resignation from a group is simple. Just call the resign method of the MembershipService object. The credentials used to join the group are destroyed as a part of this process:

```
membership.resign();
```

Pipe Binding Protocol API

The pipe binding protocol is a mix of capabilities that includes the routing of connections and the interfaces for communicating between peers. In other words, the pipe binding protocol describes how we create connections between peers and how we send information.

The Pipe Binding API, as opposed to the JXTA protocol specification, goes a step further by adding the programmatic structure for your application to make connections to send and receive messages. In addition, the API works as a framework for extension to create different types of pipes and different control models.

What Are Pipes?

Pipes can be compared to sockets or streams, in other words, just a channel between computers to transfer data. The difference is that you assume that the P2P network has a few things different from a normal network in that you assume that the connection is not necessarily direct and that there are many protocols that can be used. The *pipe binder* is a layer above the messy network that hides everything from the developer and adds capabilities that the network does not have via the base protocols alone.

One example of additional capabilities is the ability to cross a firewall. It is rather simple to use HTTP to cross a firewall to connect a server to a client. However, what about connecting two peers, each behind their own firewalls? Suddenly the problem is a little more difficult. Now imagine connecting a dozen clients together at the same time with each one behind its own firewall. Now the problems are almost impossible by normal means. But, by hiding the complexity in the protocol, along with using other JXTA protocols like the peer resolver and peer endpoint router, even the most convoluted interconnection of peers can be simply accessed with a simple pipe abstraction.

So, think of a pipe API as a second cousin to Java's stream API. There are a few differences, but many of the patterns you would normally use are the same. There are also a few extra functions to make our lives easier in a P2P network.

From our prior discussions, remember that there are different types of pipes. These can be asynchronous, encrypted, and other types. The API allows us to select the type we are requesting. Note that the default type of pipe is asynchronous and unidirectional.

The Pipe Service

The pipe service is obtained from your group via the following in the PeerGroup class:

```
PipeService getPipeService();
```

The class that is returned implements the PipeService interface. The UML diagram in Figure 3.16 shows the interface and the methods it contains. There are three types of methods in the interface—input pipe creation, output pipe creation, and a method to remove output pipe creation listeners (OutputPipeListener).

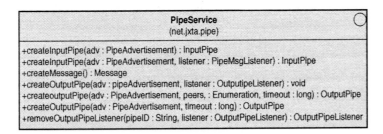

FIGURE 3.16 UML of PipeService interface.

PipeAdvertisement

Both input and output pipe creation methods use a pipe advertisement to create the pipe. The type of pipe is specified in the advertisement. The UML for the PipeAdvertisement is shown in Figure 3.17.

A pipe advertisement contains several pieces of information that will be used to find the pipe and to create the pipe. Specific implementations of the advertisement will contain additional information if required.

To find a pipe, the name is usually used, but the ID ensures that you have found a specific pipe.

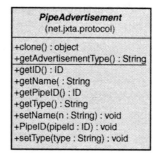

FIGURE 3.17   UML of PipeAdvertisement class.

The type of pipe is the most important for creation. There are many different types, and the initially supported types are propagate, secure, and non-blocking (these pipe types are explained fully in Chapter 2).

InputPipe

The InputPipe interface (shown in Figure 3.18) has a close method and two methods for receiving messages. The poll method waits for messages up to a certain timeout value. The waitForMessage method will wait indefinitely for a message.

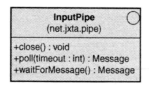

FIGURE 3.18   UML of InputPipe interface.

As you might guess, waiting for messages and polling for them will take a bit of work and possibly threads to process messages appropriately. The good news is that you can use the `PipeMsgListener` to listen to messages. We will cover `PipeMsgListener` later in this section.

`OutputPipe`

The `OutputPipe` interface, shown in Figure 3.19, is simpler as the `InputPipe` interface. The only two methods are `close` and `send`.

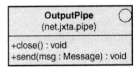

FIGURE 3.19   UML of `OutputPipe` interface.

One Way Pipes?

The initial representation of pipes are one way. The direction of a pipe flows from an output pipe on one peer to an input pipe on another peer. There are implementations of two way pipes, but they are really a wrapper around two pipes created in opposite directions.

The reason for pipes being one way is because of the nature of the P2P network. If the only pathway is via HTTP, full bi-directional capability is not easily created. Remember that HTTP is a response/request protocol. In fact, any bi-directional HTTP pipe is, by definition, a simulation.

Because many peers will be behind firewalls or other barriers, the most logical medium is HTTP. By creating an underlying protocol that can always be deconstructed into messages, the designers have ensured that most peers can be accessed. This also means that you can communicate to multiple peers using the same messages but different protocols. This may seem inefficient, but connectivity was preferred over speed.

The Pipe Process

Pipes are created in a specific order. The process is that the listener must open an input pipe before the talker creates an output pipe. If there is no input pipe available, an output pipe will fail because it cannot connect. This is very similar to a socket that needs to have a listener opened before another machine can connect to it.

The following is a sequence of events for a peer that waits for others to communicate with it:

1. Group advertises pipe advertisement.

2. Listener peer creates an input pipe from advertisement.

3. Talk peer creates output pipe addressed to the listener peer.

4. Talk peer sends message on pipe.

5. Listener peer receives message.

The following is the opposite:

1. Peer wanting information opens an input pipe.

2. Peer wanting information advertises the pipe.

3. Peer with data opens an output pipe to the input pipe.

4. Peer with output pipe sends data.

Connecting Pipes

There are two ways to connect pipes. First is a blind pipe and the second is a peer-addressed pipe. A blind pipe is no different from a stream opened on a port to accept the first caller to a server. A listener pipe is always blind and will accept a connection from any peer. Output pipes can be both blind and specifically addressed.

You may at first be uncomfortable with blind pipes, but they are not different from how we dealt with sockets in the traditional client server world. The one difference is that the resources are group based and not peer based in P2P. The peer you connect to in many P2P applications is not important. For example, a group of peers sharing storage or processing would not care who connected to what peer, only that they connected to a peer within the group that guarantees a resource.

Blind Output Pipe

Calling the following method in the pipe service creates a blind output pipe. The parameters are only the advertisement and a timeout that defines how long to wait for a connection. The timeout is the number of milliseconds to wait or, if -1, to wait forever:

```
OutputPipe createOutputPipe ( PipeAdvertisement adv
                        , long timeout)throws IOException;
```

This method will block until the pipe connects to an input pipe or the timeout occurs. If you look at the implementation, actual behavior will depend on the type of pipe in the pipe advertisement. For example, if the type is unspecified or if the advertisement type is `PipeService.UnicastType`, a non-blocking unicast pipe is created. Because there is no endpoint specified, the system just looks for the same pipe advertisement published by another peer and attempts a connection.

If the type of pipe is a propagate pipe, all peers in the group that have open input propagate pipes will simply listen for messages because you are not specifying a peer.

Propagate is much more a construct than a physical connection like the unicast pipe. There is not a specific search for peers with the same pipe, because messages are delivered by routing and not by a specific connection. The OutputPipe object returned would send messages to any peer that has an equivalent input pipe.

Remember that unicast and propagate pipes are unreliable. This means that you need to have code that accounts for dropped messages.

Blind Output Pipe with Listener

The method for creating a blind output pipe with a listener is a little different from one that directly returns a pipe. The key difference is that as peers are found, the listener is called with a new output pipe. The listener interface and the event class are shown in Figure 3.20.

The following is a simple interface that allows you to create output pipes as input pipes appear on other peers:

```
void createOutputPipe ( PipeAdvertisement adv
                    , OutputPipeListener listener)throws IOException;
```

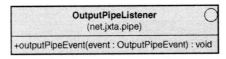

OutputPipeListener
(net.jxta.pipe)

+outputPipeEvent(event : OutputPipeEvent) : void

OutputPipeEvent
(net.jxta.pipe)

+getOutputPipe() : OutputPipe
+getPipeID() : String
+getQueryID() : int
+OutputPipeEvent(source : Object, outputpipe : OutputPipe, pipeID : String, queryID : int)

FIGURE 3.20   UML of OutputPipeListener interface and OutputPipeEvent class.

Addressed Output Pipe

With an addressed pipe, you are looking to connect with a specific peer. The create method will block until that peer is connected. If the peer cannot be found within a specific time, the creation fails.

The following method signature from the PipeService class adds an Enumeration of peers. Be careful to only pass in multiple peers if the pipe is a type of propagate pipe.:

```
OutputPipe createOutputPipe ( PipeAdvertisement adv
                        , Enumeration peers
                        , long timeout) throws IOException;
```

Blind Input Pipe

Input pipes are a bit different from output pipes because they are not addressed. In other words, they are always blind. The following method signature from the `PipeService` class returns an input pipe object. To receive a connection, you need to call the `waitForMessage` method that blocks until an output pipe on another peer attempts to connect.

```
InputPipe createInputPipe (PipeAdvertisement adv) throws IOException;
```

Blind Input Pipe with Listener

The signature for the next input pipe type allows you to specify a message listener. Note that this is not a listener for pipes but for messages. There is no need to process multiple output pipes connecting to the input pipe. The input pipe is only created to listen to one connection. If you want to accept messages on another peer, you need to create a new input pipe:

```
InputPipe createInputPipe ( PipeAdvertisement adv
                          , PipeMsgListener listener) throws IOException;
```

The UML of the listener and the listener event in Figure 3.21 shows how simple the system is. The listener's only method is `pipeMsgEvent`, which passes a `PipeMsgEvent` that, in turn, passes the `Message` object received.

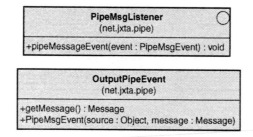

FIGURE 3.21   UML of `PipeMsgListener` interface and `PipeMsgEvent` class.

Unicast input pipes are simply waiting for messages sent to the propagate pipe's ID. For this reason, this method should return as soon as the pipe is initialized. Note that there may not ever be a corresponding propagate output pipe and the listener may never be called.

With the listener, there is no need to process messages by waiting. Instead, the listener is called every time a message is received. To remove a PipeMsgListener, close the input pipe.

CAUTION

The pipeMsgEvent method in your implementation of the PipeMsgListener must be thread safe. This method could easily become a bottleneck if the method is synchronized causing the thread to block for the entire run time of the method. Use synchronized blocks inside the method around shared objects. The method should be callable as soon as possible to process as many messages as possible.

Removing the Output Listener

To stop accepting requests for output pipes, you need to remove the listener. After the listener is removed, the output pipe is no longer available. The following is the signature for the removeOutputPipeListener method:

```
OutputPipeListener removeOutputPipeListener(String pipeID
                                    ,OutputPipeListener listener);
```

Messages

Messages are meant to be very simple containers of data. In the following lines, the message is created in the context of the pipe service. The data is created by adding a tag called Test and setting it with the raw bytes created from the "Hello, World!" string:

```
Message msg = peerGroup.getPipeService ().createMessage ();
msg.setBytes ("Test", "Hello, World!".getBytes ());
```

Bidirectional Pipes

The BidirectionalPipeService is an optional service that you can use to create bi-directional pipes. As we discussed when talking about one-way pipes, a bi-directional pipe is really two one-way pipes in complementary directions. The BidirectionalPipeService class and accompanying classes are shown in Figure 3.22.

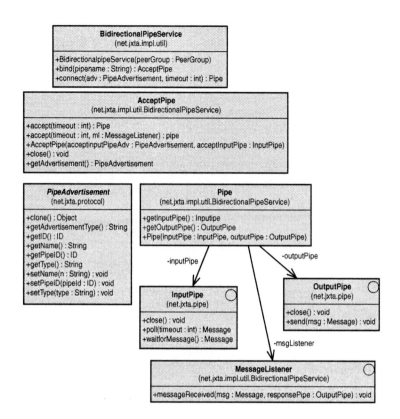

FIGURE 3.22   UML of `BidirectionalPipeService` and related classes and interfaces.

Wire Pipes (One-to-Many)

The `Wirepipe` class is used to create a pipe that will broadcast a copy of each message to each of a list of specified peers. Only peers that have accepted the pipe will receive messages.

Reliable Pipes

This `ReliablePipeService` class provides reliable message-delivery pipes. Each of the messages will be received in the order that they were sent, and the message is guaranteed to reach its destination. Reliable pipes can also be encrypted.

Peer Endpoint Protocol

Peer endpoint routing is not really a public API. Endpoint routing is used to enable pipes or simplistic messaging, such as that found in the peer info, peer resolver, and pipe binding protocols.

The EndpointService class provides a front-end API and environment to all endpoint protocols. Applications can use the Endpoint API directly to control or examine the topology of the JXTA network. The Endpoint API would normally be used to help implement a new endpoint protocol.

We will only touch on a few aspects of this protocol. The more interesting functionality to most JXTA developers is how routes are formed.

Use in Applications

In Chapter 2, we talked about the many reasons for routing in JXTA. You do not need to worry about using the actual protocol in your application. For example, the pipe binding protocol uses the Peer endpoint protocol to build routes. As a result, there is no need to supply the pipe with a route, just the other endpoint.

There are reasons for using the protocol directly if you are writing your own implementation of a pipe or other method of P2P communication. Knowing the protocol is also very important for understanding how routes are built.

Accessing the Service

To access the endpoint service, you get the service from your peer group as in the following line:

```
EndpointService getEndpointService();
```

The EndpointService interface (shown in Figure 3.23) contains multiple and very useful methods:

- addEndpointProtocol—This method allows us to add a new type of communication protocol.

- addFilterListener—Used to add a listener to filter endpoint messages.

- addListener—Used to listen for messages to a specific endpoint address.

- demux—Used to de-multiplex a message. Given an incoming message this method calls the appropriate listener by the destination returned by the getDestAddress() method of the message.

- getEndpointProtocolByName—This is a convenience method used to fetch an endpoint protocol.

- getEndpointProtocol—Returns an enumeration of endpoint protocols.

- getGroup—Returns the group of which this service is a member.

- GetMessenger—Creates an EndpointMessenger given an EndpointAddress. The messenger is used to send messages to the specific address defined by the EndpointAddress.

- newEndpointAddress—Creates a new endpoint at a specific URI.

- newMessage—Creates a message to be used to send a message to an endpoint.

- ping—Used to determine if a peer exists.

- propagate—Used to continue sending the message to other peers.

- removeEndpointProtocol—Uses to remove a protocol that is no longer valid.

- removeEndpointListener—Used to remove the endpoint listener.

- removeEndpointFilterListener—Used to remove the endpoint filter listener.

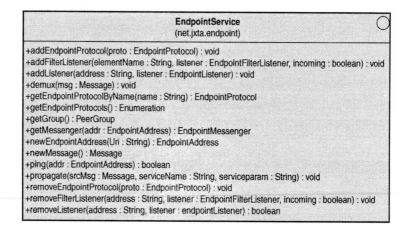

FIGURE 3.23   UML of EndpointService interface.

Filter Listener

The filter is a fun and useful part of the endpoint API. What the system allows you to do is snoop on any of the messages in the system. You simply specify an XML tag name, the listener, and a Boolean that specifies whether you are interested in oncoming or outgoing messages.

The following is the method from the `EndpointService` interface:

```
void addFilterListener(String elementName, EndpointFilterListener listener
                    , boolean incoming) throws IllegalArgumentException;
```

There is also an equivalent remove method:

```
void removeFilterListener( String address
                            , EndpointFilterListener listener
                            , Boolean incoming);
```

The listener is easy to use, as you can see by the UML diagram in Figure 3.24. The method gives you the message, the source address, and the destination address. Of course, the purpose of the listener is to filter messages. Consequently, the return value is a message. Normally, you would either modify the message or return a `null` if the message is to be blocked.

| EndpointFilterListener |
| (net.jxta.endpoint) |
| +processincomingMessage(message : Message, srcAddr : endpointAddress, dstAddr : EndpointAdress) : Message |

FIGURE 3.24   UML of `EndpointFilterListener` interface.

EndpointRouterMessage

One of the more interesting messages to listen for with the `EndpointFilterListener` is the `EndpointRouterMessage`. The message is used to build a path between gateway peers to connect endpoints. By looking for these messages, you can determine the route.

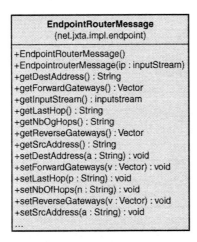

| EndpointRouterMessage |
| (net.jxta.impl.endpoint) |
| +EndpointRouterMessage() |
| +EndpointrouterMessage(ip : inputStream) |
| +getDestAddress() : String |
| +getForwardGateways() : Vector |
| +getInputStream() : inputstream |
| +getLastHop() : String |
| +getNbOgHops() : String |
| +getReverseGateways() : Vector |
| +getSrcAddress() : String |
| +setDestAddress(a : String) : void |
| +setForwardGateways(v : Vector) : void |
| +setLastHop(p : String) : void |
| +setNbOfHops(n : String) : void |
| +setReverseGateways(v : Vector) : void |
| +setSrcAddress(a : String) : void |
| ... |

FIGURE 3.25   UML of `EndpointRouterMessage` interface.

The messages that are passed between peers are the `EndpointRouterQuery`, `EndpointRouterAnswer`, and the `EndpointRoute` messages. Note that the `EndpointRouter` class is the source of these messages.

The query is used to request a route, and the answer is a response that contains a route to the destination peer. Note that there is no guarantee that there is a route to the peer, and you may not get the answer message.

The DTD specification for the `EndpointRouterQuery` message is as follows:

```
<!ELEMENT EndpointRouterQuery    (Credential,
                                  Dest,
                                  Cached)>
<!ELEMENT Credential     #PCDATA>
<!ELEMENT Dest           #PCDATA>
<!ELEMENT Cached         #PCDATA>
```

The DTD specification for the `EndpointRouterAnswer` message is as follows:

```
<!ELEMENT EndpointRouterAnswer   (Credential,
                                  Dest,
                                  RoutingPeer,
                                  RouterPeerAdv,
                                  Gateway)>
<!ELEMENT Credential     #PCDATA>
<!ELEMENT Dest           #PCDATA>
<!ELEMENT RoutingPeer    #PCDATA>
<!ELEMENT RouterPeerAdv  (PeerAdvertisement)>
<!ELEMENT Gateway        #PCDATA>
```

The DTD specification for the `EndpointRoute` message is as follows:

```
<!ELEMENT EndpointRoute  (Src,
                          Dest,
                          TTL,
                          Gateway)>
<!ELEMENT Src       #PCDATA>
<!ELEMENT Dest      #PCDATA>
<!ELEMENT TTL       #PCDATA>
<!ELEMENT Gateway   #PCDATA>
```

ping

Another useful method is ping. The method, shown next, simply takes an endpoint address and returns a Boolean value of true if the address can be reached:

```
boolean ping (EndpointAddress addr);
```

The ping method is not as useful as the ping you are used to in normal networking. This ping does not return any useful information; it only lets you know that can reach the peer. The actual processing may also be much different. For example, the ping method may return true if the peer knows about the peer in some endpoint protocols. In HTTP, you do not ping the client because you really can't do so. Remember that the HTTP client must initiate the connection. If you did this, you have no reasonable guarantee that the client will check the gateway any time soon. So, for the sake of time and effort, you assume you can talk to an HTTP endpoint if you find its gateway.

Given how an HTTP ping works, the quality of the ping method may seem suspect compared to a traditional network ping that always connects to a machine if successful. However, the usefulness of ping is that it is implemented by each of the protocols. This essentially gives you a transmission protocol-independent ability to test for an endpoint. In JXTA, this is the primary goal, so other aspects, such as the actual connection or timing, is less important. Simply put, ping is less a network ping than a test for existence according to the protocol implemented by the endpoint.

Depending on the protocol of the endpoint, you may be able to sniff a returning ping message with the filter listener. You should look at the specific implementation of the protocol to understand what the message looks like.

If you are looking for a traditional ping, you will need to implement it yourself. Your ping will only work with peers in your group with your ping code.

EndpointMessenger

One method of the EndpointService interface that is very useful for applications is getMessenger. The getMessenger method takes an endpoint and returns an object that implements an EndpointMessenger interface. The EndpointMessenger (UML seen in Figure 3.26), has two methods—close and sendMessage. Messages sent via the sendMessage method are processed by an EndpointListener that will be covered in a moment.

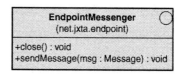

FIGURE 3.26   UML for `EndpointMessenger` interface.

The EndpointMessenger should seem very familiar to you from the previous discussion of output pipes. The simple fact is that a pipe can use the `EndpointMessenger` code implemented by the endpoint.

To get an endpoint messenger, you must first create an endpoint address. You do this with the following method in the `EndpointService`:

```
EndpointAddress newEndpointAddress (String uri);
```

The URI in this case is a unique string. The URI consists of a unique identifier that should be distinguishable between groups and services. For example, you could use the peer group ID and a service name like `Message Queue`. You could further refine the address by concatenating the peer group id, the service name, and a third parameter, such as a sequence number. In this way, you could create multiple addresses on a single endpoint. This is similar to how you would implement a type of pipe and create multiple pipe connections.

To retrieve the messenger, you supply the `EndpointAddress` object you created with the `newEndpointAddress` method, as seen by the following method signature from the `EndpointService` interface:

```
EndpointMessenger getMessenger (EndpointAddress addr) throws IOException;
```

Where Is the Router?

You might ask, if this is the endpoint router, where is the router? The router is deep in the bowels of this API and is actually a part of the platform as a module. The `getMessenger` method eventually results in the execution of methods to obtain a route between peers. The UML for the `EndpointRouter` is shown in Figure 3.27.

You can access the `EndpointRouter` by calling the `loadModule` method on your peer group. The following is an example that creates a router for a peer group:

```
EndpointRouter router;
router = peerGroup.loadModule( "net.jxta.impl.endpoint.EndpointRouter"
                    , Platform.refRouterProtoSpecID
                    , PeerGroup.Both);
```

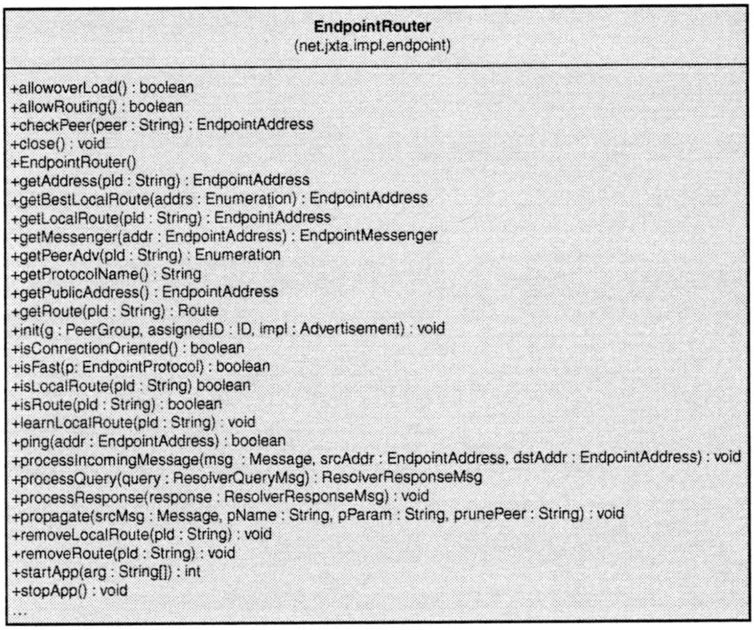

FIGURE 3.27   UML of EndpointRouter class.

NOTE

Note that there is no need to access the router in your code. The router is access via other classes in the JXTA API.

Endpoint Listener

There is another listener interface you can use. The addListener method in the EndpointService interface adds an incoming message listener to a specifically named address that is usually formed by concatenating the name of the invoking service and a parameter unique to that service across all groups.

The listener is called when you send a message through an EndpointMessenger to an EndpointAddress constructed with matching serviceName and serviceParam.

The address parameter is really the same string used to create the EndpointAddress. Although the parameters are called two different things, uri and address, they are the same thing (expect the parameter names to be one or the other in a future version).

The following is the method signature from the `EndpointService` interface:

```
public void addListener( String address
                      , EndpointListener listener
                      ) throws IllegalArgumentException;
```

The method may throw an `IllegalArgumentException` if the address is deemed incorrect by the protocol.

The `EndpointListener` interface is shown in Figure 3.28.

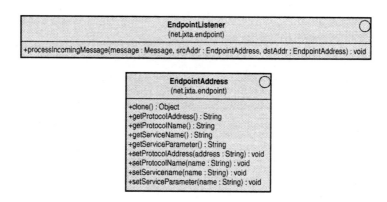

FIGURE 3.28   UML of `EndpointListener` interface and `EndpointAddress` class used to process endpoint messages.

Summary

The key areas of the JXTA API are the peer group, discovery, and pipes. In addition, the peer resolver API can be used for generic queries. Other APIs may be useful, but are less frequently used in most applications. You can also debug by using the listener interfaces of discovery, resolver, and endpoint APIs. We did not cover the authentication service in the peer group API because it had not been implemented.

You now have an overview of the JXTA core API. We have covered a lot of ground. In the following chapters, we will cover much of the API in more depth, in the context of applications and advanced examples.

4

JXTA Shell

By Darren Govoni

The term *shell* historically refers to an encapsulating layer or interface around a kernel or core as it is sometimes called. Its primary role is to provide an interface boundary to a user or other programs. Traditionally, shells provide scripting languages that can batch together many of the common commands one would execute by hand from an interactive shell interface. Internally, there will be an API such that programs can call out to the shell and use some of the mechanisms the shell provides, such as environment space and process execution. As such, the user has interactive access to the core services of the operating system and can load, execute, and unload applications and modules as needed.

This chapter will introduce you to the JXTA shell and various aspects of it such as installing, running, using, and so on. It is not intended to be a complete primer on the JXTA shell, but it will help you get started using it nonetheless.

Why Shell?

The JXTA shell defines a local environment (or execution context) through which peer applications can run and interact. Just as you use your desktop operating system to run and manage your files and applications, JXTA shell allows you to control P2P applications and services. Unlike the desktop, the JXTA platform extends to other computers.

The process of building, running, and debugging P2P applications can be complicated for a variety of reasons. P2P systems are *distributed systems*, and distributed systems are hard to instantiate and meter in controlled environments. Typically, processes scattered across a network need to be simultaneously monitored, measured, or managed to effectively understand the collective behavior of a system.

The shell provides a common looking glass through which JXTA shell applications can be controlled and executed. Running and testing applications becomes much easier, allowing you to access and combine them in a single context. This speeds development considerably. Finally, because most developers are familiar with other shell-like interfaces, such as DOS or Unix shells (such as bsh, csh, tcsh), the JXTA shell should be a familiar metaphor. Note that the JXTA shell itself is a JXTA application and not a mandatory aspect of using JXTA.

Installation and Troubleshooting

Now we will introduce you to installing the shell and work through some potential problems you might encounter while configuring and possibly running the JXTA platform.

Installing the Shell

Installing the shell is quite straightforward and easy. The installation procedure is subject to change as the JXTA platform and installation processes evolve. These steps are meant as guidelines to follow; more specific actions might be needed to complete the installation.

NOTE

For the most up-to-date information on installing and configuring the shell, refer to
http://shell.jxta.org.

Following are steps and resources for the "quick and easy" installation. More details about this process can be viewed at http://download.jxta.org/easyinstall/install.html.

After you have downloaded the requisite install file, open a DOS or shell window (or what have you) and change the directory (cd) to the home directory of the downloaded file. Table 4.1 indicates the execute command for each platform you should see.

TABLE 4.1   Platform-Specific Commands of Executing Installation File

Platform	Without VM	With VM
Windows/DOS	JXTAInst_VM.exe	JXTAInst.exe
Solaris	sh ./JXTAInst.bin	sh ./JXTAInst_Sol_VM.bin
Linux	sh ./JXTAInst.bin	sh ./JXTAInst_LNX_VM.bin
Unix	sh ./JXTAInst.bin	Download the latest J2SE from java.sun.com

For other flavors of Unix, the following procedure might be required:

1. After downloading, type

   ```
   jre -cp JXTA_Demo.zip install
   ```

2. If that doesn't work, try

   ```
   jre -classpath [path to]classes.zip:JXTA_Demo.zip install
   ```

3. If that doesn't work either, on sh-like shells, try

   ```
   cd [to directory where JXTA_Demo.zip is located]
   CLASSPATH= [path to]classes.zip:JXTA_Demo.zip
   export CLASSPATH
   java install
   ```

   Or for csh-like shells, try

   ```
   cd [to directory where JXTA_Demo.zip is located]
   setenv CLASSPATH [path to]classes.zip:JXTA_Demo.zip
   java install
   ```

> **NOTE**
>
> Command syntax may vary from what is listed.

For generic platforms, you should download the demo archive, change the directory to where it is stored, and add JXTA_Demo.zip to your CLASSPATH. Then execute Java using the Java main class called install.

Running the Shell

After you have installed the shell, running it should be simple. For the Windows platform, there is a jxta.exe file located in the shell/shell directory beneath the root of your installation. Other platforms may vary on the executable name that should reside in the same place.

If all goes well, you should see the JXTA Configurator screen (hereto referred to simply as the Configurator) as JXTA boots for the first time. From this window, you need to configure important aspects of your JXTA peer.

The Configurator is divided into four sections—Basics, Advanced, Rendezvous/Routers, and security. For typical network configurations, you will likely only need to supply your peer name on the Basics Settings portion of the Configurator. For situations where there is a NAT, firewall, or proxy, you will need to use the Advanced Settings. The Rendezvous/Routers section should be used for more advanced configuration where you have specific peers that help you connect to the JXTA network. The Rendezvous/Routers section is most often used to create a local P2P network or a test network of peers on a single machine. Lastly, the Security tab will ask you for a login name and password to identify you and protect your peer from unauthorized access.

After you have selected OK, configuration files and directories will be written to disk and the platform will boot. Before the platform fully boots, you will be presented with a security login dialog that requests the name and password you chose in the Configurator dialog. After entering the proper login name and password, you should soon see the JXTA Shell console appear. It might take a few moments to initially come up as it attempts to determine aspects of your network necessary for proper function.

Common Problems and Solutions

Considering the possible variations in your platform and network configuration, the following sections will highlight some likely problems you might have to address. You will get an overview of the configuration process for the JXTA platform, the pertinent files in this process, and some guidelines and troubleshooting tips when problems might be encountered.

Configuration Files

When any JXTA application is started, the base platform will attempt to resolve some configuration settings. When you run the shell for the first time, you will not have any default settings, and JXTA will display a dialog window that will allow you to set mandatory and optional settings (see Figure 4.1). The Configurator will also be displayed if certain files are not present.

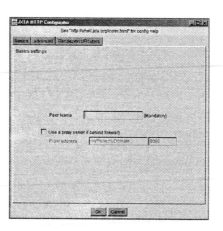

FIGURE 4.1   JXTA Configurator.

The important configuration file involved in starting the JXTA platform (and therefore the shell) is the `PlatformConfig` file. If the `PlatformConfig` file is not present, the JXTA Configurator is presented and the `PlatformConfig` file is created. The `PlatformConfig` file is an XML file that records your network and JXTA platform configuration specific to your peer. This file is required for JXTA to boot properly.

NOTE

You will likely see the Configurator if your network address or other aspects of your network configuration have changed, possibly because you rebooted or changed networks entirely.

It's difficult to pinpoint exactly the types of problems you might encounter. Generally, the boot process is robust. Because there can be problems with certain network configurations, the following are some actions to follow in case you're experiencing difficulty getting the shell or platform to boot and/or execute properly:

NOTE

Sometimes JXTA applications may not seem to work, but are actually just slow to respond. The discovery of remote peers and services may take several minutes to complete. Be careful to wait long enough for things to happen.

- Anomalies may appear if your configuration is corrupt or not set correctly. If this is suspected, try removing the `PlatformConfig` file and restart.

- Anytime you suspect a configuration file is corrupt or you have changed your configuration settings, it's a good idea to also remove the `cm` directory in your platform root directory (see the "Caching" section, later in this chapter).

- Another problem might occur when the configuration points to a router or rendezvous that is currently offline. You can help prevent this problem by running a shell on another machine (or on the same machine using different ports) to ensure a connection.

- Because JXTA is being developed openly and is subject to frequent change, the JXTA managers maintain a development P2P network to help mitigate affects. This network uses different routers and rendezvous. Whether you are using the code from the code in development or from the released branch, the configuration should automatically select the routers and rendezvous that are compatible.

- The network will not be static while JXTA undergoes fine tuning. Beware that if you are using either the development or the production applications, a new release will cause the production routers and rendezvous to switch to those with an incompatible protocol. You should make sure you are running with the most up-to-date platform code.

Firewalls

JXTA is designed to work with firewalls, which is to say from either side. If you are running JXTA behind a firewall, you will need to configure the HTTP transport mechanism in the JXTA Configurator. In most cases, this is done by enabling the HTTP transport (checking the box titled Enabled under the HTTP setting section of the dialog in the Advanced section). At least one active HTTP router is needed to discover remote peers and should be provided automatically as well.

In either event, the Configurator can download an active list for you. This is done by clicking the Download Gateways and Rendezvous Lists button on the Rendezvous/ Routers section of the Configurator dialog. Otherwise, you can find a list of active routers by visiting http://shell.jxta.org/quick.html#install.

If you are behind a firewall, you might also be required to use your HTTP proxy server (within your network) to gain visibility beyond your LAN. The JXTA Configurator might auto-recognize your proxy server and enable it for you; otherwise, you will have to select the Use a Proxy Server box in the Basics Settings section. If you do this manually, be sure to provide the precise IP address and port on which the proxy is listening. Check with your system administrator to find the address and port of your HTTP enabled proxy server.

> **NOTE**
>
> Be sure to know these details about your network before configuring the Advanced settings in the JXTA shell, because it will determine whether you have visibility to other JXTA peers and networks. Beware of personal firewalls too, which can be very restrictive.

If you have followed these guidelines and are still experiencing problems, it is possible that some of the default HTTP routers are not functioning. One possibility is that the default list has become outdated or the routers are experiencing difficulty. In this case, you should select the Advanced portion of the Configurator and designate additional HTTP routers that can forward traffic to and from your peer (providing you know of some!). A list of reliable HTTP routers can always be retrieved from http://www.jxta.org.

Rendezvous Peers

As mentioned before, rendezvous peers are designed to facilitate long-range discovery of peers, typically residing on different networks or subnets. Within the Configurator, you can specify a list of rendezvous addresses. These will be required if you are behind a firewall.

The entire list is used by the platform, so all indicated rendezvous are eligible. As with HTTP routers for communication through firewalls and across networks, a list of rendezvous peers can be dynamically downloaded through the Advanced section using the Download Gateways and Rendezvous Lists button to update your tables.

There are two main types of rendezvous characterized by their supported transport mechanisms—namely, TCP/IP and HTTP. In either case, you must indicate both the IP address and port on which the rendezvous is running; otherwise, your peer will not see the rendezvous and other peers.

If you cannot see other peers or groups you feel should exist, one or some of the rendezvous you are using might be inoperable. Double-check your list of rendezvous or check `http://platform.jxta.org/java/rendezvous.html` for a list of active rendezvous.

If you find that the rendezvous server address you are using is not one of those listed at `http://shell.jxta.org/quick.html#install`, remove your `PlatformConfig` file and re-run JXTA using the JXTA Configurator to add new routers or rendezvous from the Rendezvous/Routers section. Running `peerconfig` within the shell and restarting has the same effect.

NAT

Network Address Translation (NAT) is designed to mask IP address details within your network from the outside world. If you are behind a NAT device, you will need to enable the HTTP transport for your peer or rendezvous. For most intents and purposes, JXTA's handling of NATs is identical to firewalls. If you also use a proxy server, you must configure it within the Configurator as well. See the "Firewalls" section, later in this chapter, for more details.

Caching

The cache management system provided by JXTA makes use of the `cm` directory in your peer root directory. It is recommended that, whenever your configuration changes, you remove this directory to avoid any stale references or ID collisions, especially when testing peer services.

> **NOTE**
>
> When the platform boots successfully, it will recreate the `cm` and `pse` directories.

Reconfiguring

Whenever you feel you need to reconfigure your settings and have already configured and run the shell, use the `peerconfig` command within the shell and then restart JXTA. The `peerconfig` command is explained in more detail next.

Release Notes and Updates

Finally, it is a good idea to consult the release notes located at `http://shell.jxta.org/release.html` that may contain changes to shell installs or configures for the version you have downloaded. Additional updates will also be available at `http://www.samspublishing.com`.

Configuring Multiple Peers on One Machine

If you intend to write JXTA peer services and applications, it is inevitable you will want to run and test them in a multi-peer environment. One way of doing this is to simply use multiple machines on a network. Conveniently, you might choose to run multiple peers on a single machine. In this case, you must follow a few simple steps:

1. Ensure that you have *separate* installations of JXTA residing in *separate* top-level directories. That is, do not locate one installation in a sub-directory of another to avoid any possible conflicts.

2. When you run each JXTA shell and see the JXTA Configurator dialog appear, select the Advanced tab and ensure that the TCP and HTTP ports do not conflict with other peers. By default, they will try to be 9701 and 9700, respectively. If you have done this properly, you should be able to boot JXTA within each installation directory without any conflicts.

3. If you are able to boot multiple shells on the same machine but cannot see other peers on your machine, try removing the cm directory in each shell directory and restarting the shell. If the problem persists, delete the PlatformConfig file and make sure the Manual check box in the TCP and HTTP settings sections is not selected. This will force JXTA to auto-detect these settings and that might solve your problem.

Shell Commands

The JXTA shell comes equipped with a variety of useful commands for interacting with the JXTA platform and JXTA shell applications. Many of these commands resemble the ones you've used in Unix, such as man, who, whoami, history, and so on. In addition to those, other commands specific to JXTA allow the shell user to create messages, pipes, and advertisements and manipulate them in interesting ways, all from a single shell console. This ability, along with the ability to extend the shell by adding your own commands or applications, makes it quite a powerful tool for building P2P systems.

Table 4.2 highlights some of the default shell commands.

TABLE 4.2 Common Shell Commands

Command	Description
cat	Display the content of an environment variable.
chpgrp	Change the default peer group.
clear	Clear the shell's screen.
env	Display all environment variables.
exit	Exit the shell.

TABLE 4.2   Continued

Command	Description
exportfile	Export a shell variable into an external file.
get	Extract a message tag body from a pipe message.
grep	Search for matching patterns.
groups	Discover and list peer groups.
history	Recall previous issued commands.
importfile	Import an external file into a shell variable.
join	Join a new peer group.
leave	Leave a peer group.
man	Online man page about commandsmkadv
	Make a new pipe or peer group advertisement.
mkmsg	Make a new pipe message.
mkpgrp	Make a new peer group.
mkpipe	Make a new pipe.
more	Browse or page through a Shell object.
peerconfig	Reset the peer configuration.
peers	Discover and list peers.
put	Put a new tag body into a pipe message.
recv	Receive a pipe message.
rdvstatus	Show connected rendezvous peers.
search	Search a shared advertisement in a peer group.
send	Send a pipe message.
setenv	Set the value of an environment variable.
share	Share an advertisement in a peer group.
shell	Fork a new shell.
talk	Instant messaging talk command.
version	Display version and build info.
wc	Count lines, words, and characters.
who	Display member identity in a peer group.
whoami	Display peer and peer group information.

You will find a few of these commands useful immediately, so they are discussed in the following sections. More detailed explanations of these and other commands can always be found at http://shell.jxta.org.

The peers Command

peers [-r][-p *peerName*][-n limit][-a *TagName*][-v *TagValue*][-f]

The peers command tells you what peers are currently visible to your peer, which is to say, your shell platform peer. If your list of rendezvous servers is current and there are active servers with registered peers, you should begin to see lists of peers.

```
JXTA>peers
peer0: name = vunix
peer1: name = vu
peer2: name = cq
peer3: name = bensondemo
JXTA>
```

If you do not see any peers right away, issue peers -r, which sends a peer discovery message across the JXTA network through rendezvous servers and possibly other peers. This request is asynchronous and propagates through peers, gathering advertisements for peers and delivering them to your local cache. As such, peer discovery will occur over a period of time. Typing peers at various intervals should reveal a growing list of visible peers (providing more peers are being discovered).

If you do this and still do not see any peers, you might not be connected to a JXTA rendezvous host. Refer to the previous suggestions on configuring rendezvous. In addition, issuing the rdvstatus command will provide details about your active rendezvous connections.

The peerinfo **Command**

peerinfo [-p *peerid*][-r] [-l][-f]

The peerinfo command can be used to get information about JXTA peers. Regardless of whether the peer is in a specific group or at a concrete location, peerinfo can request and display information about a peer or many peers. For example,

```
JXTA> peerinfo -r
peer info message sent
JXTA> peerinfo -l
stored peerinfo0
JXTA> cat -p peerinfo0
<?xml version "1.0"?>
<!DOCTYPE jxta: PeerInfoAdvertisement>
<jxta:PeerInforAdvertisement>
      <sourcePid>
            jxta://5969795949393934949493030292929393932
      </sourcePid>
      <targetPid>
            jxta://5969393939292921919043949303943929290
      </targetPid>
      <uptime>
            512
```

```
      </uptime>
</jxta:PeerInfoAdvertisement>
JXTA>
```

The groups Command

```
groups [-r][-p peerName][-n limit][-a TagName][-v TagValue][-f]
```

Group discovery is identical to peer discovery in the command usage and basic operation. Issuing groups -r will issue a group discovery message that finds group advertisements across the JXTA network:

```
JXTA>groups -r                    // send out a network request for group ads
group discovery message sent
JXTA>groups                   // still no groups seen
JXTA>groups                   // now some groups are showing up
group0: name = JxtaWire.
group1: name = ANewGroup
JXTA>
```

You will notice that both peers and groups are prefixed with unique local identifiers such as peer0, peer1, and group0, group1, and so on. These entities are actually uniquely identified with special JXTA UUIDs that are typically not human friendly. As such, a way of indicating with precision the peer or group you might perform an operation on is useful. Furthermore, because peers can have the same human readable name, it is necessary to employ this mechanism locally.

The rdvstatus Command

```
rdvstatus
```

rdvstatus indicates the status of your rendezvous connections. It is necessary to have active rendezvous connections to discover peers, groups, and services outside your local network. The shell console output of rdvstatus is as follows:

```
JXTA>rdvstatus
======= Rendezvous status ======
This peer is connected to the following rendezvous:
Rendezvous id: jxta://59616261646162614A78746150325033760AAE534B1E42F6AAC2A29
➥1225F52E00000000000000000000000000000000000000000000000000000000000000301

This peer is not a rendezvous
JXTA>
```

The `peerconfig` Command

`peerconfig` is used when you need to reconfigure your peer. This command removes relevant configuration files. When you reboot JXTA, the Configurator is then displayed.

Using the Shell

Using the shell is easy. It's no different than DOS in that it provides a blinking cursor and prompt from which to enter commands. Fortunately (or unfortunately, depending on who you are), most of us are acquainted with this metaphor and it shouldn't be intimidating. As you'd expect, typing a command causes that particular JXTA application to run. Like a true shell architecture, the commands are actually tiny applications that run in the shell's context. This context provides things like environment variables and resource bindings to separate it from other co-existing contexts. Therefore, it's important to know that the commands you run when using the shell are actually JXTA shell applications.

Starting Out

For a complete listing of shell commands bundled with shell, use the man command that produces output like the following:

```
    JXTA> man
The following is the list of commands available:
  cat        Display the content of an environment variable
  chpgrp     Change the default peer group
  clear      Clear the shell's screen
  env        Display all environment variables
  exit       Exit the Shell
  exportfile Export a Shell variable into an external file
  get        Extract a message tag body from a pipe message
  grep       Search for matching patterns
  groups     Discover and list peer groups
  history    Use history to recall previous issued commands
  man        Use man to display man pages about commands
  importfile Import an external file into a Shell variable
  join       Join a new peer group
  leave      Leave a peer group
  man        On-line man page about commands
  mkadv      Make a new pipe or peer group advertisement
  mkmsg      Make a new pipe message
  mkpgrp     make a new peer group
  mkpipe     Make a new pipe
```

```
more        Browse or page through a Shell object
peerconfig  Peer configuration
peers       Discover and list peers
put         Put a new tag body into a pipe message
recv        Receive a pipe message
rdvstatus   Show connected rendezvous peers
search      Search a shared advertisement in a peer group
send        Send a pipe message
setenv      Set the value of an environment variable
share       Share an advertisement in a peer group
Shell       Fork a new Shell
talk        Instant messaging talk command
version     Display version and build info
wc          Count lines, words, and characters
who         Display member identity in a peer group
whoami      Display peer and peer group information

JXTA>
```

Additional information about individual commands can be obtained by using man <cmd>.

> **NOTE**
>
> Comments have been added to the output and will not actually appear in your console.

The following session transcript demonstrates some basic activities, such as searching for peers, groups, creating a group, and joining that group:

```
JXTA>peers                    // displays peers visible to me at this moment
peer0: name = vunix
peer1: name = vu
peer2: name = cq
peer3: name = bensondemo
peer4: name = ecerami
peer5: name = peer1           // This is the name of my peer
peer6: name = rdv4 coloc linux
peer7: name = ajoukiller
peer8: name = dI_lab1
JXTA>groups                   // no groups appear to be visible at the moment
JXTA>groups -r                // send out a network request for group ads
group discovery message sent
JXTA>groups                   // still no groups seen
```

```
JXTA>groups                        // now some groups are showing up
group0: name = JxtaWire.
group1: name = ANewGroup
JXTA>mkpgrp mynewgroup                  // make my own group 'mynewgroup'
JXTA>groups                        // more group advertisements arrive
group0: name = ANewGroup
group1: name = fred
group2: name = vunix
group3: name = JxtaWire.kdroom
group4: name = MDE
group5: name = cookie
group6: name = mynewgroup          // notice my new group
JXTA>join mynewgroup                  // joining my group
Enter the identity you want to use when joining this peergroup (nobody)
1Identity : mypersona
JXTA>peers
peer0: name = vunix
peer1: name = vu
peer2: name = cq
peer3: name = bensondemo
peer4: name = ecerami
peer5: name = peer1
peer6: name = rdv4 coloc linux
peer7: name = ajoukiller
peer8: name = dI_lab1
JXTA>
```

stdin, stdout, stdgroup

Like traditional operating system shells, the JXTA shell initializes a stdin and stdout
through which shell commands can send and receive input and output, and these
are maintained in the shell environment. In addition to these standard I/O objects,
the shell provides stdgroup that refers to the group in which the shell is running.

Pipes

Commands can be linked together using shell pipes that connect the stdout used by
one shell command to the stdin used by the next shell command, separated by the
pipe. Using re-direction operators > and <, the cardinality of inputs to outputs can be
manipulated for any given command sequence.

The standard format for all commands including these operators is as follows:

command [< *pipe*] [>*pipe*] *options arguments* ;

where

> redirects the output

< redirects the input

; is a command separator

This can produce a variety of ad hoc I/O flows between shell applications. The following example pipes the output of man to the input of wc (word count), which then outputs to the default stdout that is the console:

```
JXTA> man | wc -w
        76
JXTA>
```

The | operator is a shortcut for flowing the output to the input in a left to right fashion on the command line.

Piping can also be done in both directions. For example,

```
command1 <> command2
```

is equivalent to

```
command1 >p1 <p2 ; command2 <p1 >p2
```

Where p1 and p2 persist the I/O between each command execution. For example,

```
cat >p1 afile ; grep <p1 someword
```

Pipes are useful for a variety of purposes, but they mainly serve to flow data between applications that are executing. As such, pipes can flow data from other applications, variables, environment objects, or data streams, such as files.

Environment

Another important aspect about the shell is the environment it maintains. The *environment* is a collection of variables available to all shell applications over time.

To see the current variable in the environment, use the env command. Setting variables is done with the = operator. For example,

```
JXTA> myvar = mkmsg
```

assigns a new message to the variable named myvar. mkmsg is a command that creates a new message. The resulting environment space is as follows:

```
JXTA>env
stdin = Default InputPipe (class net.jxta.impl.shell.ShellInputPipe)
SHELL = Root Shell (class net.jxta.impl.shell.bin.Shell.Shell)
History = History (class net.jxta.impl.shell.bin.history.HistoryQueue)
Shell = Root Shell (class net.jxta.impl.shell.bin.Shell.Shell)
stdout = Default OutputPipe (class net.jxta.impl.shell.ShellOutputPipe)
consout = Default OutputPipe (class net.jxta.impl.shell.ShellOutputPipe)
consin = Default InputPipe (class net.jxta.impl.shell.ShellInputPipe)
stdgroup = Default Group (class net.jxta.impl.peergroup.ShadowPeerGroup)
instjars = Installed Jar Files (class java.lang.String)
myvar = Message (class net.jxta.impl.endpoint.MessageImpl)
JXTA>
```

Using the shell can be simple and straightforward, yet it is a powerful environment and tool for manipulating JXTA entities, data, and applications. For details beyond the scope of this chapter, refer to the technical documentation at
http://www.jxta.org/project/www/docs/TechShellOverview.pdf.

Adding Shell Commands

Adding new commands to the shell is simple. The shell environment provides a set of useful base classes and interfaces with which to work. For the purpose of adding new commands, you must extend net.jxta.impl.shell.ShellApp. This class implements the core JXTA Application interface used by all JXTA peer applications. It also provides hooks into the shell's environment, including access to the input and output facilities as well as the environment variable space.

Listing 4.1 presents the everlasting Hello World example in the form of a JXTA shell application. The classname is hello, which corresponds to the command name in the shell.

LISTING 4.1   Hello Shell Command Source Code

```
package net.jxta.impl.shell.bin.hello;

import net.jxta.impl.shell.*;

import java.io.*;
import java.util.*;

import net.jxta.pipe.*;
import net.jxta.document.*;
import net.jxta.protocol.*;
import net.jxta.endpoint.*;
```

LISTING 4.1   Continued

```java
/**
 * Our first shell command
 */
public class hello extends ShellApp {

    /**
     * For access to the shell environment
     */
    ShellEnv env;

    public hello() {
    }

    /**
     * Called when the shell application stops running.
     */
    public void stopApp () {
    }

    /**
     * Called when the shell application is launched in the shell.
     */
    public int startApp (String[] args) {

        env = getEnv();

        if(args.length==2 && "-store".equals(args[0])) {

            // Create a new shell object and add it to the environment
            // variable space
            env.add("helloname", new ShellObject(null,args[1]));
            println("stored name");
        }
        if(args.length==0) {
            // Retrieve the shell object with label 'helloname'
            // If it's not null use it
            ShellObject nameObj = env.get("helloname");
            if(nameObj==null) {
                println ("Hello World!!");
            } else {
                println("Hi "+(String)nameObj.getObject()+"!");
            }
        }
```

LISTING 4.1   Continued

```
            // Return no error
            return ShellApp.appNoError;
    }


    /**
     * Returns a description of this command.
     */
    public String getDescription() {
        return "Says hello to the world!";
    }


    /**
     * Called to trigger help (e.g. when doing a 'man hello')
     */
    public void help() {
        println("hello [-store name]");
    }
}
```

The shell command applications reside exclusively in the net.jxta.impl.shell.bin package. Therefore, the source file path is net/jxta/impl/shell/bin/hello/hello.java. The main class of any command takes the following format:

net.jxta.impl.shell.bin.<cmd>.<cmd>.class

where <cmd> is the name of your command.

Create a jar file of your new command called <cmd>.jar and use the shell command instjar <path_to_jar> to install it in the shell.

For convenience, you can create or edit the .jshrc file in your shell startup directory and add the following line:

instjar <path_to_jar>

where <path_to_jar> is the fully qualified path to the jar file. After you have taken these steps, reboot the shell and type your command at the prompt.

What follows is a complete transcript of the installation and execution of our shell command:

```
JXTA>instjar C:\jxtanew3\tests\hello.jar
JXTA>hello
Hello World!!
JXTA>hello -store you
stored name
JXTA>hello
Hi you!
JXTA>
```

Summary

In this chapter, you learned what the shell is and why the shell is used to add and access P2P services. The shell console provides a portal through which anyone can interact with P2P services and applications, debugging and exploring the state of their P2P network.

You also should have a sense for how the shell is installed and configured for your particular platform. The chapter also covered common pitfalls as well as a few transcripts from basic shell sessions.

Some of the common starter commands were discussed as well as some programming aspects about the shell, such as stdin, stdout, the environment, and using pipes. Although the chapter only touched the surface on these subjects, you should feel ready to dig deeper into these areas.

There will be new commands added to the shell by many other programmers and companies. Participate in the related mailing lists at www.jxta.org to keep posted on current developments regarding the shell and shell extensions.

The shell is a great platform for testing and experimenting with JXTA. By using the shell, you can create and test new services quickly by using the provided shell API. Because it was designed for testing and exploration, you should think about the shell as your first stop when designing any new P2P service.

5

JXTA `ping` Command

By Darren Govoni

In Chapter 4, "JXTA Shell," you were introduced to aspects of the JXTA shell, including its purpose, general use, and adding a simple shell command. Now you will take a closer look at shell application programming by building a useful command for pinging JXTA peers.

`ping`

The `ping` command is designed to work much like traditional ping, which sends message packets to a remote host identified by an IP or DNS address. Ping then waits for replies from the host and measures the amount of time involved in the roundtrip. We will extend this simple model of ping in a number of ways, which should give you a better understanding of programming the pertinent facilities in JXTA. Our version of the `ping` command provides the following additional features:

- Ability to ping multiple peers in sequence

- Ability to do anonymous pings

- Asynchronous operation

- Client and server modes

Our `ping` will allow you to specify multiple peers on the same command line. It will then attempt to ping each peer. This is reasonable now that we operate asynchronously. `ping` will not have to wait for long periods before proceeding to the next peer, and all peers can have ping requests sent to them in sequence.

Anonymous pings are ping requests sent to special propagate pipes where the peer names are not known in advance. All peers listening on the propagate pipe will respond when they receive a ping request. As ping replies arrive from various peers, they are handled automatically by threaded handlers.

Our JXTA ping must operate asynchronously and, in fact, that is a feature of this program. In peer networks, latencies can be higher than traditional networks and whether a given peer is alive or not cannot be restricted to a particular time window. If the timeout period is shorter than the roundtrip time for a ping request, it will always time out and the peer will not reveal it is indeed alive. Indeed, all of JXTA is founded on the notion of unreliable, asynchronous messaging at its core layers, just like network protocols.

Command Overview

Before we get into the design and code details of our JXTA ping command, let's discuss its command line format and how it compares and contrasts to original ping.

Traditionally, the ping command appears as follows:

```
ping <host address>
```

where <host address> is an IP or DNS address. Ping requests are delivered across Internet Communication Messaging Protocol (ICMP) and processed by TCP/IP endpoint stacks, so they operate below application layer communication mechanisms.

The original ping utility provides useful timing information about the response of a particular host and the network connectivity to and from it. Our ping command, however, is an application and uses the JXTA facilities to simulate traditional ping. Nonetheless, the information returned by our ping will be useful in assessing latencies between peers using the JXTA protocols and determining if peers are alive (which is to say, listening for ping requests). It will tell us how long it takes a given peer to respond to our message.

Our version takes the following format:

```
ping [-listen] [-propagate] [<peername> <peername> …]
```

As noted earlier, you can supply more than one *peername* to ping. For pings to be heard, however, a peer must be set up to run in server mode making the peer *pingable*. To do this, you must issue the following variation:

```
ping -listen
```

This should return you to the JXTA prompt immediately because it spawns a handler thread to listen on a message input pipe for this particular peer. As ping requests arrive on the pipe, they are replied to. You must use the -listen option before your peer can be pinged.

Project Overview

The following list represents the phased approach we will take with this mini-project. Although, not always applicable to larger projects, this waterfall model is useful for our discussion and most of you are probably familiar with it already:

- Requirements

- Design approach

- Implementation

- Install

- Test

Requirements

We've already touched on the basic requirements for our `ping` command. Table 5.1 lists them more formally.

TABLE 5.1   Project Requirements

Requirement #	Description
1.0	Can ping one or more peers identified by name.
1.1	Can anonymously ping peers listening on a common pipe.
1.2	Server and client provided by same command.
1.3	Does not block. Operates asynchronously at all times.

Unique numbers for each requirement make it easy to verify them separately and record the results. We will refer to these requirement numbers at various times in our discussion.

Design Approach

For this project, you'll implement the core facilities in a somewhat de-coupled, framework-like manner. Should you care to extend, customize, or utilize the ping framework in other contexts, it should be easier to do so.

As noted in requirement 1.2, the `ping` command provides facilities for both the server and client portions, to use somewhat dated terms. This model is needed because both the *pingee* (the server) and the *pinger* (the client) need to have some statically known method of identifying one another and completing the ping roundtrip. Lest we build entirely separate programs to do this, we chose to combine them for simplicity because there was a common design to both the client and server portions.

The server listens in the background for ping requests arriving over a special pipe. When they arrive, it broadcasts a notification event to local listeners who then process the inbound message in interesting ways. These background pipe handlers will continue to run even after the initial ping -listen command has returned. This is necessary because ping requests can arrive at any time. The background handlers are stored in the shell environment space and should be visible by executing env in the shell.

Ping clients send requests to ping servers directly (by name) or via propagate broadcast (anonymously). Before sending a ping request, the client installs a background listener to handle inbound responses from various peers (on its own pipe). When a response arrives on this client pipe, a notification event is also broadcast to client event listeners locally, where it can be used or displayed in a variety of ways. The high-level diagram in Figure 5.1 conveys the basic elements involved in our design.

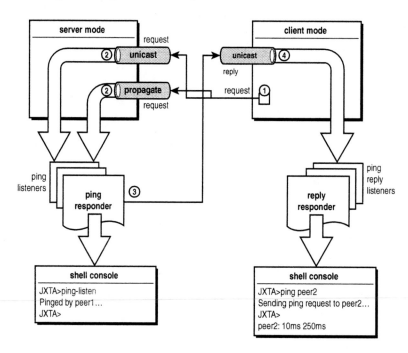

FIGURE 5.1   Ping high-level design.

Implementation

Because there are two essential roles in the operation of the ping command, we will focus our implementation discussion on each role separately, noting the pertinent classes, interfaces, and behaviors in each. Because there is only one command, per requirement 1.2, we will refer to these as modes, such as server *mode* and client *mode*, for the sake of our discussion.

Server Mode

The server design is straightforward and based on a simple thread and event model. To receive ping requests, the server publishes two pipes that can be discovered and used by client pingers. One pipe represents a unicast pipe unique to the peer who created it. In our simple ping program, this pipe is identified by name, which is inherited from the peer's name. For example, if the peer's name were pier, the pipe would be named ping.pierserver. Although not a globally unique mechanism, it is the same mechanism used by peer names, which is equally not globally unique nor intended to be.

WARNING
....
For our purposes, this technique is sufficient, but a stronger approach will be needed for broad scale use where peer names might conflict.

The other pipe (in reality a pipe advertisement) published by the server is a propagate pipe. This pipe is always named ping.pingprop and is discovered or published by all peers executing ping -listen. Anonymous pings (requirement 1.1) allow you to send requests across a propagate pipe without knowing exactly which peers might receive it. All peers currently listening for ping requests on the ping.pingprop propagate pipe should receive the same ping request and will respond independently, reflecting their true time differences. As we indicated earlier, these responses will arrive on the client over time. Some responses may never arrive (and they would not be responses in that case!).

Just prior to publishing the pipe advertisements, the ping command will create two objects of class PingHandler. There is one PingHandler for each pipe because ping requests can arrive on either. Ping requests will arrive over the peer pipe (unicast) or the anonymous pipe (propagate). Each PingHandler spawns a thread to wait for messages on the input pipe and hence requirement 1.3 is achieved.

The ping command adds the primary ping class PingPeer (which implements PingListener and provides much of the core coordination of ping) as a listener of both PingHandlers. PingPeer receives internal events when ping requests arrive and is responsible for parsing the inbound message and responding to it. In this fashion, the core duties of the ping workflow are defined by PingPeer, which uses the ping framework to define our ping behavior.

This listener model approach allows application programs to register their own user classes as listeners for ping requests/replies and react in specialized ways.

Listing 5.1 shows the AbstractPingHandler class, which is the base class for specialized ping handlers.

LISTING 5.1   AbstractPingHandler Class Source Code

```java
package net.jxta.impl.shell.bin.ping;


import java.io.*;
import net.jxta.exception.*;
import net.jxta.discovery.*;
import net.jxta.endpoint.*;
import net.jxta.pipe.*;
import net.jxta.peergroup.*;
import net.jxta.document.*;
import net.jxta.id.*;
import net.jxta.protocol.*;
import java.util.*;

/**
 * This abstract class factors out the common behavior of all ping
 * handler types. Namely, creating a thread, listening on a particular
 * pipe and dispatching the pipe Message and timestamp to an abstract method.
 */
public abstract class AbstractPingHandler implements Runnable {

    InputPipe pipe;
    Thread thread ;

    public AbstractPingHandler(InputPipe pipe) {
        this.pipe = pipe;
    }

    public void abort() {
        thread.interrupt();
    }

    /**
     * Spawn a thread and wait for a ping message to arrive.
     */
    public void waitForMessage() {
        thread = new Thread(this);
        thread.start();
```

LISTING 5.1   Continued

```
    }

    public void run() {
            Message msg = null;

            long timestamp;

            while(true) {
                try {
                    msg = pipe.waitForMessage();
                    // Arrival timestamp
                    timestamp = new Date().getTime();
                    if (msg == null) {
                        if (Thread.interrupted()) {
                            pipe.close();
                            return;
                        }
                    }
                } catch (Exception e) {
                    e.printStackTrace();
                    pipe.close();
                    return;
                }
                deliverMessage(msg,timestamp);
            }
    }

    /**
     * This key method is abstractly declared in AbstractPingHandler which
     * delegates to subclasses here.
     * @param msg The Message object received on the pipe
     * @param timestamp The timestamp the message was received on the pipe
     */
    protected abstract void deliverMessage(Message msg, long timestamp);

}
```

The thread creation and pipe message listening occur in this abstract base class via
the waitForMessage() method. How a message is handled (parsed and processed) is
deferred to concrete classes at runtime via the abstract method:

```
public abstract void deliverMessage(Message m, long timestamp);
```

The timestamp is provided automatically and immediately after message arrival because it is used in calculating trip latencies and must be precise. Concrete subclasses of AbstractPingHandler will provide implementations of deliverMessage() to parse and handle the message appropriately. This paves the way for ping protocol enhancements, tailored responses, or custom behaviors.

PingHandler is the server-side concrete subclass of AbstractPingHandler and is seen in Listing 5.2.

LISTING 5.2   PingHandler Class Source Code

```
package net.jxta.impl.shell.bin.ping;

import java.io.*;
import net.jxta.exception.*;
import net.jxta.discovery.*;
import net.jxta.endpoint.*;
import net.jxta.pipe.*;
import net.jxta.peergroup.*;
import net.jxta.document.*;
import net.jxta.id.*;
import net.jxta.protocol.*;
import java.util.*;

/**
 * A concrete implementation of AbstractPingHandler that listens for only
 * inbound ping requests.
 */
public class PingHandler extends AbstractPingHandler implements Runnable {


    // PingListeners
    Vector listeners = new Vector();

    public PingHandler(InputPipe pipe) {
        super(pipe);
    }

    /**
     * This key method is abstractly declared in AbstractPingHandler which
     * delegates to subclasses here.
     * @param msg The Message object received on the pipe
     * @param timestamp The timestamp the message was received on the pipe
```

LISTING 5.2   Continued

```
    */
    protected void deliverMessage(Message msg, long timestamp) {
        Enumeration enum = msg.getNames();
        if ((enum == null) || (!enum.hasMoreElements())) {
            // Empty message
            return;
        }
        byte[] buffer = null;

        try {
            buffer = msg.getBytes("ping");
            String message = new String(buffer);

            // Parse values out of ping message
            StringTokenizer st = new StringTokenizer(message,":");
            String name = st.nextToken();
            String timestr = (String)st.nextToken();
            long ostamp = new Long(timestr).longValue();


            PingEvent pr = new PingEvent(this,name,ostamp,timestamp);

            // notify listeners
            notifyListeners(pr);
        } catch (Exception e) {
            e.printStackTrace();
            pipe.close();
        }
    }
    /**
     * Notify interested listeners that a PingEvent has occurred and send the
     * ping event.
     */
    private void notifyListeners(PingEvent event) {
        for(int i=0;i<listeners.size();i++)
            ((PingListener)listeners.elementAt(i)).pingEvent(event);
    }

    public void addPingListener(PingListener ppml) {
        listeners.addElement(ppml);
    }
```

LISTING 5.2   Continued

```
    public void removePingListener(PingListener ppml) {
        listeners.removeElement(ppml);
    }

}
```

In addition to the threaded handling of inbound ping requests, the ping framework must notify interested listeners that a *ping event* has occurred and provide them a facility for examining the event data. Beyond the concrete PingHandler class, listeners will receive packaged ping event information from PingHandler. In this way, listeners are not burdened with how ping events are created or how the protocol messages are implemented. These can then change with minimal disruption.

The listener interface is called PingListener and appears in Listing 5.3.

LISTING 5.3   PingListener Interface Source Code

```
package net.jxta.impl.shell.bin.ping;

/**
 *
 * Listener interface to receive PingEvents
 */
public interface PingListener extends java.util.EventListener {

    /**
     * Callback invoked when a ping event occurs
     * @param event The PingEvent
     */
    public void pingEvent(PingEvent event);
}
```

> **NOTE**
>
> We extend the java.util.EventListener and java.util.EventObject classes where necessary because they are required superclasses in conformance with the JavaBean introspection guidelines. This will allow JavaBean component editors to see implementation classes using these event mechanisms as true JavaBeans.

When the pingEvent() method is called by a concrete implementation of AbstractPingHandler, a PingEvent object is forwarded. PingEvent contains all the interesting data relating to ping requests (inbound) as defined by your framework.

PingEvent provides access to two kinds of timestamps—one stamped on the client just before it sent the ping request, and one stamped by AbstractPingHandler when it receives a ping request on the server. Timestamps are long value types representing milliseconds since some fixed point.

The latter timestamp is created immediately when a ping message arrives. The timestamp and the inbound Message object are then sent to concrete implementations via deliverMessage() where PingEvent objects can be created and delivered to listeners.

In addition to timestamps, the PingEvent provides the time differential, which represents the delta in milliseconds between the two timestamps—that is, departing and arriving timestamps. PingEvent is shown in Listing 5.4.

LISTING 5.4 PingEvent Class Source Code

```
package net.jxta.impl.shell.bin.ping;

import java.util.*;

/**
 * Provided to PingReplyListeners when a ping reply is received by
 * a PingReplyHandler. This represents the initial ping leg and not
 * the reply.
 *
 * This event object holds two timestamps. One representing the sending
 * time and one representing the receiving time. Plus the differential
 * time.
 *
 */
public class PingEvent extends java.util.EventObject {

    //timestamp of ping arrival
    long timestamp = 0;

    // name of peer who sent this message
    String name = "";

    // timestamp when ping left
    long ostamp = 0;

    /** Creates new PingEvent */
    public PingEvent(Object source, String name, long ot, long t) {
        super(source);
```

LISTING 5.4   Cotinued

```
        this.name = name;
        this.ostamp = ot;
        this.timestamp = t;
    }


    /**
     * @return This method returns the timestamp of the origin of the ping
     * message, which is to say, the ping sender.
     */
    public long getOriginTimestamp() {
        return ostamp;
    }


    /**
     * @return Returns the timestamp when the ping message was received.
     */
    public long getTimestamp() {
        return timestamp;
    }


    /**
     * @return The name of the peer who sent the ping message
     */
    public String getPeerName() {
        return name;
    }


    /**
     * @return Returns the time differential between the sender
     * and receiver of this leg of a ping.
     */
    public long getDifferential() {
        return timestamp-ostamp;
    }
}
```

Client Mode

The client side of the design is a mirror image and in some places an extension of
the design of your server. Both the client and server modes operate in an asynchronous threaded fashion using pipe listeners and event notification.

When you ping another peer either explicitly or anonymously, ping will create a pipe advertisement and a handler to listen for ping replies that will arrive on that pipe. The handler is only created once and is stored in the shell environment. Subsequent invocations of ping will see if a handler currently exists and will create one only if it does not. Therefore, the handler will continue to run in the background, handling replies as they arrive.

Pinged peers receive a ping-formatted message, referred to as the *ping request*, which takes the following format:

```
<pingclientname>:<dispatch timestamp>
```

<pingclientname> is the name of the pinging client (the pinger). Ping replies extend the ping request format as such:

```
<pingservername>:<differential>:<timestamp>
```

<pingservername> tells the ping client who is replying. *<differential>* is the calculated time the ping request took to arrive at the ping server (pingee) from the client (pinger), and *<timestamp>* is the timestamp of the outbound ping reply *from* the ping server. Using these fields, the ping client can calculate the reply trip of the ping as well as the total trip time.

Where the server mode utilizes the PingHandler class to handler inbound ping request messages, the client mode uses PingReplyHandler. Both PingHandler and PingReplyHandler provide concrete implementations of AbstractPingHandler. Additionally, PingReplyListener is the callback interface applied to PingReplyHandler and awaits PingReplyEvents when ping replies are received. The symmetry between client and server in this regard provides a much simpler design that is better understood and extended. Listing 5.5 shows the PingReplyHandler class.

LISTING 5.5   PingReplyHandler Class Source Code

```
package net.jxta.impl.shell.bin.ping;


import java.io.*;
import net.jxta.exception.*;
import net.jxta.discovery.*;
import net.jxta.endpoint.*;
import net.jxta.pipe.*;
import net.jxta.peergroup.*;
import net.jxta.document.*;
import net.jxta.id.*;
```

LISTING 5.5   Continued

```java
import net.jxta.protocol.*;
import java.util.*;

/**
 * This handler class listens on a supplied pipe for ping reply messages
 * and notifies its listeners when one does.
 */
public class PingReplyHandler extends AbstractPingHandler implements Runnable {

    Vector listeners = new Vector();

    public PingReplyHandler(InputPipe pipe) {
        super(pipe);
    }

    /**
     * Notify listeners of a ping reply event.
     * @param event The PingReplyEvent
     */
    protected void notifyListeners(PingReplyEvent event) {
        for(int i=0;i<listeners.size();i++)
            ((PingReplyListener)listeners.elementAt(i)).pingReply(event);
    }

    public void addPingReplyListener(PingReplyListener ppml) {
        listeners.addElement(ppml);
    }

    public void removePingReplyListener(PingReplyListener ppml) {
        listeners.removeElement(ppml);
    }

    /**
     * This key method is abstractly declared in AbstractPingHandler which
     * delegates to subclasses here.
     * @param msg The Message object received on the pipe
     * @param timestamp The timestamp the message was received on the pipe
     */
    protected void deliverMessage(Message msg, long timestamp) {
            Enumeration enum = msg.getNames();
            if ((enum == null) || (!enum.hasMoreElements())) {
              // Empty message
                return;
```

LISTING 5.5   Continued

```
        }
        byte[] buffer = null;

        try {
            buffer = msg.getBytes("reply");
            String message = new String(buffer);
            StringTokenizer st = new StringTokenizer(message,":");

            // The peer's name
            String peername = st.nextToken();

            // Time it took for original ping request to reach peer.
            long time = new Long(st.nextToken()).longValue();

            // Time the ping was received on the peer
            long tstamp = new Long(st.nextToken()).longValue();

            PingReplyEvent pr =
                new PingReplyEvent(this,time,tstamp,timestamp,peername);
            notifyListeners(pr);
        } catch (Exception e) {
            // No user information
        }
    }
}
```

Listing 5.6 shows the interface used to receive PingReplyEvent objects when ping replies arrive on the client-side pipe. Using the event delivered by the pingReply() method callback, listeners can understand properties of the reply message.

LISTING 5.6   PingReplyListener Class Source Code

```
package net.jxta.impl.shell.bin.ping;

/**
 * This callback interface represents listeners notified by PingReplyHandler
 * objects when ping replies arrive.
 * @see PingReplyHandler
 */
public interface PingReplyListener extends java.util.EventListener {

    /**
```

LISTING 5.6   Continued

```
    * Callback invoked  when a ping reply message
    * is received.
    * @param event The PingReplyEvent
    * @see PingReplyEvent
    * @see PingReplyHandler
    */
    public void pingReply(PingReplyEvent event);


}
```

PingReplyEvent is seen in Listing 5.7. PingReplyEvents are passed to
PingReplyListeners by PingReplyHandlers.

LISTING 5.7   PingReplyEvent Class Source Code

```
package net.jxta.impl.shell.bin.ping;

import java.util.*;

/**
 * Extends PingEvent to include the first leg differential
 * as a message component.
 */
public class PingReplyEvent extends PingEvent {


    long time = 0;

    public PingReplyEvent(Object source, long diff, long otime,
                                        long atime, String name) {
        super(source,name,otime,atime);
        this.time = diff;
    }

    /**
     * @return Returns the time differential between the sender
     * and receiver of the previous leg of a ping.
     */
    public long getPriorDifferential() {
        return time;
    }


}
```

Remaining Classes

In addition to the core classes involved in the client and server modes of ping, a few other classes are needed to complete the project. The source code for these classes can be seen in Listings 5.8 through 5.11.

Listing 5.8 represents the focal point of the ping behavior. The PingPeer class sets up the ping framework classes and responds to their events according to the ping work-flow you've created—namely, request-response. It also defines what the ping request and response protocols look like.

LISTING 5.8   PingPeer Class Source Code

```
package net.jxta.impl.shell.bin.ping;

import net.jxta.impl.shell.*;

import java.io.*;
import java.util.*;

import net.jxta.exception.*;
import net.jxta.discovery.*;
import net.jxta.endpoint.*;
import net.jxta.pipe.*;
import net.jxta.peergroup.*;
import net.jxta.document.*;
import net.jxta.id.*;
import net.jxta.protocol.*;
import java.util.*;


/**
 *
 * This class provides all the core capability of our ping implementation
 * on top of the ping framework. This class provides the protocol format,
 * and ping workflow (e.g. request-response). It does this by instantiating
 * the appropriate handlers and implementing the appropriate interfaces and
 * then filling in the missing work (i.e. protocol format, workflow etc.)
 */
```

LISTING 5.8   Continued

```java
public class PingPeer implements PingListener, PingReplyListener {

    DiscoveryService discovery;
    PipeService groupPipe;
    PeerGroup group;
    private static final int WaitingTime = 2000;
    private static final int  MAXRETRIES = 5;
    String myname = "";
    Vector replyListeners = new Vector();
    Vector listeners = new Vector();
    InputPipe cPipeIn = null;
    InputPipe sPipeIn = null;
    InputPipe pPipeIn = null;
    ShellEnv env;

    private static final String PING_PREFIX = "ping.";
    /** Creates new PingPeer */
    public PingPeer(DiscoveryService d, PeerGroup group, ShellEnv env)
      throws PingException {
        discovery = d;
        groupPipe = group.getPipeService();
        this.group = group;
        myname = group.getPeerName();
        this.env = env;
        setup();
    }

    /**
     * When a reply to a ping arrives, this callback is invoked.
     * @param event The callback event
     */
    public void pingReply(PingReplyEvent event) {
        notifyReplyListeners(event);
    }

    /**
     * Called when a ping message is received.
     * @param event The callback event
     */
    public void pingEvent(PingEvent event) {
```

LISTING 5.8   Continued

```
    String servname = event.getPeerName();
    long otstamp = event.getTimestamp();

    String replyStr = myname+":"+event.getDifferential()+
                        ":"+event.getTimestamp();
    replyToPing(replyStr,servname);
    notifyListeners(event);
}

public void reset() {
    // Unimplemented
}

/**
 * Builds and sends a reply to a ping event
 * @param reply Reply string to send
 * @param clientName Name of client to reply to as indicated in their
 * ping message
 */
private void replyToPing(String reply, String clientName) {

    // Find pipe for the client pinging me
    PipeAdvertisement pipeAd = findPeerPipe(PING_PREFIX+
                        clientName+"client");

    OutputPipe pipeOut = null;
    try {
        try {
            pipeOut = groupPipe.createOutputPipe(pipeAd,  50000);
            if (pipeOut == null) {
                return;
            }
        } catch (Exception e) {
            return;
        }
        Message msg = null;
        msg = groupPipe.createMessage();
        long timestamp = new Date().getTime();
        InputStream ip = new ByteArrayInputStream(reply.getBytes());
        MessageElement me = msg.newMessageElement("reply",
                        new MimeMediaType("text/plain"),  ip);
        msg.addElement(me);
```

LISTING 5.8   Continued

```
            pipeOut.send(msg);
            pipeOut.close();

    } catch (Exception e) {
    }

}

/**
 * Initialize the client by creating initializing it's inbound listening
 * pipe and publishing it. Also, create a PingReplyHandler and store it
 * in the environment so it can be found in future ping invocations and
 * not recreated in that case.
 */
private void setup() throws PingException {
    PipeAdvertisement adv = null;


    ShellObject ph3Obj = env.get("pr3");
    if(ph3Obj==null) {
        // Build an advertisement for my input pipe
        // and publish it, but only once
        try {

            adv = createPipeAd(PING_PREFIX+group.getPeerName()+
                                "client",PipeService.UnicastType);
            if(adv==null) throw new PingException();
            // Not really using the bundles, but could
            PipeBundle pb = new PipeBundle(adv,groupPipe);

            // This is my client pipe waiting to hear back from
            // pinged peers
            cPipeIn = pb.getInputPipe();

        } catch( Exception all ) {
            throw new PingException();
        }

        PingReplyHandler pr3 = new PingReplyHandler(cPipeIn);
        pr3.addPingReplyListener(this);
        pr3.waitForMessage();
```

LISTING 5.8   Continued

```
            env.add("pr3",new ShellObject("pr3",pr3));
            try {
                // So republish the ad for the client reply pipe in case
                // it gets lost  which means it won't work the rest of the
                // shell session.
                discovery.publish(adv, DiscoveryService.ADV);
                discovery.remotePublish(adv, DiscoveryService.ADV);
            } catch (Exception e) {
                throw new PingException();
            }
        }

    }


    /**
     * install and run the ping listeners.
     */
    public void listen() throws PingException {

        PipeAdvertisement adv = null;
        PipeAdvertisement adv1 = null;

        try {

            /**
             * Create the unicast input pipe to this peer
             */
            adv = createPipeAd(PING_PREFIX+group.getPeerName()+"server",
                                        PipeService.UnicastType);
            PipeBundle pb1 = new PipeBundle(adv,groupPipe);
            sPipeIn = pb1.getInputPipe();

            /**
             * Create the propagate input pipe to this peer
             */
            adv1 = findPeerPipe(PING_PREFIX+"pingpropserver");
            if(adv1 == null)
            adv1 = createPipeAd(PING_PREFIX+"pingpropserver",
                                        PipeService.PropagateType);
            PipeBundle pb2 = new PipeBundle(adv1,groupPipe);
            pPipeIn = pb2.getInputPipe();
```

LISTING 5.8   Continued

```
            /**
             * Build PingHandlers for the unicast and propagate inbound pipes
             * When a ping message arrives on either pipe, the            *
pingEvent(PingEvent e) method is invoked.
             */
            ShellObject ph1Obj = env.get("ph1");
            if(ph1Obj==null) {
                PingHandler ph1 = new PingHandler(sPipeIn);
                ph1.addPingListener(this);
                ph1.waitForMessage();
                env.add("ph1",new ShellObject("ph1",ph1));
            }
            ShellObject ph2Obj = env.get("ph2");
            if(ph2Obj==null) {
                PingHandler ph2 = new PingHandler(pPipeIn);
                ph2.addPingListener(this);
                ph2.waitForMessage();
                env.add("ph2",new ShellObject("ph2",ph2));
            }
            /**
             * Publish the pipe advertisements.
             */
            discovery.publish(adv, DiscoveryService.ADV);
            discovery.remotePublish(adv, DiscoveryService.ADV);
            discovery.publish(adv1, DiscoveryService.ADV);
            discovery.remotePublish(adv1, DiscoveryService.ADV);
        } catch (Exception e) {
            throw new PingException();
        }
    }

    /**
     * Send a ping request across the supplied pipe advertisement.
     * @param adv The pipe advertisement corresponding to a peer
     * that has run 'ping -listen' to receive ping requests.
     */
    public void ping(PipeAdvertisement adv) throws PingException {
        OutputPipe pipeOut;

        try {
```

LISTING 5.8   Continued

```
            pipeOut = groupPipe.createOutputPipe(adv, 50000);
            if (pipeOut == null) {
                throw new PingException();
            }
            Message msg = null;
            msg = groupPipe.createMessage();
            long timestamp = new Date().getTime();

            // We've defined our protocol in a compact string format
            // It could easily be done using message elements and probably
            // should -- a good side project for the reader.
            String data = new String(myname+":"+timestamp);
            InputStream ip = new ByteArrayInputStream(data.getBytes());
            MessageElement me = msg.newMessageElement("ping",
                            new MimeMediaType("text/plain"),  ip);
            msg.addElement(me);
            pipeOut.send(msg);
            pipeOut.close();

        } catch (Exception e) {
            throw new PingException() ;
        }
    }

    /**
     * Send a ping request across a pipe named 'pingpropagate' which
     * is published to be a propagate pipe. The ping request should then be
     * received by all input pipes bound to the ad.
     */
    public void propagate() throws PingException {
        ping("pingprop");
    }

    /**
     * Send a ping message to a peer listening on an input pipe represented
     * by the supplied advertisement.
     * @param adv The pipe advertisement of the peer to ping.
     */
    public void ping(String name) throws PingException {

        OutputPipe pipeOut = null;
        try {
```

LISTING 5.8   Continued

```
                PipeAdvertisement adv = findPeerPipe(PING_PREFIX+name+"server");
                ping(adv);

        } catch (Exception e) {
            throw new PingException() ;
        }
    }

    /**
     * Find a pipe advertisement by name
     * @param name Name of pipe
     * @return The PipeAdvertisement
     */
    public PipeAdvertisement findPeerPipe(String name) {

        // Look to see if I have a valid ad locally
        PipeAdvertisement pipeAd = getLocalPipe(name);
        if(pipeAd==null) {
            // Search for remote ad and store it in local cache
            discovery.getRemoteAdvertisements(null, DiscoveryService.ADV,
                                PipeAdvertisement.NameTag, name,2,null);
            int i=0;
            while (true) {
                try {
                    pipeAd = getLocalPipe(name);
                    if (pipeAd!=null){
                        return pipeAd;
                    }
                    if(i>MAXRETRIES) break;
                    Thread.sleep(WaitingTime);
                    i++;
                } catch (Exception e) {
                    // Just drop out if an error occurs
                    // Ok for our purposes
                }
            }

        } else return pipeAd;


        return null;
    }
```

LISTING 5.8   Continued

```
private PipeAdvertisement getLocalPipe(String name) {
    Enumeration enum = null;

    try {
        enum = discovery.getLocalAdvertisements(DiscoveryService.ADV,
                               PipeAdvertisement.NameTag, name);

        if ((enum != null) && (enum.hasMoreElements())) {
            PipeAdvertisement adv = null;

            while (enum.hasMoreElements()) {

                try {
                    adv = (PipeAdvertisement) enum.nextElement();
                } catch(Exception e) {
                    continue;
                }
                if(isValid(adv,name)) {
                    return adv;
                }
            }
        }

    } catch (Exception e) {
        // Ok for our purposes
    }
    return null;
}


/**
 * Determine if a given advertisement is indeed valid.
 */
private boolean isValid(PipeAdvertisement adv, String name) {

    if (adv == null) return false;
    if (adv.getName() == null) return false;
    if (adv.getName().equals(name)) return true;
    return false;
}

/**
 * Helper method to create input pipe advertisements.
```

LISTING 5.8   Continued

```
    * @param name Name of pipe
    * @param type Type of pipe
    * @return The PipeAdvertisement
    */
   private PipeAdvertisement createPipeAd(String name, String type) {
       PipeAdvertisement adv;

       try {
           // Create a pipe advertisement for this pipe.
           adv = (PipeAdvertisement)
           AdvertisementFactory.newAdvertisement(
                           PipeAdvertisement.getAdvertisementType() );
           // Associate pipe id with group id, creating a new id.
           // (PeerGroupID) group.getPeerGroupID()
           adv.setPipeID( IDFactory.newPipeID(
                           (PeerGroupID) group.getPeerGroupID()) );
           // Use peer name here
           adv.setName(name);
           adv.setType(type);
           return adv;
       }
       catch( Exception all ) {
           return null;
       }
   }


   /**
    * Notify listeners of a ping reply event.
    * @param event The PingReplyEvent
    */
   protected void notifyReplyListeners(PingReplyEvent event) {
       for(int i=0;i<listeners.size();i++)
           ((PingReplyListener)replyListeners.elementAt(i)).pingReply(event);
   }

   public void addPingReplyListener(PingReplyListener ppml) {
       replyListeners.addElement(ppml);
   }

   public void removePingReplyListener(PingReplyListener ppml) {
       replyListeners.removeElement(ppml);
   }
```

LISTING 5.8   Continued

```
/**
 * Notify interested listeners that a PingEvent has occurred and send the
 * ping event.
 */
private void notifyListeners(PingEvent event) {
    for(int i=0;i<listeners.size();i++)
        ((PingListener)listeners.elementAt(i)).pingEvent(event);
}

public void addPingListener(PingListener ppml) {
    listeners.addElement(ppml);
}

public void removePingListener(PingListener ppml) {
    listeners.removeElement(ppml);
}

}
```

PingException is a generic exception class thrown within the ping framework. Currently, it offers no useful information other than its type. It is seen in Listing 5.9.

LISTING 5.9   PingException Class Source Code

```
package net.jxta.impl.shell.bin.ping;

/**
 * This class is a provisional exception class that needs to
 * be more thoroughly designed to meet specific needs. It will
 * be thrown whenever an failure occurs in the ping framework.
 */
public class PingException extends java.lang.Exception {

    /**
     * Creates new <code>PingException</code> without detail message.
     */
    public PingException() {
    }


    /**
     * Constructs an <code>PingException</code> with the specified
     * detail message.
```

LISTING 5.9   Continued

```
     * @param msg the detail message.
     */
    public PingException(String msg) {
        super(msg);
    }
}
```

PipeBundle is a convenient class for encapsulating a pipe advertisement and the acts
of retrieving input and output pipes associated with that advertisement. Listing 5.10
contains the source for PipeBundle.

LISTING 5.10   PipeBundle Class Source Code

```
package net.jxta.impl.shell.bin.ping;

import java.io.*;
import net.jxta.exception.*;
import net.jxta.discovery.*;
import net.jxta.endpoint.*;
import net.jxta.pipe.*;
import net.jxta.peergroup.*;
import net.jxta.document.*;
import net.jxta.id.*;
import net.jxta.protocol.*;
import java.util.*;


/**
 * This class bundles a pipe advertisement with its input
 * and output pipes and their creation methods.
 */
public class PipeBundle {

    private PipeAdvertisement ad;
    private PipeService ps;
    private InputPipe iPipe = null;
    private OutputPipe oPipe = null;

    /** Creates new PipeBundle */
    public PipeBundle(PipeAdvertisement ad, PipeService ps) {
        this.ad = ad;
```

LISTING 5.10   Continued

```
        this.ps = ps;
    }


    /**
     * Returns the input pipe associated with this PipeBundle
     */
    public InputPipe getInputPipe()  {
        try {
            if(iPipe==null)
                return (iPipe = (InputPipe)ps.createInputPipe(ad));
            else return iPipe;
        } catch (IOException e) {
            return null;
        }
    }


    /**
     * Returns the output pipe associated with this PipeBundle
     */
    public OutputPipe getOutputPipe()  {
        try {
            if(oPipe==null)
                return (oPipe = (OutputPipe)ps.createOutputPipe(ad, 50000));
            else return oPipe;
        } catch (IOException e) {
            return null;
        }
    }


    /**
     * Returns the advertisement associated with this PipeBundle
     */
    public PipeAdvertisement getAdvertisement() {
        return ad;
    }


}
```

Listing 5.11 represents the shell command application class ping. This class is loaded
and executed by the shell context when you enter it on the command line. Because
it is a shell application class, it extends net.jxta.impl.shell.ShellApp.

LISTING 5.11   ping Class Source Code

```java
package net.jxta.impl.shell.bin.ping;

import net.jxta.impl.shell.*;

import java.io.*;
import java.util.*;

import net.jxta.exception.*;
import net.jxta.discovery.*;
import net.jxta.endpoint.*;
import net.jxta.pipe.*;
import net.jxta.peergroup.*;
import net.jxta.document.*;
import net.jxta.id.*;
import net.jxta.protocol.*;
import java.util.*;

/**
 * The ping command class. This class essentially takes the input
 * and coordinates the execution of PingPeer.
 */
public class ping extends ShellApp  implements PingListener,
                                              PingReplyListener {

    private DiscoveryService discovery=null;

    private ShellEnv env = null;
    PingPeer pingPeer;

    public ping() {
    }


    /**
     * Invoked by shell to formally stop this application.
     */
    public void stopApp() {
    }

    /**
     * Invoked by shell to formally start this application.
```

LISTING 5.11   Continued

```
*/
    public int startApp(String[] args) {

        try {
            env = getEnv();
            discovery= group.getDiscoveryService();
            //flushAds();
            pingPeer = new PingPeer(discovery,group,env);

            // Notify me when certain events happen so I can respond
            // in my own way
            pingPeer.addPingReplyListener(this);
            pingPeer.addPingListener(this);

            if(args.length == 1 && "-listen".equals(args[0]))
                pingPeer.listen();
            else if(args.length == 1 && "-propagate".equals(args[0])) {
                println("Send propagate ping request...");
                pingPeer.propagate();
            } else if(args.length>0) {
                List list = (List)Arrays.asList(args);
                pingPeers(list);
            }
            else {
                help();
            }
            return 0;
        } catch (PingException e) {
            return 1;
        }
    }




    /**
     * This method takes the list of peers provided on command line
     * looks up their corresponding unicast ping pipes, and pings them.
     */
    private void pingPeers(List names) {
        Iterator it = names.iterator();

        while(it.hasNext()) {
```

LISTING 5.11   Continued

```
            String name = (String)it.next();
            println("Sending ping request to "+name+" ...");
            try {
                pingPeer.ping(name);
            } catch (PingException pe) {
                println("ping exception: "+name);
            }
        }

    }


    /**
     * Flush current cache of advertisements.
     */
    private void flushAds() {
        try {
            discovery.flushAdvertisements(null,DiscoveryService.ADV);
        } catch (IOException e) {
        }
    }

    /**
     * Callback invoked when a ping reply message
     * is received.
     * @param event The PingReplyEvent
     * @see PingReplyEvent
     * @see PingReplyHandler
     */
    public void pingReply(PingReplyEvent event) {
        long pdiff  =  event.getPriorDifferential(); // first leg duration
        long diff   =  event.getDifferential(); // second leg duration
        long tstamp =  event.getTimestamp(); // time event was received
        long ostamp =  event.getOriginTimestamp(); // time event dispatched
        String pname = event.getPeerName();
        println("");
        // display reply data.
        println(pname+": "+pdiff+"ms "+diff+"ms ");
    }

    /**
```

LISTING 5.11   Continued

```
    * Callback invoked when a ping event occurs
    * @param event The PingEvent
    */
   public void pingEvent(PingEvent event) {
       println("");
       println("Pinged by "+event.getPeerName()+"....");
   }


   /**
 * Description method implementation. Displayed next to command during a 'man'.
 */
   public String getDescription() {
       return "Send a ping request to another peer and
                             receive a response if it is alive.";
   }


   /**
 * Help method implementation. Invoked when 'help ping' is typed.
 */
   public void help() {
       println("NAME");
       println("    ping  - Send a ping request to another peer and
                             receive a response if it is alive.");
       println(" ");
       println("SYNOPSIS");
       println(" ");
       println("    ping [-listen] [-propagate] <peername>");
       println(" ");
       println("DESCRIPTION");
       println(" ");
       println("'ping' is a command that can be used to determine if ");
       println("remote peers that are listening for pings are 'alive'.");
       println("Ping will receive ping responses asynchronously ");
       println("and the times involved in the ping messages are");
       println("recorded and displayed.");
       println(" ");          println("EXAMPLE");
       println(" ");
       println("    JXTA> ping -listen");
       println("    JXTA> ping");
   }


}
```

Figure 5.2 shows us the complete UML class diagram of the framework abstractions and implementation classes.

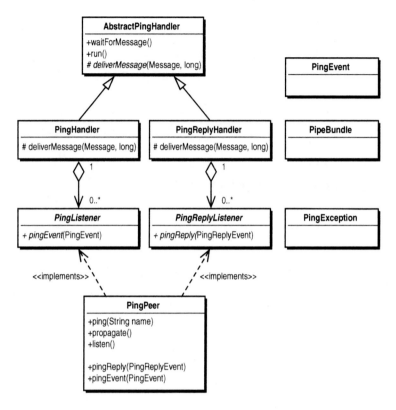

FIGURE 5.2   UML class diagram of all classes and interfaces.

Install

Installing `ping.jar` is identical to the example in Chapter 4. Use the following command to install `ping.jar`:

```
JXTA> instjar <path>/ping.jar
```

where *<path>* is the absolute path to `ping.jar`.

To avoid typing this every time you launch shell, add the command to the .jshrc file in your shell directory (or create it). You might want to do this for ping -listen as well.

Test

Testing the ping command is easy. Should you want to run ping on a single machine, you might want to run multiple shell peers on a single machine, which you learned in Chapter 4. Having done this, ensure that the ping.jar is installed in each shell. Otherwise, you can simply ping yourself, which is to say, the single peer you choose to use.

If you choose to run multiple shells, you can run ping in each. To set this up, execute ping -listen in each shell so that they can receive ping requests. From any shell, you can issue ping <peername> commands to ping that peer. After a moment, you should get a reply that looks like the following:

```
JXTA>
peer1: 10ms 250ms
```

The first time indicated (10ms) is the time it took for the peer request to go from the pinger to the pingee. The second time (250ms) is the total time for the ping request-response roundtrip. The name before the colon represents the name of the peer replying, therefore, it took 10 milliseconds for our ping request to reach the peer named peer1 and 250 milliseconds from the time we sent the request to the time the reply was received. If you see replies for all peers you pinged, requirement 1.0 (ping one or more peers) is satisfied.

To test requirement 1.1 (anonymous pings), you must issue ping -propagate, which sends the ping request across the JXTA propagate pipe published by listening peers. If you do this and all peers currently listening for pings respond in time, the requirement is satisfied.

Because both listening and pinging are initiated from the single ping command, requirement 1.2 (client and server embodied in same program) is satisfied. Lastly, requirement 1.3 is achieved because the ping command does not wait for replies itself but rather returns you to the JXTA prompt.

Any variety of pings should work, providing the pinged peers have executed ping -listen. You may also test ping against peers that are not currently online, in which case, no reply should be received. Figure 5.3 shows a screen shot of some sample ping trial runs on a single desktop.

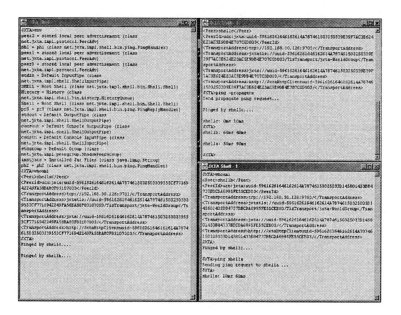

FIGURE 5.3   Ping console screen shots.

Further Improvements to Ping

At the time of this writing, the JXTA platform was undergoing numerous API improvements. One particular class, PipeMsgListener, is useful to our ping design in that it defines a callback interface when pipe messages arrive on a specific pipe. Registering a PipeMsgListener at the time of pipe creation would free us from having to implement the listener and thread model as we have done here. Therefore, a good exercise would be to modify ping to use this new mechanism.

Another ping improvement project would be to add a GUI console such that you could ping peers using a mouse and keep the responses isolated in a nice table, outside of the shell console.

And finally, for the bold at heart, ping could also be used to bridge the actual ping protocol so that JXTA ping could work for JXTA peers and Internet hosts as well!

Summary

This chapter dove deeper into designing and implementing a somewhat useful shell command called ping. From this project, you should have gained knowledge in a few key areas.

- Asynchronous operation

- Threaded pipe handling

- Shell environment space

- Framework approach

Asynchronous operation is a fundamental aspect of JXTA P2P programming and there are many ways to provide it, one of which we've demonstrated in this project. It's important to remember that peer networks are not reliable for the most part. They compensate for fine-grained reliability with course-grained redundancy and adaptation.

Our threaded handlers were critical to achieve the asynchronous operation because they ran quietly in the background and only woke up when messages arrived. You can use this approach in other applications, not just shell commands.

You also saw, once again, how to use the shell environment to store shell objects. In this case, you stored your ping handlers. Subsequent invocations of ping would notice whether handlers were already present in the environment and would only create them if they weren't. The environment is ideal for shell applications that need to share information or processes across invocations.

Lastly, we chose to provide the core facilities of ping through a flexible set of abstractions that can allow you to define variations of ping or attach listeners to ping events. This framework approach is more useful for larger more general problem categories than ping, but for our purposes, it served as a useful design mechanism that you can use in your own projects.

NOTE

To acquire the project files for our ping example, please visit www.samspublishing.com.

6

Working with Groups

By Navaneeth Krishnan

Perhaps the most interesting feature of the peers in a P2P network is their ability to dynamically aggregate into cooperative unions called *peer groups*. Peer groups become particularly important in enterprise and collaborative computing applications. The increasing significance of peer groups brings up the related issue of an efficient strategy for peer group management. In this chapter, we will delve into how JXTA offers a simple solution to the peer group management issue. We will also build a simple Group Manager application and, in that process, explore the various steps involved in group management.

Importance of Peer Groups

One of the key areas where peer-to-peer technologies are expected to make a great impact, and are already doing so, is that of *collaborative computing*. Consider the example of an enterprise application that enables employees to exchange information, such as documents, in real-time with each other, additionally serving as a channel to conduct conferences and brainstorm sessions.

Such applications normally classify its users into *work groups*, with groups of managers exchanging confidential documents, groups of architects exchanging design strategies, and groups of developers exchanging code samples. Consequently, collaborative computing applications are sometimes referred to as *groupware*.

These applications could be easily designed by mapping the work group to JXTA peer groups. But this is just one way of looking at peer groups.

The JXTA specification illustrates three common situations where peer groups are formed:

- *Scoping*—This is similar to the previous example—different kinds of people form groups based on some common characteristics between them. The grouping is to achieve some common goal. Scoping can also mean something other than providing an application level identity. There can be peers in the network who are specialized in certain areas, such as file sharing and so on, and expose this to other peers.

- *Security*—In the previous example, the groups also provide a mechanism to create a secure environment. Grouping all managers in one group can ensure that they can freely exchange information among themselves and ensure that only other managers are involved in such exchanges. Of course, this depends a lot on the security of the membership service to these groups.

- *Monitoring*—Peer groups can be used to enable easy monitoring of individual peers in the group. This will be particularly important in enterprise P2P applications where a system administrator may need to remotely monitor or control peers in the network.

Importance of Peer Group Management

Traditionally, systems have relied on central authorities for management and administration. For example, a corporate intranet may use a central repository in the form of an Oracle database to store valid user names and passwords. All applications that need to authenticate users can always do so by using this repository. This method is simple and straightforward, but such a strategy is not possible in a *pure* P2P network.

Notice the emphasis on the word *pure*. A P2P network *can* use a centralized repository for authentication. In fact, a lot of applications available today work this way. But doing so adds a bit of centralization to the network. What happens if the point of centralization fails?

In contrast to a centrally managed system, management in a decentralized system can be overly complex. This is mainly due to dynamic and the ad hoc nature of the network. Lack of a single point of control for the entire system can be quite a challenge to overcome.

However, the concept of peer groups can reduce the severity of these restrictions to some extent. Because the services running on any peer are dependent on the peer groups which it belongs, a well-organized peer group management plan will aid in managing the network as a whole.

Types of Peer Group Management

Various strategies can be adopted to successfully manage peer groups. The actual strategy (or combination) adopted depends on the requirements of the system that you are designing.

Managing Peer Membership

All JXTA peers join interested peer groups by using the membership service exposed by these groups. The role of the membership service is to help authenticate a peer that is joining the group.

This is the easiest place to impose a management policy. Applications can be so designed so that only peers conforming to certain guidelines become members of the peer group. We will have a detailed look at how this is done in the later parts of this chapter (Refer to the "Peer Membership Management" section).

Of course, not all groups need to enforce a policy for membership. The JXTA platform recognizes this need by providing a NullMembershipService. It is a membership service that requires no real authentication (Windows users may be able to draw parallels between this and the null login used by the NetBios protocol that helps to find other computers and shared files in Windows networks).

However, this is only an "entry level" policy because it is used only at the time of membership. After a peer has successfully joined a group, it may try to flout some of the group policies, and these actions cannot be controlled by the membership service. The first mechanism is to validate rights via credentials

Still, there is a way to overcome this limitation. The membership service can choose to set a fixed expiration period for membership. This will force the peer to periodically refresh its membership to the group. This can act as a routine review mechanism.

Peer Credibility Rating

Peer credibility plays a lot of importance, especially in publicly available peer-to-peer networks. Credibility determines the integrity or the trustworthiness of a peer. Public networks should be managed in such a way that credible peers have an edge over the not-so-credible peers, thereby encouraging every peer to increase its credibility to benefit more from the network.

The point is to reduce the number of undesirable entities (peers) in the network by reducing the exposure that they get from the network. The undesirable entities can be subdivided into three categories:

- *Leechers*—Leechers are bent on taking more from the network than they contribute. Many users in the Napster network tend to download significantly more music files than they share (if they share at all) for others to download. They are the classic example of leechers in a network.

- *Spammers*—Spammers are those who use the network for unsolicited messages, advertisements, and so on that serve no purpose to others. Traditionally, e-mail and news have served as popular channels for spam. Today, it seems to be catching popular instant messaging networks, such as Yahoo and AOL, mainly due to their large user base.

- *Malevolent peers*—This is a category of peers who are bent on reducing the net worth of the network. There can be many reasons for this. For example, it is widely discussed that record companies, who feel threatened by music file sharing networks, intentionally insert low-quality versions of popular music files. This is done to reduce the worth of the network and draw users away from it.

Rating of the peers in a group requires the maintenance of logs and statistics that can be used to arrive at the rating. A well-defined rating mechanism must also be determined.

The easiest way to achieve this would be to use a logging service that logs the interested statistics corresponding to a peer. Interested statistics could be storage space offered, CPU cycles shared, and so on. These could be used to determine the peer's credibility at any point.

Active Monitoring

In sensitive networks, it may be necessary to keep an active watch on the activities of a peer. Active monitoring will help identify any signs of problems in the network.

It is possible that the peers in a network may indulge in a variety of malicious activities, such as:

- Attempting to hijack the network

- Attempting a denial of service attack

- Attempting to spoof its identity

While active monitoring can provide a fast incident response in such cases, there will be a performance overhead using this method.

Peer Membership Management

Group membership management can have different manifestations depending on the actual application that you are building. If you are building a network where a peer group specializes in file sharing, you may not need to place any restrictions on peers joining and leaving the group. On the other hand, if the group represents employees of an organization from different global locations discussing their company strategy, you would want to place proper restrictions to ensure that only legitimate peers can join the group.

Because JXTA is designed to be as generic as possible, it is difficult to enforce any specific scheme for management without a specific implementation. Therefore, JXTA approaches this problem by proposing a well-defined process by which peers can associate and disassociate from peer groups. The Peer Membership Protocol (PMP) does this. It suggests a generic procedure by which memberships to groups can be established, leaving the details of the actual mechanisms to the implementations.

To illustrate our ideas, we will do two things. First, we will build a generic Group Manager. The Group Manager should be such that you should be able to plug in any membership service of your liking, including the default membership service provided by the JXTA binding. Second, we will build our own membership service to illustrate how a membership service must behave.

The Student Analogy

For explaining the concept of group membership management, let's take a real life analogy. Consider a student interested in joining a university for graduate studies. The interested student is a peer seeking membership in a group, and the collection of all students already studying in the university can be thought of as the peer group. Let's take a quick look at the various steps involved in this process.

Locating the Group Membership Service

A student may have many universities from which to choose. The first step is to identify the university that the student chooses to join. Next, the student must try to locate the point of contact for all admissions to the university. Generally, universities have an Admissions office to satisfy this requirement.

Likewise, the first step toward obtaining a membership in a peer group is to locate the appropriate peer group. In a network, there may be many existing groups. Each group will have a group membership application *Authenticator* that is responsible for the membership services of the group. Any peer desiring to join the group must first locate the authenticator.

Applying to the Group

After the university admissions office has been identified, an interested student is expected to submit a preliminary application form (usually called a pre-app). The purpose of the pre-app form is to restrict applications to only those candidates who satisfy the minimum requirement for admissions. This acts as the first level of filtering. Students who don't have a basic eligibility need not go through the long process of application submission and evaluation to realize that they are not eligible. The university Admissions office evaluates the pre-app form and sends an application form to the student if he/she is found to be eligible.

Similarly, after the interested peer finds the membership service of the group, it sends an *apply* request. The apply request consists of an *authentication credential*. A credential is any piece of data that can be used to identify a peer. The authentication credential can be regarded as an unsigned credential; that is, it represents the peer even before it interacts with the membership service (refer to Chapter 8, "JXTA and Security," for more about signatures). If the application is successful, the membership service in turn sends an *authenticator* to the applying peer. The authentication credential is comparable to the pre-app form, and the authenticator is comparable to the application form.

Joining the Group

After the student receives the application form, he/she is expected to fill it out and submit it to the Admissions office. The Admissions office in turn evaluates the student's application form. When the office deems the student fit to join the university, it sends an invitation letter to the student.

Similarly, after the peer receives the authenticator, it is expected to fill it out and send it back to the membership service. The membership service evaluates the authenticator and sends back a credential. The credential is equivalent to the invitation letter sent to the student. The possession of this credential implies that the peer has been successfully admitted to the peer group.

Resigning from the Group

At any point, the student may decide to leave the university. In this case, he/she can do so by contacting the concerned authorities.

A peer can leave a peer group by sending a cancel membership message. A peer is considered to have left the peer group when this request has been accepted.

Renewal of Membership

A peer can also renew its membership to a group. While this does not make much sense in our student example, it becomes particularly important if the peer group membership policy decides that all memberships have a validity period, for whatever reasons, one of which could be to serve as review period, as previously explained.

The peer sends a *renew* message to request a membership renewal. The membership can be considered renewed if a successful acknowledgment is sent by the membership service.

Using the Peer Group Manager

The Group Manager is a class that can be used by any JXTA application for simple group management functions, such as the following:

- Creating new peer groups

- Plugging in a membership service for the group

- Providing a simple ability to join, authenticate, renew, and resign from the group

- Providing a simple user interface for the authentication process

The com.sams.jxta.groups package contains four classes. The com.sams.jxta.groups.GroupManager class is our implementation of the Group Manager. The com.sams.jxta.groups.AuthenticatorBean class is a helper class used by the Group Manager to provide a simplistic user interface in the form of a dialog, as you will see later in the "Completing the Authenticator" section. The remaining two classes represent the exceptions that we have defined for the Group Manager, namely GroupManagerException and GroupManagerAuthenticationException. The UML design diagram of the Group Manager is shown in Figure 6.1.

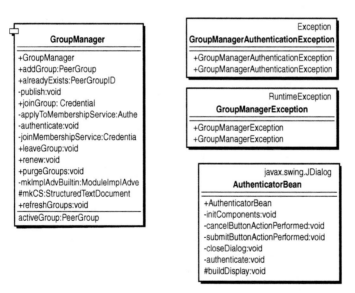

FIGURE 6.1   UML Design of *GroupManager*.

The membership service that you will be building can be found in the com.sams.jxta.groups.student package on the book's Web site. The class that makes use of the Group Manager is com.sams.jxta.groups.student.StudentDemo. This class can be run using the included batch file. We will introduce the remaining classes as we encounter them.

NOTE
To acquire the project files for this book's examples, please visit www.samspublishing.com.

Before we go any further, it is important to note that the example that we will be dealing with will not involve any remote authentication. In other words, both our peer and the group authenticator are on the same machine, simplifying our study.

Deciding on a Parent Peer Group

The first step is to decide on a parent for the peer group that you are going to create. As you saw in Chapter 2, "Overview of JXTA," by virtue of being a module, any peer group can be loaded only in the context of another peer group, the platform peer group forming the base of this hierarchy. Consequently, the Group Manager takes a pre-existing group in its constructor. We refer to this group as the *parent peer group*. This group will form the base of your hierarchy. The constructor of the Group Manager is as follows:

```
public GroupManager (PeerGroup parent)
```

This parent can be any peer group.

The StudentDemo class demonstrates the use of the Group Manager. This class is designed to be a module by itself. The GroupManager is instantiated in its init() method:

```
public void init(PeerGroup parentGroup,ID assignedID,
                            Advertisement implAdv)
                          throws PeerGroupException {

    GroupManager manager = new GroupManager(parentGroup);
...
}
```

This example uses the net peer group as the parent group. This is done for two reasons:

- The net peer group already offers all the basic services required to get started. Being a child can benefit our peer group because any child can use its parent's services. For example, because the net peer group already has a discovery service, our peer group can use this itself without any changes. As a result, you are spared from a great deal of code.

- Because many common applications available today (like the JXTA shell) use the net peer group, the application that you are writing can interoperate to a limited extent with these applications. For example, a JXTA shell user can discover the groups that we publish.

The code that instantiates the net peer group appears in Listing 6.1.

LISTING 6.1   `StudentDemo.java runJXTA()` Method

```
private void runJXTA(){
    PeerGroup netPeerGroup = null;
    try {
        netPeerGroup = PeerGroupFactory.newNetPeerGroup();
    } catch (PeerGroupException peerGroupException) {
        //could not instanciate the group,
        //print the stack and exit
        System.out.println("fatal error : group creation"+ "failure");
        peerGroupException.printStackTrace();
        System.exit(1);
    }
    ModuleClassID mID = IDFactory.newModuleClassID();
    ModuleSpecID moduleSpecID = PeerGroup.refMembershipSpecID;
    ModuleImplAdvertisement adv =
    (ModuleImplAdvertisement)
        AdvertisementFactory.newAdvertisement
            (ModuleImplAdvertisement.getAdvertisementType());
    adv.setModuleSpecID(moduleSpecID);
    adv.setCompat(StdPeerGroup.stdCompatStatement);
    adv.setCode("com.sams.jxta.groups.student.StudentDemo");
    adv.setUri("http://www.jxta.org/download/jxta.jar");
    try{
        netPeerGroup.loadModule(mID,adv);
    } catch (Exception e) {
        e.printStackTrace();
    }
}
```

The factory `net.jxta.peergroup.PeerGroupFactory` creates the net peer group. After creating the net peer group, you create a `ModuleImplAdvertisement`. This is done by using another factory—`net.jxta.document.AdvertisementFactory`. This advertisement will represent your `StudentDemo` module, so you set the corresponding attributes of the advertisement.

Creating and Publishing a New Peer Group

The `GroupManager` exposes an `addGroup()` method that can be used to create a new peer group. This method not only creates a new peer group but also publishes it. The `addGroup()` method is shown in Listing 6.2.

LISTING 6.2   GroupManager.java addGroup() Method

```
public PeerGroup addGroup(String groupName,
                          String groupMembershipClassName,
                          String groupDescription,
                          ModuleImplAdvertisement advertisement,
                          boolean conditional){

    // The first thing we do is to see if a group already
    // exists by this name.
    PeerGroupID oldPeerGroupID = alreadyExists(groupName);
        if(oldPeerGroupID != null && conditional==true)
            throw new GroupManagerException("A Group "+
➥"by this name already exists with id :"+oldPeerGroupID);

    // If no Advertisement is provided, we create a
    // fresh advertisement.
    if (advertisement == null){
        // We use the existing advertisement of the
        // standard peer group
        // and add our service along with the other
        // standard services
        try{
            // This is used as a base to create the
            // new advertisement upon
            advertisement = parent.getAllPurposePeerGroupImplAdvertisement();
            StructuredDocument paramDoc = advertisement.getParam();
            // The Param document used to make the
            // StandradPeerGroup Advertisement
            StdPeerGroupParamAdv paramAdv = new StdPeerGroupParamAdv(paramDoc);
            // List of all the available standard services
            Hashtable services = paramAdv.getServices();
            // Make a ModuleImplAdvertisemnet for the
            // membership service
            ModuleImplAdvertisement moduleAdv =
                MkImplAdvBuiltin
➥(PeerGroup.refMembershipSpecID,groupMembershipClassName,
```

LISTING 6.2   Continued

```
                                     groupDescription);
              // Add this service along the other        // standard services
              services.put(PeerGroup.membershipClassID, moduleAdv);
              paramAdv.setServices(services);
              advertisement.setParam
➡((net.jxta.document.TextElement)paramAdv.getDocument(

➡new net.jxta.document.MimeMediaType(DOCUMENT_MIME_TYPE,[ccc]
DOCUMENT_BASE_TYPE)));
          }catch(PeerGroupException peerGroupException){
              LOG.error("Error in creating Advertisement",peerGroupException);
                  throw new GroupManagerException(peerGroupException.getMessage());
          }catch(Exception genericException){
              LOG.error("Error in creating"+ "Advertisement",genericException);
                  throw new GroupManagerException(genericException.getMessage());
          }
      }


    // initialize but to no start the application
    // this is done by the join command
    PeerGroup peerGroup = null;
        try {
            // create a PeerGroup ID
            PeerGroupID peerGroupID = null;
            if(oldPeerGroupID != null)
                peerGroupID = oldPeerGroupID;
            else
                peerGroupID =
➡new net.jxta.impl.id.UUID.PeerGroupID(UUIDFactory.newUUID());
            // create the PeerGroup
            peerGroup = parent.newGroup(peerGroupID,
➡ advertisement, groupName, groupDescription);
            // initialize the peergroup
            peerGroup.init(this.parent,peerGroupID, advertisement);
```

LISTING 6.2   Continued

```
        } catch (PeerGroupException peerGroupException) {
            LOG.error("Unable to create a peer group !",peerGroupException);
            throw new GroupManagerException(peerGroupException.getMessage());
        }
        // Try to publish the advertisement
        publish(peerGroup, advertisement);
        return peerGroup;
}
```

Let us see what the code in Listing 6.2 does. The groupName is the name of the group to be created. It need not necessarily be unique. groupMembershipClassName represents the membership service of this new group by its fully-qualified classname. The group description is a string description of the group. The advertisement is the ModuleImplAdvertisement assigned to this group, if any.

Here, the user of the GroupManager is an API that is free to provide its own ModuleImplAdvertisement to be used. If this is not provided, the method creates a fresh advertisement using the mkImplAdvBuiltin() utility method. This method is shown in Listing 6.3.

LISTING 6.3   GroupManager.java mkImplAdvBuiltin() Method

```
private ModuleImplAdvertisement mkImplAdvBuiltin(
                            net.jxta.platform.ModuleSpecID specID,
                            String code,String descr) {

    String moduleImplAdvType = ModuleImplAdvertisement.getAdvertisementType();
    ModuleImplAdvertisement implAdvertisement = (ModuleImplAdvertisement)
                AdvertisementFactory.newAdvertisement(moduleImplAdvType);
    implAdvertisement.setModuleSpecID(specID);
    implAdvertisement.setCompat(stdCompatStatement);
    implAdvertisement.setCode(code);
    implAdvertisement.setUri(stdUri);
    implAdvertisement.setProvider(stdProvider);
```

LISTING 6.3   Continued

```
    implAdvertisement.setDescription(descr);
    return implAdvertisement;
}
```

You may have noticed a boolean variable called conditional. This is used in case there is any name conflict occurring during the addGroup operation. The addGroup method first checks whether a peer group with the given name already exists. This is done by the alreadyExists() method shown in Listing 6.4.

LISTING 6.4   GroupManager.java alreadyExists() Method

```
public PeerGroupID alreadyExists(String name){

    DiscoveryService discovery = parent.getDiscoveryService();
    Enumeration enumeration =null;
    try{
        enumeration =
            discovery.getLocalAdvertisements(discovery.GROUP, "Name",name);
    } catch(java.io.IOException ioException) {
        LOG.debug("Error in getting local advertisements ");
        return null;
    }
    // If the group already exists
    // either the  enumeration is null
    // or it does not contain any data

    if(enumeration != null && enumeration.hasMoreElements())
        return ((PeerGroupAdv)enumeration.nextElement()).getPeerGroupID();
        else
        return null;
}
```

It may be possible that a group already exists with the given name. If this is the case, you are left with two options:

- Create a fresh group, regardless of the fact that another with the same name exists.

- Throw an exception and inform the user that a group with the same name exists.

The conditional flag achieves this. If the addition of the group is a "conditional add" (conditional==true), the second option is used. In case of an "unconditional add," the first option is used.

In the case where you are to create a new group even if an old one exists with the same name, make certain that the new group uses the PeerGroupID of the old group.

The new group is then published using the publish() method shown in Listing 6.5.

LISTING 6.5   GroupManager.java publish() Method

```
private void publish(PeerGroup child,Advertisement pgAdv ) {

    //Get the Discovery Service for this group
    //Publish the New Peer in its group discovery

    DiscoveryService discovery;
    try {

        discovery = parent.getDiscoveryService();
        discovery.publish(pgAdv, DiscoveryService.GROUP);
    } catch (java.io.IOException ioException) {
        LOG.error("Could not publish the service !",ioException);
        throw new GroupManagerException(ioException.getMessage());

    }

}
```

Now, the StudentDemo class uses this addGroup() method to create a new group:

```
PeerGroup p =manager.addGroup("UniversityStudents",
➥"com.sams.jxta.groups.student.UniversityAdmissionsService"
➥,"To represent all graduate students in a University",null,false);
```

The group is named UniversityStudents. The membership service class is com.sams.jxta.groups.student.UniversityAdmissionsService. Because no ModuleImplAdvertisement is created, a null is passed to the method.

Using the joinGroup() Method

After a peer group is created, any peer desiring to join it must apply for a membership. Only after this can the peer proceed to the next step in the membership process.

To simplify the use of the GroupManager, it exposes a single method for the entire membership process:

```
public Credential joinGroup(PeerGroup newGroup,StructuredDocument credentials,
                    String authenticationMethod)
                throws GroupManagerAuthenticationException,
                ProtocolNotSupportedException;
```

Notice the parameters of this method. The newGroup is the group that has to be joined. The other two parameters are a net.jxta.document.StructuredDocument, representing the credentials, and a String, representing the authentication method. Before going into the details of these variables, following are a few words about the joinGroup() method.

The joinGroup() method encapsulates three discrete steps:

- The membership apply process

- The authentication process

- The membership join process

A failure in any of these processes will lead to a GroupManagerAuthenticationException.

Therefore, to join the new group, the StudentDemo class just needs to invokes the GroupManager's joinGroup() method:

```
try{

    StructuredDocument preAppForm =
        PreApplicationForm.createPreAppForm
➥(PreApplicationForm.DEPARTMENT_MANAGEMENT);
    manager.joinGroup(p,preAppForm,"PreApplication");

} catch(GroupManagerAuthenticationException authenticationException) {
    //
} catch(ProtocolNotSupportedException protocolException) {
    //
}
```

This takes care of all the steps for joining the membership service. Now let us look into each of these steps in detail.

Applying to the Membership Service

In the apply process, an authentication credential is sent to the membership service. On a successful apply, an authenticator is returned. This is done in the applyToMembershipService() method of the GroupManager, shown in Listing 6.6.

LISTING 6.6   GroupManager.java applyToMembershipService() Method

```
private Authenticator applyToMembershipService(PeerGroup peerGroup,
➥StructuredDocument credentials,String authenticationMethod)
                                                throws
➥ GroupManagerAuthenticationException,[ccc]
ProtocolNotSupportedException{
    Authenticator authenticator = null;
    try {

        AuthenticationCredential authenticationCredential =
                    new AuthenticationCredential
➥(peerGroup,authenticationMethod,credentials );
        MembershipService membership =
➥ (MembershipService) peerGroup.getMembershipService();
        authenticator = (Authenticator)membership.apply(authenticationCredential );

    } catch( PeerGroupException peerGroupException ) {
        LOG.error("Apply process failed !! ",peerGroupException);
        throw new GroupManagerAuthenticationException
➥(peerGroupException.getMessage());
    } catch (ProtocolNotSupportedException protocolNotSupportedException){
        LOG.error(protocolNotSupportedException);
        throw protocolNotSupportedException;
    }
    return authenticator;
}
```

Because we compared an authentication credential to a pre-application form, the classes have been designed to reflect this. Listing 6.7 shows the `PreApplicationForm` class.

LISTING 6.7   PreApplicationForm.java.java;

```
public abstract class PreApplicationForm {

    public static final String DEPARTMENT_COMPUTER_SCIENCE = "CS";
    public static final String DEPARTMENT_MANAGEMENT       = "MT";
    public static final String DEPARTMENT_ARCHITECTURE     = "AT";

    /*
     * This methods creates a Structured Document representing the PreApp form.
     * This serves as an IdentityInfo in the authentication credential.
     */
    public static final StructuredDocument createPreAppForm(String department){

        MimeMediaType type = new MimeMediaType("text","xml");
        StructuredDocument doc =StructuredDocumentFactory.newStructuredDocument
➡( type,"PreAppForm" );
        Element e = doc.createElement( "Department",department);
        doc.appendChild( e );
        return doc;

    }
}
```

The `createPreAppForm()` method creates a `StructuredDocument` representing a pre-app form. It takes a `String` argument to represent the department to which the student wants to apply. Consequently, students can create different documents according to their interests to submit to the `MembershipService`:

```
StructuredDocument preAppForm =
    PreApplicationForm.createPreAppForm
➡(PreApplicationForm.DEPARTMENT_MANAGEMENT);
```

Processing the Apply

During the creation of the group, your membership service was
com.sams.jxta.groups.student.UniversityAdmissionsService. Let us now see how
the membership service processes the apply request. Listing 6.8 shows the
UniversityAdmissionsService.java class.

LISTING 6.8   UniversityAdmissionsService.java.java;

```
public Authenticator apply( AuthenticationCredential unsubscribedCredential )
                    throws PeerGroupException, ProtocolNotSupportedException{

    String method = unsubscribedCredential.getMethod();


    if( (null != method) && !"PreApplication".equals( method ) )
        throw new ProtocolNotSupportedException(
            "Authentication method not recognized :"+
➡" Required \"PreApplication\" ");
    StructuredDocument preApForm =
            (StructuredDocument)unsubscribedCredential.getIdentityInfo();
    Enumeration enum = preApForm.getChildren();
    Element element = (Element) enum.nextElement();
    String departmentAppliedFor =(String) element.getValue();
    // Vacancies exist only in the Computer Science Department
    if(!departmentAppliedFor.equals
➡(PreApplicationForm.DEPARTMENT_COMPUTER_SCIENCE))
        throw new PeerGroupException("No Admissions to this Department(code:"
➡+departmentAppliedFor+")");
    ApplicationForm applicationForm =
➡ new ApplicationForm(this,unsubscribedCredential);
    return applicationForm;
}        .java;
```

The first thing that the method does is get the authentication method. The authentication is checked to verify that it matches the predefined String "PreApplication."

If the string does not match, a
net.jxta.exception.ProtocolNotSupportedException is thrown. What this matching does is prove that you have a credential class that is compatible with your
authentication class. The authentication is done by name instead of the class signature, because the code could be implemented in another language.

After this step, the method extracts the identityInfo element from the authentication credential. From the identityInfo, the String representing the department
applied for is extracted.

Now, the current assumption is that only the department of computer sciences has
vacancies, so the code throws an exception for all departments other than the
computer science department, in which case, it returns a
com.sams.jxta.groups.student.ApplicationForm. The return of the
ApplicationForm signals a successful apply process.

Completing the Authenticator

With a successful apply, an ApplicationForm is returned. An application form is an
authenticator and implements the net.jxta.membership.Authenticator interface.

It is up to the peer to complete the ApplicationForm and submit it to the membership service. The Group Manager provides a dialog the user can fill in to complete
the application form. The code to achieve this is as shown:

```
private void authenticate( Authenticator authenticator ){
    // The following bean looks for standard
    // bean parameters to create the
    // contents to set the authenticator.
    AuthenticatorBean viewBean = new AuthenticatorBean(null,true,authenticator,
➥"Please Enter Required Group Info");
    viewBean.setVisible(true);
}
```

It is the AuthenticatorBean that is responsible for showing the dialog to the user
and accepting inputs. The bean internally uses Java bean introspection and checks
for setter methods in the ApplicationForm.

The output of the authenticate will be as shown in Figure 6.2. Listing 6.9 shows the
main methods in the ApplicationForm.

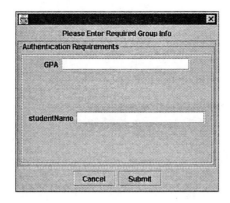

FIGURE 6.2 Completing the application form.

LISTING 6.9 ApplicationForm.java

```java
public class ApplicationForm implements Authenticator{

    private String studentName;
    private float GPA;
    private UniversityAdmissionsService admissionsService;
    private AuthenticationCredential unsubscribedCredential;

    public ApplicationForm(UniversityAdmissionsServiceadmissionsService,
                      AuthenticationCredential unsubscribedCredential){
        this.admissionsService    = admissionsService;
        this.unsubscribedCredential = unsubscribedCredential;
    }

    public String getMethodName(){
        return "ApplicationForm";
    }

    public boolean  isReadyForJoin(){
     if(studentName == null || studentName.trim().equals(""))
        return false;
     if(GPA >3.0f)
      return true;
     else
      return false;
```

LISTING 6.9   Continued

```
    }

    public void setGPA(float GPA){
     this.GPA = GPA;
    }

    public void setStudentName(String studentName){
        this.studentName=studentName;
        }
...
}
```

Note the isReadyForJoin() method of the ApplicationForm. This is a method inherited of the Authenticator interface. It can be used to query the ApplicationForm to determine whether it is completely satisfied and ready for the next step. A return value of false can indicate either an incomplete or failed authentication. Only if the isReadyForJoin() method returns true can the peer actually join the group.

The implementation of the isReadyForJoin() method uses a simple criterion for acceptance. You accept an application form if the student has a GPA (Grade Point Average) above 3 and has filled in a name (in other words, the name field is not left blank).

Joining the Group

After the authenticator is completed (the ApplicationForm is filled up), the peer sends a join request to the MembershipService.

The joinMembershipService of the Group Manager achieves this (see Listing 6.10).

LISTING 6.10   GroupManager.java joinMembershipService() Method

```
private Credential joinMembershipService(Authenticator authenticator,
➥PeerGroup peerGroup)throws GroupManagerAuthenticationException {

    Credential authenticatedCredential = null;
    // We check if the user is authentic
    if( !authenticator.isReadyForJoin() ) {
        LOG.error( "Authenticator is not ready to join");
        throw new GroupManagerAuthenticationException
➥("Authenticator is not ready to join !");
```

LISTING 6.10   Continued

```
    }

    // Since the user is authentic , we allow the
    // user to join the service. But the service may reject the
    // user as well.

    try{
        MembershipService membership =
➥ (MembershipService) peerGroup.getMembershipService();
        authenticatedCredential= membership.join(authenticator);
    } catch(PeerGroupException peerGroupException) {
        LOG.error( "Error in the Join Process",peerGroupException);
        throw new GroupManagerAuthenticationException("Error in the Join Process");
    }
    return authenticatedCredential;
}
```

The `joinMembershipService()` method checks whether the authenticator is ready to join. If this is not the case, it means an incomplete or failed authentication, and an exception is thrown.

If the authenticator is ready to join, it calls the corresponding `MembershipService`'s `join()` method with the `Authenticator` as a parameter. An `AuthenticationCredential` is returned on a successful join. A failure in the join process will throw a `PeerGroupException`. The Group Manager handles this exception by throwing a `GroupManagerAuthenticationException` back to the invoker of the method.

Processing the Join

Having seen that the `GroupManager` invokes the `join()` method of the `MembershipService`, let us look at how your `UniversityAdmissionsService` handles it (see Listing 6.11).

LISTING 6.11   `UniversityAdmissionsService.java` `join()` Method

```
public Credential join(Authenticator authenticated )throws PeerGroupException{

    ApplicationForm applicationForm   = (ApplicationForm)authenticated;
```

LISTING 6.11   Continued

```
    // We double check that the Authentication
    // is indeed successful
    if(!applicationForm.isReadyForJoin())
        throw new PeerGroupException("Application Form rejected !!");
    // this means that the person can be taken in
    InvitationLetter invitationLetter = new InvitationLetter(this);
    invitationLetters.addElement(invitationLetter);
    authenticationCredentials.addElement
➥(authenticated.getAuthenticationCredential());
    return invitationLetter;
}
```

The UniversityAdmissionsService double-checks whether the authenticator is indeed ready to join. This is important because nothing prevents the peer from calling the join method, even though the ApplicationForm is fully complete.

There can also be other conditions that the service checks before allowing the peer to actually join. For the sake of simplicity, we ignore them in this example.

After the service decides that the peer is eligible to join the group, it prepares the Credential. Thereafter, using this Credential can prove membership to the group. In this case, the Credential is an invitation letter represented by the com.sams.jxta.groups.student.InvitationLetter class.

The InvitationLetter class implements the net.jxta.credential.Credential interface, as shown in Listing 6.12.

LISTING 6.12   InvitationLetter.java

```
public class InvitationLetter implements Credential {

    private UniversityAdmissionsService admissionsService;

    public InvitationLetter(UniversityAdmissionsService admissionsService){

        this.admissionsService = admissionsService;
    }

    public MembershipService  getSourceService(){
```

LISTING 6.12   Continued

```
        return admissionsService;
    }

    public ID getPeerGroupID(){
return admissionsService.getPeerGroup().getPeerGroupID();
        }

    public ID getPeerID(){.java;
        return admissionsService.getPeerGroup().getPeerID();
        }

    public StructuredDocument getDocument(MimeMediaType as) throws Exception {

        StructuredDocument doc =
➥StructuredDocumentFactory.newStructuredDocument( as,"InivtationLetter" );

        Element e = doc.createElement( "PeerGroupID",
➥admissionsService.getPeerGroup().getPeerGroupID() );
        doc.appendChild( e );
        e = doc.createElement("TimeOfRequest",""+System.currentTimeMillis());
        doc.appendChild( e );
        return doc;
    }
}
```

The getDocument() method returns a StructureDocument representing the InvitationLetter. The document contains two pieces of information:

- The time that the document was requested
- The PeerID of the peer who has joined the group

The UniversityAdmissionsService maintains a list of all ApplicationCredentials and InvitationForms in two separate vectors called invitationCredentials and authenticationCredentials. The MembershipService requires that this information be maintained and exposed via the methods getAuthCredentials and getCurrentCredentials, respectively. This helps keep track of the various peer memberships of the peer.

Using the `leaveGroup()` Method

The `leaveGroup()` method of the `GroupManager` can be used to cancel the membership from the currently active peer group. The method is shown in Listing 6.13.

LISTING 6.13   `GroupManager.java leaveGroup()` Method

```java
public void leaveGroup(){

    MembershipService memberShipService = activeGroup.getMembershipService();
    try{
        memberShipService.resign();
    } catch(PeerGroupException peerGroupException){
        LOG.error("Exception in resign",peerGroupException);
        throw new GroupManagerException(peerGroupException.getMessage());
    }
    activeGroup = parent;
    purgeGroups();
}
```

The `GroupManager` invokes the `resign()` method of the `MembershipService` to cancel the membership. An exception can occur in this process, and it is thrown back to the invoker as a generic `GroupManagerException`.

After the resign method is successfully executed, the `activeGroup` is made to point to the parent group. In addition, all old advertisements are flushed out. This flushing out is done by the `purgeGroups()` method shown in Listing 6.14.

LISTING 6.14   `GroupManager.java purgeGroups()` Method

```java
public void purgeGroups(){
    DiscoveryService discovery = parent.getDiscoveryService();
    try{
        discovery.flushAdvertisements(null,DiscoveryService.GROUP);
    } catch (java.io.IOException ioException) {
        LOG.error("Error in purging Groups",ioException);
        throw new GroupManagerException(ioException.getMessage());
    }
}
```

The purgeGroups method gets a handle to the DiscoveryService of the parent peer group. It then uses the flushAdvertisements() method to flush all peer group Advertisements.

Processing the Leave

Let us now look at how our UniversityAdmissionsService handles a resign request (see Listing 6.15).

LISTING 6.15   UniversityAdmissionsService.java resign() Method

```
public void resign() throws PeerGroupException{
    //Destroy all records
    invitationLetters = new Vector();
    authenticationCredentials = new Vector();
}
```

The resign method is pretty straightforward. The UniversityAdmissionsService deletes all the records that it had stored about the student. This is achieved by reinitializing the invitationLetters and authenticationCredentials variables.

The StudentDemo Application

The StudentDemo Application is a simple example of how to use the GroupManager. Listing 6.16 shows the init method of the StudentDemo class.

LISTING 6.16   StudentDemo.java init() Method

```
public void init(PeerGroup parentGroup,ID assignedID,Advertisement implAdv)
                        throws PeerGroupException{

    GroupManager manager = new GroupManager(parentGroup);
    // This is to create a new University Admissions group
    // to deal with the admissions
    // of a particular university
    PeerGroup p =manager.addGroup("UniversityStudents",
➥"com.sams.jxta.groups.student.UniversityAdmissionsService",
➥"To represent all graduate students in a University",null,false);

System.out.println("Successfully created Admissions Service");

    // Try to submit a Pre-Application for the
    // Department of Management
```

LISTING 6.16   Continued

```
        try{

            StructuredDocument preAppForm = PreApplicationForm.createPreAppForm(
➡PreApplicationForm.DEPARTMENT_MANAGEMENT);
            manager.joinGroup(p,preAppForm,"PreApplication");

        } catch(GroupManagerAuthenticationException authenticationException) {

            LOG.debug("Exception :Expected behavior. University has no admissions"+
➡" for this dpt");
            LOG.debug("Message is : "+authenticationException.getMessage());
        } catch(ProtocolNotSupportedException protocolException) {

            LOG.error("Error in join !",protocolException);
        }

        // Try to submit a Pre-Application for the
        // Department of computer science
        try{

            StructuredDocument preAppForm =[ccc]
PreApplicationForm.createPreAppForm(
➡PreApplicationForm.DEPARTMENT_COMPUTER_SCIENCE);
            manager.joinGroup(p,preAppForm,"PreApplication");

        } catch(GroupManagerAuthenticationException authenticationException) {
            LOG.error("Error in join !",authenticationException);
        } catch(ProtocolNotSupportedException protocolException) {
            LOG.error("Error in join !",protocolException);
        }
    }
```

The init() method creates a GroupManager instance. The parent peer group used is actually the net peer group. The addGroup() method is used to create a new group called UniversityStudents with the membership service class as UniversityAdmissionsService.

After the successful creation of the group, the user tries to create a pre-application form to join the Department of Management. This is expected to fail during the apply process because, you may recall, we designed the service in such a way that it admits students only to the Computer Sciences Department. This failure in the apply process will lead to a GroupManagerAuthenticationException.

Next, the user tries to apply to the Computer Sciences Department. This should work, and when the authenticate method has been reached, a dialog will pop up, asking the user to fill the application form.

The user must fill the application form such that the GPA is greater than 3.0 and the name is not blank. Only in this case will the join process succeed. If this condition is not met, the join process fails.

As you can see, it has become a fairly trivial task to join and exit groups at will by using the Group Manager.

"Plugging in" the Null Membership Service

When we started designing the Group Manager, we wanted to design it in such a way that the programmer could easily plug in any MembershipService implementation. To test this, you can try to get your Group Manager to work with the null membership service provided by the platform. The class representing this service is net.jxta.impl.membership.NullMembershipService.

For this purpose, we have included another class, which is a modified version of the StudentDemo class, to make it work with the NullMembershipService. The class is com.sams.jxta.groups.student.StudentDemoNull.

The output of running the StudentDemoNull class is shown in Figure 6.3.

FIGURE 6.3   Authenticator for null membership service.

The authenticator has just one file called auth1Identity. Regardless of what you fill in here, you will be authenticated. The authentication will work, even if the field is left blank and submitted.

Summary

In this chapter, we have discussed peer groups and their importance. The peer group concept can help simplify many of the challenges faced in managing P2P networks. It becomes even more significant as the complexity of the network increases.

We have looked at various techniques that can be employed for peer group management. We have also seen peer membership management in depth by building a Group Manager and a real-life student example. Peer Membership management is an easy but powerful strategy that can be used to manage peer groups.

The examples in this chapter do not emphasize the security requirements of the system. However, this is an important requirement in real–world scenarios. There are many ways by which this can be achieved. One possible way is to add digital signatures to credentials. Digital signatures are discussed in Chapter 8.

7

JXTA Content Manager Service (CMS)

By Daniel Brookshier and Navaneeth Krishnan

Many people consider P2P synonymous with file sharing. There is a very good reason for this popular misconception. The majority of the P2P systems that exist today, such as Napster, Gnutella, and Freenet, are used for file/data sharing. These very same applications brought the P2P technology to the limelight. As a result, data sharing has become the most popular application of the peer-to-peer technology. While applications that use the peer-to-peer architecture need not be limited to file sharing, it must be admitted that data sharing is one of the most powerful ways of utilizing the peer-to-peer architecture.

Because data sharing among peers has the potential of becoming one of the basic requirements for almost all non-trivial JXTA applications, it would be logical to have something in JXTA that satisfies this necessity. This is where the JXTA Content Manager Service (CMS) comes in. The CMS acts a framework for sharing/exchanging content among JXTA peers. This chapter will introduce you to the workings of the JXTA CMS. You will also create a simple example that will illustrate the CMS API.

An Overview

CMS is a service that is a service for sharing content among multiple peers in a peer group. The service provides the ability for a peer to host content that it shares with other peers and to locate and retrieve content from others.

The first version of CMS is not as sophisticated as many other CMS systems. There is no sophisticated search mechanism or any guarantee of optimum distribution of content. However, the first implementation is extremely useful for many situations.

In addition, there is work being done to improve CMS. With additions to searching capabilities and improvements to file transfer, CMS will become better over time. The initial implementation should work for many applications as is.

Before we proceed into the actual workings of the CMS, we should cover a few concepts about content management in general.

What Is Content?

Any data that needs to be shared can be called *content*. It could be a simple text file, a music file, or even an executable class file. JXTA sometimes uses the term *codat* (Code/Data) to refer to content that can be code or data or both.

A *content identifier* is used to uniquely identify content. Because the content identifier needs to be unique, a 128-bit MD5 checksum of the actual content is used as the content identifier.

A *content advertisement* is used to provide metadata about the content. In addition to the content ID, this metadata includes the following:

- *Content name*—Any user-specified name for the content. CMS requires that all content have a content name. However, because this parameter is user specified, there is no guarantee that the content name is unique.

- *Content length*—The length of the content in bytes.

- *Mime type*—The Mime type of the content.

- *Description*—A brief textual description of the content.

All information about the content, other than its name and identifier, are optional.

Applications for Content Management

As mentioned earlier, data sharing is one of the basic services that any sufficiently complex P2P application will require. Although CMS provides only some basic functionality, it can be used as a foundation to develop content sharing applications.

Content management is more than just the sharing of information. Content management includes the right to create, edit, and access information. There is also searching, backups, publishing, archiving, indexing, and other services.

The current version of CMS simply gives you the ability to share content within a group and perform a limited search based on a document's title. This, however, is a very large first step compared to other content management systems. By distributing content, users do not have to depend on a central server or expensive software.

Most content management systems today lean toward Web-based services too. With CMS, you can transfer data to a laptop and use it at your leisure while not connected to the Internet. This is also a boon to users who are still using dialup Internet, because they do not need to stay online to access content.

CMS can also be used for sharing application data. For example, the contents of a small database can be shared. This would make it possible to use a local database instead of dealing with a centralized database that requires a large capacity as well as bandwidth to serve all of its users. The data could be used in a standalone or a distributed fashion where many peers have portions of the database. The key factor is the ability to replicate sections to ensure high availability to all peers without hampering a single peer.

In many situations, you can also tailor data that is shared. Many databases or libraries of data are not accessed in their entirety by every user. Most systems have only a small percentage that is available to a single user. By replicating only the data that a user requires, the system will work faster because there is no delay to access a server.

There are many possibilities. The key is to look at data the way users do. By limiting the scope of data to just the user's focus, only small amounts of data need to be resident on the user's PC.

There is probably room on most PCs for reasonably large amounts of data. This means there is enough room to replicate the user's data plus a sub-section of the total, so that it may be shared with other users and be used in ad-hoc queries by other peers.

Digital Rights Management

As was mentioned in the introduction of the book, rights need to be respected to ensure that your application is allowed to operate. Respecting copyrights and intellectual property is key to many data applications and especially to a content management system. If you plan to create an application that is available to the public, make sure that you have a way to confirm copyright ownership, the right to distribute, and the rights of users to use or access the information.

Privacy

At the present time, CMS is not a private network application. In the future, a system that includes encryption will probably be created, or you could use CMS as a base and create your own. At present, however, all transmissions are unencrypted.

Because CMS is group based, you can constrain searching and sharing to only those in a group. However, you should create custom membership protocols if your data is even slightly sensitive and cannot withstand the public gaze.

Peers are not anonymous. Using standard techniques, a peer host computer can easily be located. JXTA was not designed to hide its users. Data encryption is available, but creating an anonymous identity is not a JXTA feature. Sharing data in countries that do not allow free speech could easily cause the user to be located and prosecuted. The same problem of user exposure exists for users that pass copyrighted information without permission (even test files).

How CMS Works

The `net.jxta.share.CMS` class represents the Content Management Service. The `startApp` method of CMS takes a directory name as an input parameter. This directory represents the persistence directory that the service uses to store persistent information about content that is shared and other persistent state information. It is specified in a name value form *dir=<directory Name>*. If no directory name parameter is provided, the CMS service will create a default directory called cms to store the information. Information that is shared or retrieved is stored in directories specified in the API.

After a persistence directory is created, the CMS will delegate a `ContentManager` to manage the content. The `ContentManager` is a generic interface that can be used for any class capable of managing content. Its default implementation is `net.jxta.share.ContentManagerImpl`.

The CMS additionally listens to the various requests that it receives. When another peer requests a search of local content or for a copy of shared content, the Content Manager will automatically handle the request. The two types of request messages recognized by CMS are list requests and get requests.

The following paragraphs detail each of the messages the CMS protocol supports. The current version of CMS uses asynchronous pipes. Because of the pipe implementation, messages may be received out of order or not at all. In addition, as with any P2P application, peers will appear, disappear, or even refuse requests. This means you should take this into account and repeat your requests at reasonable intervals.

There is no guarantee that a piece of content will be completely transferred. A peer may simply be disconnected from the network. Remember that a peer can be a laptop or on a dialup Internet connection that is dropped on a regular basis.

List Requests—LIST_REQ

A list request (LIST_REQ request message) is a request sent to the CMS to retrieve the list of all contents that it is sharing. The CMS will have to respond to such a request with a LIST_RES message that contains the catalog of items found from the LIST_REQ message. A LIST_RES response will contain the content advertisements of all the content that is shared by the service.

The CMS uses a ListMessageProcessor to process all LIST_REQ messages.

Get Requests—GET_REQ

While the list request is used to get a list of all contents from the CMS, a GET_REQ message is used to get one particular piece of content from the list. The request comes as a GET_REQ message to the CMS. It also contains an identifier to the content that is requested. The CMS will have to respond to the GET_REQ message with a GET_RES message. The GET_RES response will contain the actual data of the content requested.

The CMS uses a GetMessageProcessor to process all GET_REQ messages.

Any client of the CMS will use these two types of messages for content exchange. A LIST_REQ can be used to retrieve a list of content available in a remote peer. Any desired content can be chosen from this list by utilizing the metadata about the content available in the advertisement. After a particular content file is identified, a GET_REQ request (which will include the content identifier) can be sent to retrieve that particular content.

Future CMS Implementations

The implementation is currently undergoing changes. The first goal seems to be to improve the search mechanism. The first implementation must open a pipe to each peer to locate files. In the future, there will be improvements to how searching is done. Such systems will probably emulate similar indexing functionality of successful systems like Gnutella.

A second problem is the choice of asynchronous pipes for file transfers. Although these pipes are a common denominator, they are also very slow. Part of the problem is that the HTTP protocol is often used. This means that there is usually a relay peer between the peers that adds extra time to the transfer.

A Simple CMS Example

One good use of CMS is simple replications of files. There are many reasons for using CMS. First is that you can share files from anywhere on the Internet. This means there is no need to be directly tied into a corporate intranet. As we have discussed, looking up documents on the Internet requires a connection. If the files are copied, once on the user's PC, there is no need to connect to the Internet each time you use the documents.

Because this is P2P, the sharing will be done with all users in a peer group. Anyone can share a document. Sharing is done by specifying a directory or a file. If a directory is chosen, all the files in the directory are shared.

Search Interval

File search and retrieval will be done automatically. We assume that all files are valuable and will request a copy of every file we find. One reason we might do this is if we have a library of user manuals that need to be on each machine.

This example has just the bare minimum. Mostly, we have just written the CMS code that we will be discussing. There are a couple of flaws and quite a few missing functions. One flaw is the interval that the system takes to look for new documents. The interval is quite high in this example because we are testing the system. Normally, the search for new documents might occur once or twice a day. Remember that we are talking about documents and not e-mail or instant messages, so new documents are rare in most cases.

The sharing of documents should be continuous. As new users are added to the group, they will need to fetch all of the documents, so they need a good chance of finding the current set of documents. If reachable peers are not sharing, there is no way to locate the documents. If we only shared when we were looking for documents, the system would probably fail, especially if there were only a small group of users. The reason is, the odds are that another peer is looking and sharing at the same time you are, proportional to the number of users. In a large network, there is a good chance you will find a peer with the data. In a small network, the chances are slim.

Security

Another problem not addressed by the example is security. In many cases, security of the data is probably not an issue. If you used group membership to limit peers, you probably have the minimum you need. If you need to keep the files secret, the easiest method is to encrypt the files before sharing. You could also use a secure pipe, but you can use stronger encryption plus use a digital signature to ensure that data is not corrupted.

Another aspect of CMS that is often overlooked are viruses. Any shared file could be infected. Any virus-free file that you re-share, could have been infected by your computer, and could then infect those with whom you share. This can be a nightmare unless you take precautions. One precaution is to scan files as they arrive.

If you can ensure everyone has the virus software, this is a good solution. The problem is that virus scanners are not always on a user's PC, and there is no standard interface to run a scanner on a new file. It could be possible within a corporate context where you have control. If your users are all over the Internet, the odds are low that you can ensure proper virus protection.

Another way to ensure that files are virus free is to have digitally signed copies. By comparing the checksum of the document and validating the signature of the sender, you can trust the sender enough to use the document. As long as you share only the signed version, others will also be able to trust the information without fear that you tampered with the file. Just be sure that the source of the files really can be trusted.

One concept that is ripe for the P2P world is a distributed virus checker. By using a set of peers that are trusted, files can be validated, signed, and then made available to the network. This is another example of a JXTA appliance that could be used to make the JXTA network more dependable and less risky. This also opens the door for a commercial application.

Another feature that needs to be added is a capability to ignore duplicate files on other peers and not request them. Because the current design uses a share directory and a directory for content from other peers, there is no problem with overwriting local documents. However, if a document is on two peers, the last document down-loaded will overwrite others with the same name. This should be easy to add because the advertisement has a checksum that can be used to look for duplicates. Some type of renaming or file management would also need to be added.

Now that we have covered what is and what is not part of our example, let's start by getting the context of the CMS.

Overall Design

The current design breaks the application into two parts—the user interface and the JXTA specific code. Figure 7.1 presents a UML diagram of the application. The UpdateCMS class implements Application and performs the bulk of the operations with CMS.

The MirrorLibrary class is used to display files and to initiate sharing of directories. We won't cover the user interface class because it is rather simple.

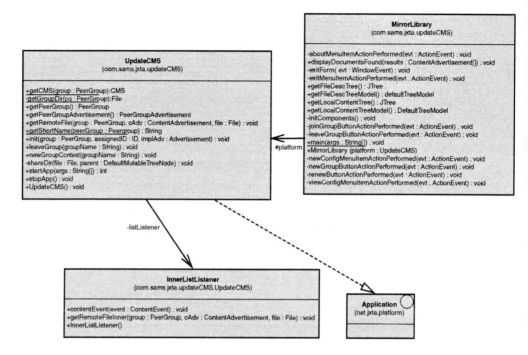

FIGURE 7.1   UML diagram of the *UpdateCMS* application.

Initializing the Content Manager

Initializing CMS is done as a JXTA service that has a self-contained application that handles input and output requests. To initialize CMS, you create an instance of CMS, call the init method, with the group you want to share documents within, and then call startApp.

The startApp method takes two directory names as arguments. The first is used to store group related files. The second directory is used by CMS for various bookkeeping functions that need to persist between sessions. When startApp is called, the system begins processing incoming requests for shared files.

The method in Listing 7.1 performs the steps required and ensures that only one copy of CMS is started per group. By matching a hash of the group ID in the cmsSessions hashtable, you can ensure that just one copy exists per group ID. CMS does not have the ability to know there is already a copy created for the given group. If you did create a duplicate service, you would start up extra threads that would be redundant. There can also be other problems, including threading issues.

LISTING 7.1   Accessing the CMS Service

```
public static CMS getCMS(PeerGroup group) {
       // check if the cms is already started
       CMS cms = (CMS)cmsSessions.get(group.getID());

       if (null == cms) {
           // create a new cms for this peergroup
           cms = new CMS();
           try {
               cms.init(group, null,group.getPeerGroupAdvertisement());
           } catch (PeerGroupException e) {
               e.printStackTrace();
           }

           cms.startApp(new File(getGroupDir(group), CMS.DEFAULT_DIR));
           if (null != cms) {
               cmsSessions.put(group.getID(), cms);
           }else{
               System.out.println("Error creating CMS object.");
               throw new RuntimeException("Error creating CMS object.");
           }
       }else{
           System.out.println("Using the old CMS.");
       }
       return cms;
   }
```

ContentManager **Class**

Figure 7.2 shows the relationship of the CMS class, the Application interface, and the ContentManager class. The ContentManager class is used as an interface to the CMS service.

Note that to access the ContentManager, you simply call getContentManger. The ContentManager class has the methods to initiate searches, get files (based on the search), share files, and unshare files. The ContentManger object returned is capable of operating in the group with which the CMS object was initialized.

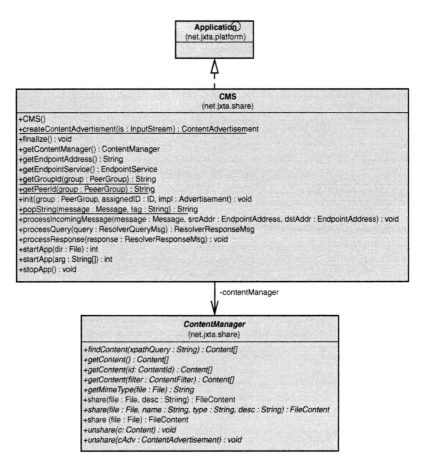

FIGURE 7.2   UML diagram relating the CMS class, ContentManager, and the JXTA Application Interface.

Sharing Content

Sharing data with CMS is relatively easy. In the following code, the ContentManager is retrieved from the CMS object. The ContentManager can then share the give file:

```
ContentManager contentManager;
cContentManager = cms.getContentManager();
contentManager.share(file);
```

Note that the shared file is only visible to members in the same group using CMS.

Sharing a Directory

The shareDir method shown in Listing 7.2 is used to recursively share a directory of files to a CMS group. There is nothing here that is too spectacular, and the only code associated to CMS is the share method at the bottom of the second if statement's true block:

LISTING 7.2   Example shareDir Method

```
private void shareDir(File file,DefaultMutableTreeNode parent){
   File files[] = null;
   try {
      if (file.isDirectory()){
         files = file.listFiles();
         //Share a default Directoryfor (int i = 0; i < files.length;i++){
         if (!files[i].isDirectory()){
            DefaultMutableTreeNode fileNode
                   = new DefaultMutableTreeNode(files[i].getName());
            parent.add(fileNode);
            // this is where we actually share the file
            contentManager.share(files[i]);
         }else{
            // it is a directory so add it to the list too
            DefaultMutableTreeNode dirNode
                   = new DefaultMutableTreeNode(file.getName());
            parent.add(dirNode);
            // Recursive call to read files in the directory
            shareDir(files[i],parent);
         }// end for
      }else{
         DefaultMutableTreeNode fileNode
                   = new DefaultMutableTreeNode(file.getName());
         parent.add(fileNode);
         // this is where we actually share the file
         contentManager.share(file);
      }
   }catch (IOException e) {
      System.out.println("ERROR: could not share ");
      e.printStackTrace();
      return;
   }
}// end of shareDir()
```

Searching for Content

To search, you need to do three things:

1. Create a listener to process results.

2. Initiate the search.

3. Retrieve content.

The CachedListContentRequest class is used as a basis for launching and managing a search. The class uses a cache to store responses and to ensure that duplicate content results are unique by ignoring those already in the cache. You override the notifyMoreResults and notifyDone methods to process events.

The notifyMoreResults method is called whenever a peer responds with a list of results from a search.

The notifyDone method is called when all peers have been notified or when the search is terminated by calling the cancel method.

The listener, in Listing 7.3, is actually a compound class that listens for and processes the results from search queries. The UML for the listener and the CachedListContentRequest class is shown in Figure 7.3.

LISTING 7.3   Inner Class ListRequestor Class

```
class ListRequestor extends CachedListContentRequest {
  boolean done = false;
  public ListRequestor( PeerGroup group, String inSubStr ) {
    super( group, inSubStr );
  }// end of constructor

  public void notifyMoreResults() {
    if (mirrorGUI != null) {
      ContentAdvertisement[] searchResults = getResults();
      // Get the files
      File saveFile;
      for(int i = 0;i < searchResults.length;i++){
        saveFile = new File(inputDir+searchResults[i].getName());
        getRemoteFile(group,searchResults[i], saveFile);
      }
```

LISTING 7.3   Continued

```
    }
  }// End of notifyMoreResults()

  public void notifyDone() {
     done = true;
     System.out.println("Requestor done");
     //lsResults = this.getResults();
  }// End of notifyDone()

  public boolean isDone(){
     return done;
  }// End of isDone()
}// end of inner class
```

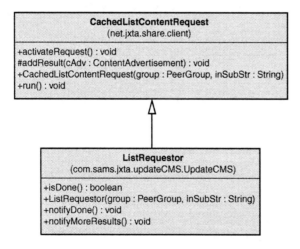

FIGURE 7.3   *CachedListContentRequest* and an example implementation.

Available in the content request via the call to the getResults method is an array of
ContentAdvertisement objects (see the UML shown in Figure 7.4). The
ContentAdvertisement is used to create a request to transfer the file from another
peer. We cover the getRemoteFile method in our example code later that does this
processing.

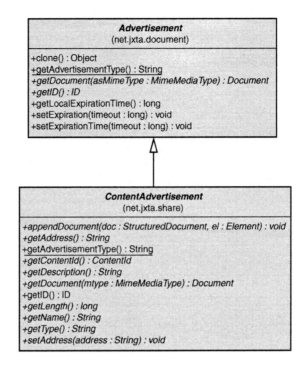

FIGURE 7.4   The `ContentAdvertisement` class.

Starting a Search

The next step is to initiate the search for the content. Normally, the process would seem simple—just send a message out to the JXTA network to look for the file you want. In fact, the command is rather simple. This is shown in the following code that looks for a file named `resume.doc`:

```
request = new ListRequestor(group, "resume.doc");
```

The request does not start to execute until you activate it with the `activateRequest` method:

```
request.activateRequest();
```

The CMS system will begin broadcasting requests to other peers after the request is activated. However, because you are in a peer-to-peer system, you can't be assured of finding your document. Peers appear and disappear on the network at random times. To find a specific document, you need to search periodically for the document.

The class shown in Listing 7.4 searches for all files in a specific group. A thread is used to repeatedly re-initiate the search based on a specific interval. The class also has the ability to stop the thread if the specific file is found.

Note that when a new request is created or the thread is canceled, the cancel method is called to terminate the code in the Content Manager that is processing incoming messages.

LISTING 7.4   Class PeriodicDocSearch, Used to Initiate a Scheduled Search Request from Peers in the Group for Files

```
class PeriodicDocSearch implements Runnable{
   ListRequestor request = null;
   boolean running = true;
   int sleepTimeMilliseconds;

   public PeriodicDocSearch(int sleepTimeMilliseconds){
       this.sleepTimeMilliseconds = sleepTimeMilliseconds;
       request = new ListRequestor(group, null);
       request.activateRequest();
   }// end of constructor

   public void stopThread(){
       running = false;
       if (request != null){
          request.cancel();
       }
   }// End of stopThread()

   public void run(){
       while (running){
          request.cancel();
          request = new ListRequestor(group, "");
          request.activateRequest();
          try{
            Thread.sleep(sleepTimeMilliseconds);
          }catch(InterruptedException ie){
             // just shut down the thread
             stopThread();
          }
       }// while running
   }// End of run()
}// end of class PeriodicDocSearch
```

Another way to search is with a `ContentFilter`. If you recall from the UML in Figure 7.1, a search method took an implementation of the `ContentFilter` interface. The interface, shown in Figure 7.5, is used to test whether an item found should be reported. Your implementation examines the input and returns `true` if the content is okay or `false` if it is to be discarded. The effect is that the system does not do a search, but asks for all content (as if the search criteria was null or an empty string). The actual elimination of items happens on the local peer.

There is development on additional search features that would distribute searching much more efficiently than the current brute force implementation.

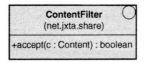

FIGURE 7.5   The `ContentFilter` interface UML diagram.

Getting Content

After you receive information about content, you need to retrieve it. Messages announcing content are content advertisements. These advertisements contain the filename and other information. In the example, you only worry about the filename. Like a listing search, the get content process includes the creation of a listener. However, the difference is that the class that downloads the file can also be used to monitor the download process and status. This is different from the list listener, because it is optional. You could override the class if you needed to add monitoring. Note that the current version starts the thread for monitoring in the constructor. The problem here is that this makes it impossible to use a listener pattern, because the thread is started before a listener could be added. So if you decide you need to monitor downloads, be sure to override the methods and have that class as an inner class communicating with its parent or some other method, because the class could begin to generate events before a listener could be added, making it possible to lose events.

The following is example code. Because you do not need to monitor downloads, you do not have a listener. All you need to do is create a `ContentRequestHandler` object with the desired group, the content advertisement found, and the destination file object:

```
public void getRemoteFile( PeerGroup group
                    , ContentAdvertisement cAdv
                    , File file){
```

```
    try {
      contentRequestHandler
                = new ContentRequestHandler(group, cAdv, file);
      //contentRequestHandler.addContentListener(contentListener);
    } catch (InvocationTargetException e) {
      e.printStackTrace();
    }
}// end of getRemoteFile()
```

The ContentListener interface is used for both incoming lists and handling the process of reconstituting a document from another peer. You have seen the InnerListListener implementation of the class. The InnerGetContentListener class shown in Listing 7.5 shows how simple retrieving the file is. The Content interface provides the original ContentAdvertisement that is used to create a file, and the getInputStream method is used to write the contents of the document. Figure 7.6 shows the UML.

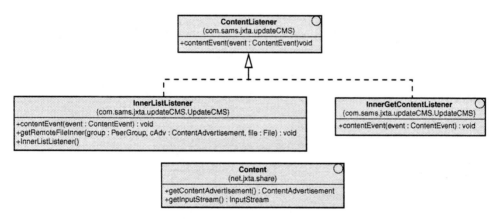

FIGURE 7.6 The ContentListener interface, InnerListListener, InnerGetContentListener implementations, and Content interface.

The ContentEvent ID is used to determine if the event has failed, completed, or is still in progress. After the transfer is complete, the file is written to the local disk. Note that this means that the file is not available to write to the local disk until it is done. The reason for this is that the contents of the file can come in any order. The ContentManager tracks all the pieces and places them into the correct order.

In the future, a transport other than asynchronous pipes will be used to reduce the overhead that is currently in the CMS service. However, asynchronous pipes are the common denominator so that most peers will be able transfer files.

LISTING 7.5   Class `InnerGetContentListener` Implements `ContentListener` to Retrieve Files from Other Peers

```
protected class InnerGetContentListener implements ContentListener {
    /** Called when a Content Handler has an event */
    public void contentEvent(ContentEvent event){
    System.out.println(event);
    switch(event.getId()){
      case ContentEvent.LOAD_FAIL:
        break;
      case ContentEvent.LOAD_DONE:
        ContentRequestHandler handler = (ContentRequestHandler)event.getSource();
        File file = handler.getFile();
        PeerGroupAdvertisement ad
            = (PeerGroupAdvertisement)group.getPeerGroupAdvertisement();
        String groupName = ad.getName();
        DefaultMutableTreeNode fileNode = new DefaultMutableTreeNode(file.getName()
                                + "("+groupName+")");
        JTree tree = mirrorGUI.getLocalContentTree();
        DefaultTreeModel model = mirrorGUI.getLocalContentTreeModel();
        model.insertNodeInto(fileNode, remoteFiles,remoteFiles.getChildCount());

        tree.treeDidChange();
        ((DefaultTreeModel)tree.getModel()).reload() ;

        break;
      case ContentEvent.LOAD_PROGRESS:
        break;
    } // End switch
}// End of inner class InnerGetContentListener
```

Summary

We have given a relatively simple overview of the JXTA CMS service. The service is quite simple and is not a full-featured content management system. It only provides simple searching and sharing without digital rights management or encryption. The service can be expanded to meet these needs.

We also covered a few applications for content managers in a peer-to-peer-system. Applications can benefit from the CMS service. Duplicating or distributing data is already a part of many applications. In some cases, the applications would work better in a P2P application instead of central servers. Servers are popular partly because of their centralized control and efficient use of resources. When the entire Internet is a resource, and applications run faster with local data, P2P content management is a better solution.

Content management can be used for documents, data, code, or any combination. In the chapter's example, content is anything that is in a specific directory. The data from other group members is automatically requested and replication. In this example, the CMS service is used to replicate all data in the peer group.

There are many more applications for content management. Depending on your requirements, you will need to add additional functionality, such as encryption and digital rights management. However, the key is that your application will be more available and probably more efficient than a traditional server-based approach.

8

JXTA and Security

By Navaneeth Krishnan

Security is unquestionably one of the major concerns in any networked environment, and peer-to-peer networks are no exception. Needless to say, the success of your application will largely depend on how well you address your security concerns. Designing a suitable security model may prove to be one of the greatest challenges to a P2P application designer.

In this chapter, we will take a look at the various security concerns that might arise when developing P2P applications. We will go into the details of how JXTA strives to provide basic security primitives to help you build secure P2P applications. Towards the end, we will look at security issues in two popular P2P networks—Freenet and Napster.

Importance of Security

The importance of security in P2P applications cannot be underestimated. In fact, security is one of the major impediments to the widespread adoption of P2P, especially in corporate environments. There are basically two reasons for this.

The first reason is purely psychological. P2P gained widespread acknowledgement due to applications like Napster, Gnutella, and so on, which were also notorious for promoting and enabling unlawful activities, such as copyright violations. This resulted in an initial "pirate-to-pirate" image for the technology, and that has been a bit difficult to get away from.

The second is purely technical. Unlike security models for centralized systems, those for decentralized ones are much harder to implement.

However, distributed security is expected to change with the growth of the technology. Security models for P2P networks are predicted to mature with time and are likely to catch up with their client/server counterparts sooner than later.

Security is Multifaceted

The word security is so broad that it can be subject to a lot of interpretations (and misinterpretations). Security needs may vary from application to application. What may be desirable in one may not be desirable in another. Consider an application that enables anonymous file sharing, such as Freenet, and compare it with an enterprise application that enables collaboration between various people in the organization. The security model for the two may be strikingly dissimilar, and desirable features could be just the opposite. While the first application may be concerned about the anonymity of its users, the second may be concerned about the authenticity of its users.

The point is that P2P as such does not dictate any security features. It is up to the applications to implement security frameworks to suit their requirement.

Security Attacks in P2P Networks

Most, if not all, of the security concerns in a traditional client/server environment hold good for the P2P environment as well. In addition, P2P applications may introduce a whole new bunch of security concerns. For example, an employee can knowingly or unknowingly share confidential information to a file-sharing network like Gnutella and thus make it publicly available to the whole world.

While the above-mentioned concern may have to do more with company policy or usage of the technology rather than the technology itself, we must understand that such concerns also exist. For our discussion, however, we will be concerned more about the technical aspects of security.

Security attacks in P2P systems (as a matter of fact, in all networked environments) can be classified into two broad categories—active and passive network attacks.

Active Network Attacks

Active attacks are those in which the attacker is an active participant. The active attacker is usually in an aggressive mode. Different types of active attacks are possible:

- *Masquerades*—These are attacks in which the attacker pretends to be someone he is not. Most often, the attacker pretends to be some valid or privileged entity.

- *Man-in-the-middle*—As the name suggests, in this type of attack, the attacker intercepts the communication between two network nodes. The attacker may intend to modify or corrupt the information flow.

- *Playback or replay Attacks*—Such an attack usually involves capturing an exchange of information between two nodes and repeating the exact steps again to make it look like another genuine conversation.

Passive Network Attacks

Passive network attacks are those in which the attackers are predominantly in an inert state. The most significant form of passive attack is eavesdropping:

- *Eavesdropping*—Generally involves the silent capture of data by the attacker.

- *Traffic analysis*—Here, the attacker not only captures the data but also tries to learn more by analyzing the data.

Usually, passive attacks are precursors to active attacks. For example, an attacker may first be passive in a network and sniff all the traffic between Peer A and Peer B. After Peer A has left, the attacker may communicate with Peer B by replaying the exact data that Peer A had initially transmitted. This is a case of an Eavesdropping as a precursor to a replay attack.

While it might not be practically possible to entirely eliminate the chances for security attacks, what needs to be done is to minimize possibility of such attacks.

JXTA Platform Security

The JXTA Java Binding by itself contains many built-in security features that can enhance applications built over it. Even though these are by no means sufficient for building a full-fledged secure application, they can potentially provide a base over which secure JXTA applications can be built.

Currently, the following security features are provided by the JXTA platform:

- TLS as a Secure Transport layer (TLS)—TLS (RFC 2246), also known as Secure Sockets Layer (SSL) V3.1, is based on public key technology. The JXTA platform provides TLS as a medium of secure communications. Applications can exploit TLS capabilities of the platform by using secure pipes, which internally use TLS, to guarantee safety against passive attacks.

- *Peer certificates*—The TLS layer requires the use of certificates to enable its functioning. Consequently, each peer generates its own certificate and acts as its own Certification Authority (CA). This certificate, called the root certificate, is used to sign service certificates that the peers issue for each service that it supports.

The root certificate is distributed along with the peer's advertisement. Therefore, every other peer can always verify that an advertisement is indeed from the peer who claims to have issued it.

- *Personal security environment*—Every peer is protected by a peer ID and password. This is used to decrypt the private key to a user's personal security environment. This acts as a first line of defense against a local attacker (an attacker having physical access to the machine running the JXTA Peer).

JXTA Security Requirements

The JXTA platform depends on the following packages and APIs for its security requirements:

- *PureTLS*—Pure TLS (`http://www.rtfm.com/puretls/`) is an open-source Java implementation of the TLS protocol. It is used to achieve end-to-end privacy between peer communications.

- *Cryptix 3*—Cryptix (`http://www.cryptix.org`) is a clean room implementation of Sun's JCE 1.1. JCE stands Java Cryptographic Extensions and provides standard interfaces for cryptographic algorithms and services. It is used by PureTLS for various algorithms.

- *Cryptix ASN.1 Kit*—ASN.1 stands for Abstract Syntax Notation One (`http://sourceforge.net/projects/cryptix-asn1`). Simply put, it is a language that allows definitions of various data types, such as integers, strings, sequences, and so on. Due to its simplistic encoding scheme, it can be used to message between different network applications. The ASN.1 kit can be used to use this notation in Java programs. It is used by the JXTA platform to support X509V3 certificates.

- *Bouncy Castle Crypto APIs*—Another open source JCE implementation used to generate certificates(`http://www.bouncycastle.org`).

The Cryptographic Toolkit

In addition to the few basic security features that come with the JXTA platform, the JXTA Security Project provides a toolkit with a basic set of security algorithms that can be used in JXTA applications.

Because JXTA is targeted for almost every device with a digital heartbeat, the security had to reflect this design philosophy. It had to be as simplistic and minimal as possible and also cater to resource-constrained environments. Therefore, the JXTA Security Toolkit was designed based on the JavaCard 2.1 security model.

JavaCard is the technology that powers Java on smart cards that may probably be the most resource constrained Java environment.

JXTA Security Suites

A *security suite* represents a full-fledged security system. It consists of various security algorithms and services that can be used by the clients of the suite. One may visualize a suite as a factory of security algorithms. Figure 8.1 shows the JxtaCrypto interface that is used to access each of the services provided in the security package. We will discuss each of these interfaces in the following paragraphs.

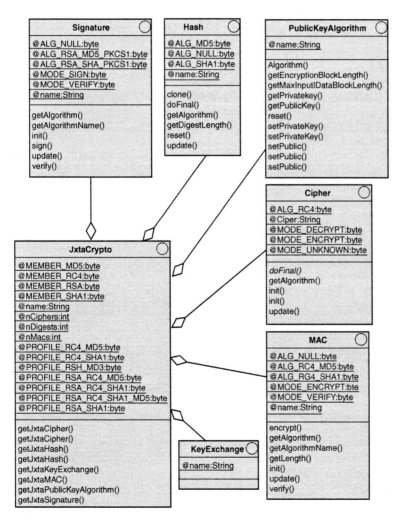

FIGURE 8.1 UML relationships of the JxtaCrypto interface and key interfaces in the JXTA Crypto package.

JXTA Security defines an interface that all suites have to adhere to, the JxtaCrypto interface is shown in the following listing. Each method returns a class that implements a standard interface. The interface is used to retrieve the supported versions of these interfaces.

```
public interface jxta.security.crypto.JxtaCrypto {
  public Cipher getJxtaCipher();
  public Cipher getJxtaCipher(byte type) throws CryptoException;
  public Hash getJxtaHash();
  public Hash getJxtaHash(byte type) throws CryptoException;
  public KeyExchange getJxtaKeyExchange();
  public MAC getJxtaMAC();
  public MAC getJxtaMAC(byte type) throws CryptoException;
  public PublicKeyAlgorithm getJxtaPublicKeyAlgorithm();
  public Signature getJxtaSignature();
}
```

The idea behind having a standard interface is that multiple implementation of the security system, probably from different providers, can be easily plugged into the system.

Nonetheless, JXTA Security also provides a default implementation of the JxtaCrypto called the JXTACrypto Suite (net.security.impl.crypto.JxtaCryptoSuite).

The JXTACrypto Suite

Being the default security suite of the JXTA platform, the JXTACrypto Suite supports various types of cryptographic operations, such as encryption, hashing, and so on. Now, each of these types of operations can be implemented using different algorithms. For example, hashing can be done using either an MD5 or an SHA algorithm. For this purpose, JXTA defines what is called an algorithm profile.

Algorithm Profiles

An *algorithm profile* can be defined as one particular combination of algorithms. This means that profiles will define one specific algorithm for encryption, one specific algorithm for hashing. For example, the PROFILE_RSA_RC4_SHA uses the RSA algorithm for asymmetric encryption, RC4 algorithm for symmetric encryption, and SHA for hashing.

For a detailed list of supported profiles, refer to Table 8.1.

TABLE 8.1   Basic JXTA Algorithm Profiles

Profile Name	Cipher	Public Key	Hash
PROFILE_RSA_SHA1	N.A.	RSA	SHA1
PROFILE_RSA_MD5	N.A.	RSA	MD5
PROFILE_RC4_SHA1	RC4	N.A.	SHA1
PROFILE_RC4_MD5	RC4	N.A.	MD5
PROFILE_RSA_RC4_SHA1	RC4	RSA	SHA1
PROFILE_RSA_RC4_MD5	RC4	RSA	MD5
PROFILE_RSA_RC4_SHA1_MD5	RC4	RSA	SHA1, MD5

Security Issues and Solutions

In this section, we will look into the details of various security issues that P2P applications can face and the relevant APIs that the Crypto Toolkit provides to address them.

To better illustrate the usage of JXTA Crypto APIs, you will build a `SecureMembershipService`. You will also reuse the `GroupManager` that you built in Chapter 6, "Working with Groups," by plugging in this membership service.

Before we proceed, it is important to note that both the peer and the membership authenticator reside on the same physical machine in this example. Therefore, secure exchanges between them may not make much sense in the real world. The intention is to make it simpler to understand the APIs. The techniques that we discuss can be easily extended to apply to remotely communicating entities.

Privacy

Privacy means that data that is transmitted from one peer to the other must not be comprehensible to any other peer in the network. The most direct way to address this issue is by encryption.

Encryption

Encryption is the process of converting data (plain text) into a nonsense form (cipher text) so that it becomes intelligible only to authorized parties. Encryption is based on *keys*. Just like keys opening real world locks, using encryption keys one can open encrypted (locked) text.

Based on the use of keys, encryption can be classified into two broad categories—symmetric encryption and asymmetric encryption.

Symmetric Encryption

Symmetric encryption is also called *single key encryption*. It is the most popularly used encryption type today and was the only one available until asymmetric encryption was introduced.

In a symmetric cryptographic algorithm, both the encryption and decryption processes use the same key. Consequently, both the sender and receiver of the message must have a shared secret key by which they encrypt and decrypt messages sent between each other. In Figure 8.2, you can see a message being passed between our users Alice and Bob. They are using a single key to encrypt and decrypt a message. Note that the key was exchanged between them via another channel. Note also that Alice handed the key directly to Bob via some method (ideally in a way that prevents others from seeing the key, because anyone can decrypt the message if they had it).

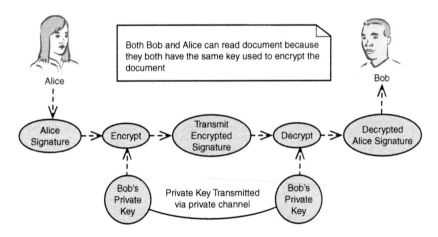

FIGURE 8.2   Symmetric encryption.

While this method is a simple but powerful way of secure communication, it has its disadvantages because of that single key. It requires a secret key be used for any pair of communicating parties. Although this is practical for small-scale communications, it is not scalable for a large-scale system where a large number of users intercommunicate if all of the pairs of users have unique keys so that no others, even in the same group, could pass secret messages. However, it is a good method if a group of users needs to send messages that can be read by anyone with a key.

The other concern is about sharing the key itself. How do a sender and a receiver share an encryption key securely in the first place? It would defeat the purpose if the insecure communication channel itself were used. Therefore, such systems depend on an out-of-band secure channel to share the key. And if such a secure channel was present, why not use that channel for data transfer as well?

However, symmetric encryption is still widely used. Compared to other forms of encryption, symmetric encryption is very fast, so it becomes increasingly important as the size of the data to be encrypted increases. Consequently, symmetric encryption is chosen when data to be encrypted is large.

Two of the most popular symmetric encryption algorithms are RC4 and DES. DES stands for *Data Encryption Standard* and was published by FIPS 46 (Federal Information Processing Standards Publication). RC4 is owned by RSA.

Symmetric Encryption Using the JXTA Crypto APIs

The JXTA Security Project defines a parent interface for all symmetric cryptographic algorithms. The init method initializes the instance of Cipher with the key and parameters. The update method performs the encryption and decryption when all input data is not available. When the message is complete, the doFinal method is called. The doFinal method performs the encryption or decryption. The getAlgorithm method simply returns a code that matches the constant used to select the algorithm:

```
public interface net.jxta.security.cipher.Cipher extends Description{
  public void init( Key theKey
                      , byte theMode) throws CryptoException;

  public void init( Key theKey
                  , byte theMode
                  , byte[] bArray
                          , int bOff,int bLen) throws CryptoException;

  public byte getAlgorithm();

  public int update( byte[] inBuff
                    , int inOffset
                    , int inLength
                    , byte[] outBuff
                            , int outOffset )throws CryptoException;

  public abstract int doFinal( byte[] inBuff
                             , int inOffset
                             , int inLength
                             , byte[] outBuff
                                     , int outOffset) throws CryptoException;
}
```

The Cipher interface extends the Description interface. The Description interface is the parent interface for all algorithms provided by the JXTA Security framework and provides an interface to get the name to control debugging.

```
public interface jxta.security.util.Description{
        String getAlgorithmName();
        public void setDebug();
        public void clearDebug();
}
```

Currently, only the RC4 algorithm is supported. This is made available by the jxta.security.impl.cipher.RC4Cipher class.

Encrypting Documents Using the EncryptedDocumentsFactory

You may recall that the first step towards joining a peer group is by invoking an apply method on the Membership Service. This is done using an AuthenticationCredential that contains an identityInfo document.

The role of the EncryptedDocumentsFactory class we have written is to provide you with this document. Not only does this class act as a factory for a StructuredDocument, it also ensures that the document is encrypted using RC4 encryption.

The class itself is simple, with just one static method. Listing 8.1 shows the EncryptedDocumentsFactory class, and Figure 8.3 shows the UML diagram.

LISTING 8.1   EncryptedDocumentsFactory.java getEncryptedDocument() Method

```
public static StructuredDocument getEncryptedDocument() throws
                              jxta.security.exceptions.CryptoException{

  // Secret shared with the Membership Service
  String sharedSecret = "Shared Secret Key";
  // This is the data which we will encrypt
  String dataToBeEncrypted = "Secret Data";
  // First build a key using the KeyBuilder
  SecretKey secretKey=( SecretKey)KeyBuilder.buildKey(KeyBuilder.TYPE_RC4
                  , KeyBuilder.LENGTH_RC4
                  , false);

  // All Keys need to have a minimum
  // length for a successful encryption

  int minimumKeyLength = secretKey.getLength();
```

LISTING 8.1   Continued

```
// If our key does not fulfill the minimum
// length requirement,
// we need to pad zero byte values with it
// and make it long enough
byte[] keyArray;
if(sharedSecret.length()<minimumKeyLength){
  // In this case we have to pad the
  // key such that it has the minimum key length.
  // The new byte[] ensures that all bytes are
  // initialized to 0X00
  keyArray = new byte[minimumKeyLength];
              System.arraycopy( sharedSecret.getBytes()
                 , 0
                 , keyArray
                      , 0
                 , sharedSecret.length());
} else {
  // The key is more that the required length.
  // Hence no concerns
  keyArray =sharedSecret.getBytes();
}
// Set the secret key with our value
secretKey.setKey(keyArray, 0);
// From the JXTACrypto Suite , get the RC4 cipher algorithm
JxtaCrypto crypto = new JxtaCryptoSuite(JxtaCrypto.MEMBER_RC4
                                     , null
                                     , (byte)0
                                     , (byte)0);
Cipher rc4Algorithm = crypto.getJxtaCipher();

//Initialize the Algorithm with the key and required mode
rc4Algorithm.init(secretKey, Cipher.MODE_ENCRYPT);
// Create a new byte[] to store the output
byte[] outputBuffer = new byte[dataToBeEncrypted.length()];
// The actual encryption is done by this method
rc4Algorithm.doFinal( dataToBeEncrypted.getBytes()
                   , 0
                   , dataToBeEncrypted.length()
                   , outputBuffer
                   , 0);
String encryptedData = new String(outputBuffer);
```

LISTING 8.1   Continued

```
LOG.debug("ENCRYPTED DATA => "+encryptedData);
// Now we have successfully encrypted the method name.
// Return a Structured Document using this method name
MimeMediaType type = new MimeMediaType("text","xml");
StructuredDocument doc
        = StructuredDocumentFactory.newStructuredDocument(type,"Apply");
Element e = doc.createElement( "Data",encryptedData);
doc.appendChild( e );
return doc;
}
```

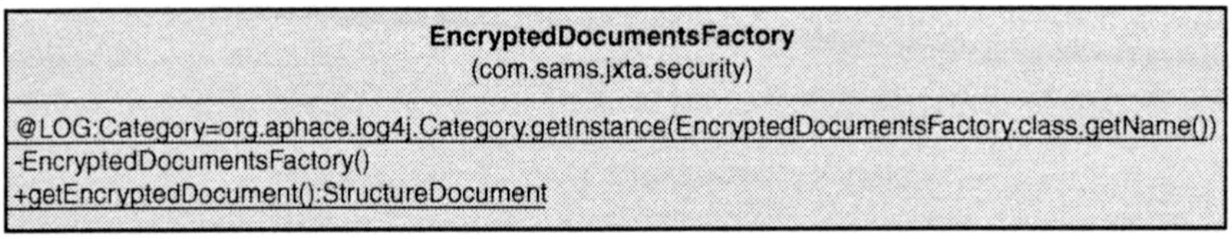

EncryptedDocumentsFactory (com.sams.jxta.security)
@LOG:Category=org.aphace.log4j.Category.getInstance(EncryptedDocumentsFactory.class.getName()) -EncryptedDocumentsFactory() +getEncryptedDocument():StructureDocument

FIGURE 8.3   The UML for the `EncryptedDocumentsFactory` class.

Note how the `jxta.security.impl.cipher.KeyBuilder` class is used to generate an RC4 secret key. This key is just a placeholder containing no data. You need to initialize the key with some data.

The key generation routine used in Listing 8.1 is a bit eccentric. You have used the `sharedSecret` string to generate the data required to initialize the key:

```
secretKey.setKey(keyArray, 0);
```

However, this is never the case in real-world cryptographic systems. Symmetric keys are always generated randomly, and the strength of the encryption will depend on how strong the random number is. It should not be possible for an attacker to discover the key by exactly duplicating the process of random number generation.

Consequently, what you need is a generator to generate secure random numbers that can be used for encryption. The `JRandom` class fulfills this need:

```
public class jxta.security.impl.random.JRandom extends java.util.Random
```

It can be used to generate pseudo-random (theoretically, these are not "random") data. The initial seed—the input random data that the generator takes—should be set to better values to get more secure numbers. The `JRandom` class can be used as shown:

```
try{
  JRandom jrandom = new JRandom();
} catch(CryptoException crypto){
   // Handle error
}
byte[] randomData = new byte[10];
// Fill the array with random data
jrandom.nextBytes(randomData);
```

Decrypting RC4 Encrypted Documents

The RC4 encrypted document is decrypted by the membership service
SecureMembershipService shown in Listing 8.2 and Figure 8.3.

LISTING 8.2   SecureMembershipService.java apply() Method

```
public Authenticator apply( AuthenticationCredential unsubscribedCredential )
    throws PeerGroupException, ProtocolNotSupportedException{

  String sharedSecret = "Shared Secret Key";
  String method = unsubscribedCredential.getMethod();
  if( (null != method) && !"Apply".equals( method ) )
      throw new ProtocolNotSupportedException(
  "Method not recognized : Required \"Apply\" ");
  // First Extract the "Data" from the document
  StructuredDocument doc =
      (StructuredDocument)
        ➥unsubscribedCredential.getIdentityInfo();
  Enumeration enum = doc.getChildren();
  Element element = (Element) enum.nextElement();
  String encrypteddata =(String) element.getValue();

  // Now to decrypt this data, we must use the shared secret
  try{
    // First build a key using the KeyBuilder
    // with RC4 as the algorithm
    SecretKey secretKey
        =(SecretKey)KeyBuilder.buildKey ( KeyBuilder.TYPE_RC4
                                        , KeyBuilder.LENGTH_RC4
                                        , false);
    // All Keys need to have a minimum length
    // for a successful encryption
    int minimumKeyLength = secretKey.getLength();
```

LISTING 8.2   Continued

```
// If our key does not fulfill the minimum
// length requirement, we need to pad zero byte values
//  with it and make it long enough
byte[] keyArray;
if(sharedSecret.length()<minimumKeyLength){
  // In this case we have to pad the key such that it has the
  // minimum key length. The new byte[] ensures that all bytes are
  // initialized to 0X00
  keyArray = new byte[minimumKeyLength];
  System.arraycopy( sharedSecret.getBytes()
                  , 0
                  , keyArray
                  , 0
                  , sharedSecret.length());
} else {
  // The key is more that the required length.
  // Hence no concerns
  keyArray =sharedSecret.getBytes();
}
// Set the secret key with our value
secretKey.setKey(keyArray, 0);
// From the JXTACrypto Suite , get the RC4 cipher algorithm
JxtaCrypto crypto = new JxtaCryptoSuite( JxtaCrypto.MEMBER_RC4
                                       , null
                                       , (byte)0
                                       , (byte)0);
Cipher rc4Algorithm = crypto.getJxtaCipher();

//Initialize the Algorithm with the key and required mode
rc4Algorithm.init(secretKey, Cipher.MODE_DECRYPT);
byte[] encrypteddataArray =encrypteddata.getBytes();
        byte[] decryptedData = new byte[encrypteddataArray.length];
rc4Algorithm.doFinal( encrypteddataArray
                    , 0
                    , encrypteddataArray.length
                    , decryptedData
                    , 0);
String decryptedString = new String(decryptedData);
LOG.debug("DECRYPTED STRING IS =>"+ decryptedString);
```

LISTING 8.2   Continued

```
    if(!decryptedString.equals("Secret Data")){
                    throw new PeerGroupException ("Data not properly encrypted
     !");
    }
  } catch(jxta.security.exceptions.CryptoException cryptoException){
    LOG.error("Error in Apply Process",cryptoException);
        throw new PeerGroupException("Failure in Apply");
  }
return new SecureAuthenticator(this,unsubscribedCredential);
}
```

As you may have noticed, the same doFinal method of the Cipher class was used for both encryption and decryption. It all depends on how the algorithm is initialized. For encryptions, initialization is done in the MODE_ENCRYPT. For decryptions, a MODE_DECRYPT is used.

Asymmetric Encryption

Asymmetric encryption or *public key encryption* is increasingly becoming popular as a secure means of many-to-many communication. It relies on two different keys (therefore, asymmetric) for secure interactions. Every participating user has a pair of keys generated by an algorithm. The keys have a unique mathematical property that any message encrypted by one can only be decrypted by the other.

The user is free to designate one of these as a public key and the other as a private key. The public key is used to represent the user and can be widely distributed on whatever channels the user wants. The user keeps the private key confidential. Any sender who wants to communicate with the user can use the users' public key to encrypt the message. Rest assured, only the user will be able to decrypt the message. Similarly, if the user wants to respond to another user, he or she can encrypt the other party's public key for encrypting the message. This can go a step further, and the user can encrypt the message with his or her private key and the receiver's public key to ensure that not only does the proper person receive the message but also for the receiver to recognize the source of the message.

An example of how this type of encryption works is shown in Figure 8.4. First, our user Alice encrypts the document meant for Bob with Bob's public key. The message is transmitted and Bob decrypts the message with his private key. The process is identical for users, other than Alice, that have access to Bob's public key. The decryption can only be done by Bob—as long as Bob does not let anyone copy his private key.

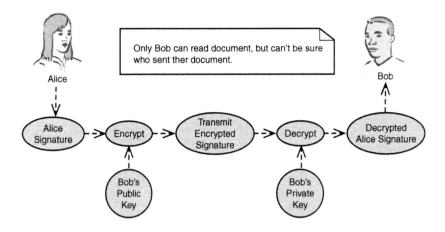

FIGURE 8.4   Asymmetric encryption (public key encryption).

Because the encryption is reversible (that is, the private key can be used to encrypt and the public key to decrypt, messages can be created that essentially prove they came from the owner of the key). In other words, as shown in Figure 8.5, if the message is encrypted by Alice using her private key, Bob can decrypt it using Alice's public key. If, as shown in this figure, the document is encrypted first with Bob's public key and then Alice's private key, the document is only decryptable by Bob and, because only Alice's public key can encrypt these contents, only Alice could have sent the message.

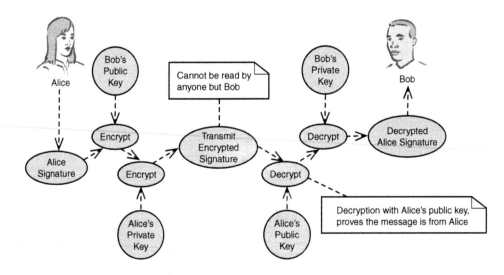

FIGURE 8.5   Asymmetric authentication.

The approach solves the main problem with symmetric key encryption caused by the exchange of what is here a private key because the private keys are never exchanged. The question of how to securely transmit private keys does not arise. The encryption/decryption processes does have a downside because it consumes more processing time and memory for calculations than symmetric key encryption. Unless you are transferring large amounts of data, the time to run the algorithms is livable for most applications (seconds to a few minutes depending on your hardware and the size of the message).

One good approach is to use a combination of symmetric and asymmetric keys. Public key encryption can be used to securely exchange a set of symmetric keys. After this is done, symmetric encryption can be used to encrypt all subsequent exchanges, so you can benefit from the best of both worlds. SSL and TLS, for example, use such an approach.

Asymmetric Encryption Using the JXTA Crypto APIs

All public key algorithms implement the PublicKeyAlgorithm interface shown in the following code. The methods are categorized into the setters and getters for the keys, a rest to reset the keys and the algorithm (this is not a typo—the method name is capitalized) method that is used to decrypt or encrypt a message.

```
public interface jxta.security.publickey.PublicKeyAlgorithm
                                        extends Description {
   public void reset();
   public int getMaxInputDataBlockLength();
   public int getEncryptionBlockLength();
   public void setPublicKey() throws CryptoException;
   public void setPublicKey(Object publickeyData)
   public void setPublicKey(byte[] nModulus)
   public void setPrivateKey() throws CryptoException;
   public void setPrivateKey(Object privatekeyData) throws CryptoException;
   public Object getPublickey() throws CryptoException;
   public Object getPrivatekey() throws CryptoException;
   public byte[] Algorithm(byte[] data,int offset,int length,
                      byte type,boolean encrypt) throws CryptoException;

}
```

The JXTA platform supports RSA with PKCS#1 padding. *Padding*, which is the process of adding random data to the data to be encrypted, is usually used to reduce the effectiveness of attacks against the encrypted dat. By adding padding, all the messages have the same length and the attackers cannot find any information about the data because "Hello" has the same length as "Hi everybody."

Hashing

A hash function is used to compact data in such a way that it is verifiable but non-reversible. In other words, a given piece of information must always hash to the same value but, using this value, it must be very difficult to reconstruct the original information. Another criterion for a hash function is that it must be highly improbable (practically impossible) to find two pieces of information that produce the same hash result. In addition, a good hash algorithm gives very different hash messages for any two pieces of data that are very similar.

Hashing can be considered as an encryption routine without a corresponding decryption routine. At first glance, you may tend to doubt the usefulness of such a function. Why would you want to encrypt, if there is no way to decrypt?

The answer is straightforward. Hashes can act as a powerful way of verification. Hashes can act as data fingerprints, being practically unique for all kinds of data.

Even though hashes cannot be used as a direct encryption routine, they are extremely useful for authentication. One of the simplest examples of using a hash function can be found in most operating systems. Almost all operating systems, including flavors of Unix and Microsoft Windows, use hashes for user authentication. Passwords are not stored directly; only their hashes are stored. Whenever a user tries to log in, his or her password is taken and hashed. This is then compared with the stored result to authenticate him or her. The advantage is that even if one has access to the password file, it is practically impossible to retrieve the user passwords (unless the ID and password are found in other ways via keyboard snooping or other means—no solution is perfect).

Hashing Using the JXTA Crypto APIs

All hashing algorithms in JXTA are implementations of the Hash interface:

```
public interface jxta.security.hash.Hash extends Description
```

Currently, JXTA supports two different hashing algorithms—MD5 and SHA-1 (shown in the following code fragment). SHA-1 produces a 160-bit (20 byte) message digest. Although slower than MD5, this larger digest size makes it stronger against brute force attacks. MD5 is a 128-bit (16 byte) message digest makes it a faster implementation than SHA-1.

```
public class MD5Hash implements jxta.security.hash.Hash ;
public class SHA1Hash implements jxta.security.hash.Hash ;
```

Using the MD5Hash Algorithm

The `SecureAuthenticator` class in Figure 8.6 is the authenticator used by the
`SecureMembershipService` (Figure 8.7) in the `isReadyForJoin` method shown in
Listing 8.3. This class demonstrates the use of the `MD5Hash` algorithm. The user is
prompted to fill up the authenticator by providing a password. The class is designed
to accept only one password that, incidentally, has the value `password`. The user's
password is then hashed and compared to the MD5 of the valid password. The user
is allowed to join only if the password is correct.

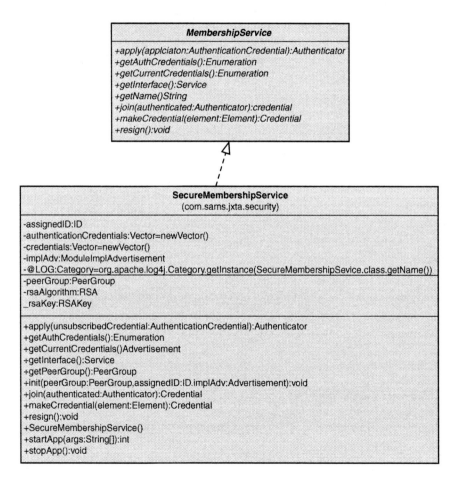

FIGURE 8.6   UML for the *SecureMembershipService* class.

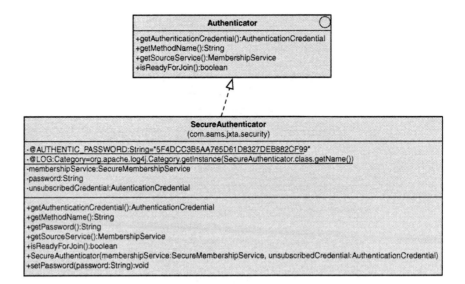

FIGURE 8.7   UML for the *SecureAuthenticator* class.

LISTING 8.3   SecureAuthenticator.java isReadyToJoin() Method

```
public boolean  isReadyForJoin(){
  // we calculate the MD5 hash of the password
  // entered by the user
  // and compare it with the AUTHNETIC_PASSWORD.
  try{
    // Now to create the MD5 hash ,first get
    // a suite with the MD5 Algorithm
    JxtaCrypto crypto = new JxtaCryptoSuite( JxtaCrypto.MEMBER_MD5
                                   , null, (byte)0, (byte)0);
    // Now get the Hash Object
    Hash hash = crypto.getJxtaHash();
    // Get the digest length of the Hash
    int digestLength = hash.getDigestLength();
    byte[] passwordInBytes = password.getBytes();
    // Calculate the length needed by the output byte array
    int outputLength = (password.length() < digestLength
                        ? digestLength : password.length());
    // Create a new array to hold the output
    byte[] outputBytes = new byte[digestLength];
    // This is where the actual hashing is done
    hash.doFinal(passwordInBytes, 0, passwordInBytes.length, outputBytes, 0);
    // Base64 encode the result
    String finalPass
        = new String(jxta.security.util.Util.hexEncode(outputBytes));
```

LISTING 8.3   Continued

```
    // Compare it with the AUTHENTIC_PASSWORD
    // If they match , the authenticator is ready to join
    if(finalPass.equals(AUTHENTIC_PASSWORD))
    return true;
    else
    return false;

  } catch(CryptoException cryptoException){
    LOG.error("Exception in creating MD5 Hash",cryptoException);
  }
  return true;
}
```

Authentication

Authentication is an important requirement in almost all secure systems. It must be possible to

- Verify that the sender of the data is indeed who he claims himself to be.

- Ascertain that the data sent has not been modified in transit by a malevolent entity.

- Disclaim or repudiate messages that have not been received or sent by a particular entity.

Encryption may by itself provide authentication in some cases. Consider a readable text message encrypted by using the private key of the sender. The recipient can decrypt the message using the sender's public key. The recipient can also be ensured that it is, indeed, the same entity that sent the message, because no one else possess the private key to encrypt the text message. If an invalid key had been used to generate the encrypted data, it would not convert to the readable message after decryption.

This view is a bit short sighted because we have only considered an example of a readable message. What if the message itself is an arbitrary block of meaningless data? Trying to decrypt such an encrypted message with any key will lead to another block of data. How do you know that this is indeed legitimate?

From these discussions, you can safely assume that encryption will, indeed, provide authentication if the data transmitted and received is human-readable.

There are two major approaches to ensure authentication in secure systems—Message Authentication Code (MAC) and Digital Signatures.

Message Authentication Codes

A Message Authentication Code, popularly referred to as MAC, is a simple way to ensure authentication. MAC relies on symmetric key encryption; in other words, it assumes that both the sender and the receiver share a common secret key.

A simple way of generating a MAC is:

1. Concatenate the message with the secret key (or combine them in some other way.

2. Hash the resultant data to get the MAC.

3. Attach the MAC to the message to be sent.

The receiver can, in turn, receive the message and the MAC, recalculate the MAC from the message and secret key, compare it with the received MAC, and verify its authenticity.

MAC Algorithms in the JXTA Crypto Suite

All MAC algorithms are implementations of the MAC interface, shown in the following code. The init method sets the keys and type of encryption, while the encrypt method is used to create signatures. The verify method is used to verify a MAC for the inBuff against the signature in sigBuff. The update method is used to update the inBuff. Of course, getAlgorithmName and getAlgorithm are used to identify what the MAC implementation is supporting.

```
public interface jxta.security.mac.MAC extends Description {
  public String getAlgorithmName();
  public byte getAlgorithm();
  public int getLength();
  public void init( byte theMode
                  , Key theKey
                  , byte[] privateKey)throws CryptoException;
  public void update( byte[] inbuf
                    , int offset
                    , int length) throws CryptoException;
  public int encrypt( byte[] inbuff
                    , int offset
                    , int inLength,byte[] macBuff
                    , int macOffset)throws CryptoException;
  public boolean verify( byte[] inBuff
                       , int inOffset
                       , int inLength
                       , byte[] macBuff
                       , int macOffset
                       , int macLength) throws CryptoException;
}
```

JXTA supports two different types of MACs profiles in addition to the basic profiles:

- MACs using RC4 encryption and SHA1 hashing, denoted by an algorithm profile ALG_RC4_SHA1.

- MACs using RC4 encryption and MD5 hashing, denoted by the algorithm profile `ALG_RC4_MD5`.

You can get an instance of the MAC algorithm by using

```
JxtaCrypto crypto = new JxtaCryptoSuite( JxtaCrypto.PROFILE_RC4_SHA1
                                       , null
                                       , (byte)0
                                       , MAC.ALG_RC4_SHA1);
MAC mac = crypto.getJxtaMAC();
```

Digital Signatures

Digital signatures are another form of authentication. Many popular systems available today, such as Pretty Good Privacy (PGP), are based on digital signatures. Digital signatures, in turn, rely on the concept of asymmetric encryption. Figure 8.8 shows how Alice can create an encrypted signature that Bob can decrypt with Alice's public key to prove the signature was from Alice.

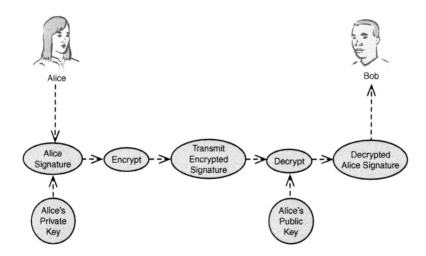

FIGURE 8.8   The example of the digital signature process.

Digital signatures can be used to sign documents by including the document in the signature or encrypting an already encrypted document (as in Figure 8.5). Alternatively, and most widely used, a checksum of a document is calculated and the checksum stored in the signature. after the receiver decrypts the signature, the checksum found in the message is compared to the checksum of the transmitted document. This is simple and fast because only a small checksum is processed with the crypto algorithms. Besides acting as a signature, this sum also proves that the document has not been modified since the document was signed.

Data can be digitally signed using the following simple steps:

1. Calculate the hash of the message to be signed.

2. Encrypt this hash with the private key.

3. The encrypted data obtained is the digital signature and can be attached with the document.

Signing Using the JXTA Crypto APIs

JXTA offers two algorithm profiles for digital signatures. AlG_RSA_SHA1_PKCS1 uses the RSA algorithm with PKCS#1 padding as the encryption algorithm and SHA1 as the hash algorithm. ALG_RSA_MD5_PKCS1 also uses RSA algorithm with PKCS#1 as the encryption algorithm but uses MD5 for the hashing.

All signature algorithms implement the Signature interface shown in the following vode. The methods are used to access information about the algorithm and to initialize it. The sign and verify methods are used to sign and verify messages:

```
public interface Signature extends Description{
  public String getAlgorithmName();
  public byte getAlgorithm();
  public void init(byte theMode) throws CryptoException;
  public void update(byte[] inbuf,int offset,
      ➡ int length)  throws CryptoException;
  public byte[] sign(byte[] inbuff, int offset,
      ➡ int inLength) throws CryptoException;
  public boolean verify(byte[] inBuff,int inOffset,
      ➡      int inLength,byte[] sigBuff,int sigOffset,
      [ccc]int sigLength) throws CryptoException;
}
```

The Secure Credential

On a successful apply to your SecureMembershipService, a SecureCredential is returned to the peer. We refer to the credential as secure because it contains a digital signature that can be verified by the peer. Figure 8.9 shows the UML diagram of the SecureCredential class. Listing 8.4 illustrates how the credential is signed in the createSignedMessage method.

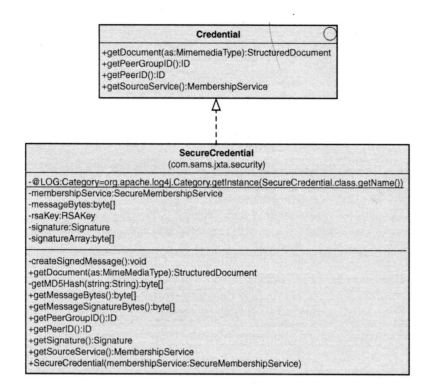

FIGURE 8.9 The UML for the `SecureCredential` class.

LISTING 8.4 SecureCredential.java createSignedMessage() Method

```
private void createSignedMessage(){
  String date = DateFormat.getDateTimeInstance().format(new java.util.Date());
  String message = "Membership since "+date;
  LOG.debug("Message is = "+message);
  // Get the MD5 Hash of the message
  messageBytes = getMD5Hash(message);
  System.out.println("MESSAGE =>"+new String(messageBytes));
  // Next step is to sign the message
  // For this we use the RSA Algorithm
  try{
    rsaKey = (RSAKey)KeyBuilder.buildKey(KeyBuilder.TYPE_RSA,
                    KeyBuilder.LENGTH_RSA_512,false);
```

LISTING 8.4   Continued

```
JxtaCrypto suite = new JxtaCryptoSuite( JxtaCrypto.PROFILE_RSA_SHA1
                                      , rsaKey
                                      , Signature.ALG_RSA_SHA_PKCS1
                                      , (byte)0);
RSA rsaAlgorithm = new RSA(rsaKey);
LOG.debug("Setting Public Key");
// This method computes a public key
rsaAlgorithm.setPublicKey();
LOG.debug("Setting Private Key");
// This method computes a private key
rsaAlgorithm.setPrivateKey();
//Get the data for both public and private keys
RSAPublickeyData publicKeyData
                  =(RSAPublickeyData)rsaAlgorithm.getPublickey();
RSAPrivatekeyData privateKeyData
                  =(RSAPrivatekeyData)rsaAlgorithm.getPrivatekey();
// Get a signature Object for the actual signing
signature = suite.getJxtaSignature();
signature.init(Signature.MODE_SIGN);
signatureArray = signature.sign(messageBytes, 0, messageBytes.length);
} catch (CryptoException cryptoException){
LOG.error("EXCEPTION IN SIGNING MESSAGE",cryptoException);
} catch (Exception exception){
LOG.error("EXCEPTION IN SIGNING MESSAGE",exception);
}
}
```

First, the KeyBuilder is used to create an RSAKey. Then you create a suite with the profile PROFILE_RSA_SHA1. The setPublicKey and setPrivateKey methods are called to compute the public and private keys, respectively.

After this is done, a Signature object is obtained from the suite. Because in this case you are interested in signing the particular document, you initialize the signature to a MODE_SIGN mode. The actually signing is done by the sign method.

Verifying a digital signature is also very similar to the signing process, except for the fact that the Signature object is initialized to a verify mode (MODE_VERIFY).

After this is done, the verify method of the signature Object can be invoked for the actual verification. This is done by the init method of the SecurityDemo class.

Trust in P2P systems

As you have seen, JXTA provides various low-level primitives necessary to build secure P2P applications. Nevertheless, they can act only as the building blocks of your security infrastructure. It is up to you to combine these primitives to arrive at a meaningful and preferably powerful security framework for your application, depending on its requirements.

There are many tricky issues in P2P security that you might want to consider. You may recall, from our discussions on Peer Group Management in Chapter 6, the difficulties in managing P2P networks. Security concerns are no different from management concerns because security can also be considered as a integral part of management.

In the client/server world, trust has been a simple issue. People usually trust a centralized authority, such as Verisign. This will also make them trust all other entities certified by Verisign. Thus, a whole trust hierarchy can be built with each trusted entity certifying that another one can be trusted. In this example, Verisign would form the base of this hierarchy.

One problem that is hard to manage is the hierarchy and transitivity of trust. For example, in the hierachial view, you have one central authority that is not good (that is, cannot be trusted) or as with transitivity, the trust is not consistent. For example, even if we are friends, a friend of mine is not necessary a friend of yours.

Trust is a concept that is handled differently in P2P due to its lack of centralization. Because there is no central trusted authority to begin with, the whole concept of trust used in client/server networks becomes meaningless in P2P.

Many interesting approaches have been formulated to approach this issue. One approach is for each peer to rate another peer based on its interactions with it. Ratings can be signed so that they can be authenticated if required. Thus, every peer builds a *trust portfolio*, which can be analyzed at any time and the overall trust evaluated.

Poblano: A Distributed Trust Model

Poblano is a distributed trust model proposed for the JXTA platform. While Poblano is still in its emerging stages at the time of this writing, it holds a lot of promise to be a base framework for trust in JXTA applications.

Poblano divides trust into three components:

- Trust between different peers termed *PeerConfidence*

- Trust between a peer and a codat termed *CodatConfidence*

- The risk factor termed *Risk*

Poblano addresses the issue of calculating the overall trust based on these factors. It also suggests methods for processing, propagating, and updating trust relationships.

As this book went to press, the Poblano system was still being implemented. Please check the security project at `http://security.jxta.org/` for the most up-to-date information.

P2P Security Models

The best ways to come up with a suitable security model is to analyze what your requirements are. We can start by learning from goals, failures, and successes of other applications. Let us now investigate two of the most popular P2P applications, Freenet and Napster. We will not be going into the finer details of these implementations, but will look at them from a broader security perspective.

Freenet

The idea behind Freenet first appeared in Ian Clarke's research paper "A Distributed Decentralized Information Storage and Retrieval System" in 1999. Freenet, as we know today, is an open-source realization of this idea. It is a truly decentralized information publication system.

The Freenet Philosophy

Freenet is built around one core value—freedom of speech. The objective is to make Freenet a channel for free communication that is not moderated by an external entity. Freenet believes that freedom of speech is not possible without anonymity. Also, information must be available for those who seek it and must be survivable from any forms of external control.

The Freenet architecture reflects the Freenet philosophy. The design of the Freenet system is centralized around two goals—privacy and availability.

- Privacy applies to the publisher of the information (one who inserts some content into the network) as well as the consumer of the information (one who retrieves that content from the network).

- Availability means that the information must be present on multiple and possibly unrelated nodes, so that attackers cannot target particular points in the network and make a particular content unavailable.

How Freenet Works

Any Freenet user can insert content of his or her choice into the network identified by a key, which can also be used to retrieve the data from the network. Simple as it seems, let us delve a bit deeper into how this is actually done.

Every node can accumulate data to a limit that can be configured by the user running the node. It also has a routing table to point to other nodes, based on what they are believed to contain. Keys are internally used to represent content. Therefore, the routing table is a mapping between keys and nodes.

When a user tries to insert data into a node, the node verifies if it has any content matching the key of this insert. If the key is not found, the insert request is propagated to the node that has the *nearest* key to the requested key. *Nearness* is calculated based on a predefined algorithm. This goes on until the limit specified by a hops-to-live value of the insert request. If any key clash occurs in this process, the node responds back to the requested node along with the content represented by that requested key and available at that node. If no key clash occurs, a success message is sent to the inserter's node. This is the green signal for the actual data insertion. Note that until this point, the content was never transferred. It was only the key of the content that was propagated. Only after receiving the success message is the actual data for insertion sent.

To retrieve any content from Freenet, you have to know its key. This can be done by either obtaining the key from previously publicized sources or by calculation (as you will see later). After this key is available, the user can request his or her node to retrieve the content.

The node verifies if it has a copy of this content. If it doesn't, it looks up its routing table and passes on the request to the node that has the nearest key matching the requested key. This process continues until the hops-to-live limit is hit. If a match is not found during this process, a failure message is propagated back to the requesting node. If a match is found, the content itself is passed back the same way the request came, but now each and every node stores a local copy of the content before passing it back to its requestor. It also updates its routing table to point to the original node that had the content.

Freenet Security
The security model in Freenet assumes that any node in the network can be potentially hostile, trying to eavesdrop or attack the network. Data exchange is designed to take place effectively under such intimidating conditions.

Before proceeding any further, let us first look at Freenet keys.

Keys
Freenet uses keys to represent content. Three types of keys exist in Freenet:

- A *Keyword Signed Key (KSK)* is the simplest, and is obtained from a descriptive string that the inserter assigns for the content. But it tends to be inserter agnostic; in other words, it is not possible to identify the user who inserted the content.

- A *Signed Subspace Key* (*SSK*) is used to ensure the authenticity of the author. It is generated based on the user's public key as well as a descriptive string.

- A *Content Hash Key* (*CHK*) is used in combination with the SSK as a mechanism for content revisions.

Security at the Protocol Level

All Freenet messages contain three elements:

- A transaction ID

- A hops-to-live value

- A depth value

A Freenet transaction spans end-to-end any process of requesting content or storing content. The transaction ID is randomly generated and can be considered unique for a transaction. The hops-to-live is very similar to a time-to-live (TTL) value found in IP datagrams, and the intent is to limit the lifetime of the message. Every node decrements this value before it passes the message to the next one. This ensures that endless loops do not exist. The depth value determines how deep the message has traveled to reach a particular node. Every node increases this value as it passes along the message. The intention is that when any node needs to reply to the originator with either a success or a failure, it can know what hops-to-live value to set.

Now for the interesting stuff. Even though the time-to-live value becomes 1, a node may choose to forward the message further. Of course, this is with a limited probability. Thus, the message may propagate to a few more nodes until probability works against it and it dies. The primary intention is to puzzle any casual eavesdropper trying to make some analysis based on the hop-to-live value.

For the same reasons, the initial depth is set to a small but random number so that the exact location of the requestor becomes difficult to determine.

Other Security Measures

Another possible security concern comes from the maintenance of the dynamic routing table by each node. As we have seen previously, when a node is involved in routing some requested content back to the requestor, it adds a pointer to the original source of the content into its routing table. Freenet recognizes that this can lead to a security issue, so it allows any node en-route to change this pointer to any other randomly-chosen node, including itself.

Passive Attacks on Freenet

While Freenet is designed to provide anonymity using obscurity, there are chances that the network can be eavesdropped. This can happen when an attacker compromises a large number of Freenet nodes, probably in a particular geography, enabling him to perform some advanced traffic analysis.

Active Attacks on Freenet

KSKs can be subject to dictionary attacks because they are just hashes of descriptive texts, unlike SSKs that involve digital signatures. This is a known vulnerability. It provides one more reason to use SSKs instead of KSKs.

Denial-of-service attacks are possible, although their effectiveness may vary. First, an attacker can flood the network from a node by inserting junk files with randomly generated keys. While key clashes may occur during this process and prevent the attacker from the insertion, it is possible to accomplish this. The attacker may also manipulate the depth of the insert by changing the hops-to-live value to reduce the probability of these collisions. But the limitations to this are that only a few nodes in the vicinity of the attacker's node will store this junk content.

Although requests are a way to replicate data through the network, any request from a node will make the data be stored nearer to that node. Consequently, any subsequent request for that data will not cause any replication. To be effective, the attacker will have to compromise a large number of nodes and issue insert and retrieval commands from multiple random nodes. Such a distributed denial-of-service attack is possible.

Napster

Another good example of security and trust issues can be seen on Napster. In a typical MP3 file transfer in the Napster network, any user who runs the Napster client initially connects to the Napster Index Server. The function of the index server is to maintain the list of users online at any point of time and the files shared by each user. The presence of this index server adds a bit of centralization to Napster.

When a user wants to search for a particular MP3 file, the Napster client contacts the index server. The search is run on the index server. The index server reports the list of files shared, along with identifiers to the other users sharing them. The role of the index server ends here. When the user confirms download for a particular file, the client contacts the target machine directly and downloads the file.

Security Issues in Napster

The main concern of the designers of Napster was to make it unfeasible for Napster to be used as a channel for trading possibly infected files and executables. To enforce this, all files are checked to be sure they are valid MP3 files by looking at the file headers. Only files with legal MP3 headers can be exchanged. Nevertheless, they were proved wrong with the coming of Wrapster.

Wrapster is an application that can be used to wrap any file (document, executable, and so on) into an MP3 format. This can fool Napster into believing that the file is indeed a genuine MP3 and allow it to be exchanged in the Napster network.

Wrapped files can be easily identified. They have a bit rate (a measure of sound quality usually 128Kbps) of 32Kbps and a frequency (number of sound samples per second typically 44,000Hz) of 32,000Hz. Searches can be effortlessly performed using these values to find wrapped files in the network.

Is this a serious issue? Not really, every file that is wrapped at one end has to be unwrapped at the other. This means that the other end needs a Wrapster client too. Without unwrapping, the files are unusable. Trying to execute such a file will invoke the default music player of the operating system, just like any other MP3 file would, and this will fail.

Moreover, users who are well informed enough to know how to wrap and unwrap files to disguise miscellaneous files as MP3s are seldom careless about potentially malicious files.

Even though Wrapster does not impose serious security concerns in Napster, it does provide an example of how a system can be exploited to do what it was not meant to do. Not only must your security design be good, how you implement it is crucial.

Summary

In this chapter, we have had a look at various security concerns that can arise in a P2P network. We have also looked at how JXTA addresses the security issue, both at a platform level and by providing the cryptographic toolkit that can be used by applications built over it. The Cryptographic Toolkit provides a lot of useful APIs, and examples of their use were presented.

Finally, we analyzed two popular P2P networks from a security perspective with the intent of providing valuable insight on various issues related to peer-to-peer security.

In the next chapter, we will be transmitting data to synchronize it between peers. Although we have not added this chapter's security features, because the data is of a personal of group private nature, it is a prime suspect for implementing encryption. Read on and, as an extra thought, think of where and how you would add security in the following implementation.

9

Synchronizing Data Between Peers

By Daniel Brookshier

One of the advantages of the JXTA network is the ability to communicate within a group of peers. In this chapter, we will use the resolver service to create an event calendar and address book organizer applications, similar to that of a Personal Digital Assistant (PDA), Personal Information Manager (PIM), or desktop application, such as Outlook, Netscape, Address Book, and others. The application created here is called JPDA.

Designing a PDA Organizer for JXTA

There are many different models possible for JXTA applications. A very interesting model is that of an application that shares data among many peers compartmentalized by many groups. By using the resolver service, you can write an application that is capable of such behavior. To demonstrate this model, we will show you how we created a personal data organizer that is capable of sharing data among peers.

The following are our goals:

- Synchronize within a group of people interested in a specific type of event.

- Create a simple management and display of calendar events, To-Do items, and addresses.

- Reuse the group code from Chapter 6, "Working with Groups," for group management and membership. This is also our only security and compartmentalization of shared data.

The resolver service will be used to share calendar events, To-Do lists, and addresses. Because the resolver only communicates to peers that are in the same group, we use the group to compartmentalize data. The application will be capable of being used by many other languages by using standard XML to transfer data. Specifically, we will be using XML specifications for addresses, calendar events, and To Do items with two well-known XML specifications called VCard and XCal.

Because an expert is involved, let's also consider what is *not* going to be part of this code. First, the goal is to demonstrate a P2P application that can synchronize PIM data. All that is needed is a couple of types of data, and that means only simple address and simple calendar entries. Synchronization methods will be very primitive to reduce complexity, and the display design is extremely simple and not really meant to be the final end user product.

After the project is complete, it will be added to the JXTA.org Web site for further development. This will ensure that the features left out are eventually resolved. More importantly, the application is used by anyone that wants it. This is extremely important to the success of a P2P application. Without a large group of users, the application has fewer resources. Also, if the application use is widespread, you will get higher odds that you find an address or person to book an event. Also, because people often open their calendar applications when they boot their machines, the JXTA network becomes more persistent and, thus, faster and more reliable. Simply, this type of P2P application is more successful when more users use it and the P2P network improves.

Feature Set

The application, JPDA, will have the following features. These were chosen to create a minimum starting point of a PDA or electronic organizer. They are also very minimal because the object of this exercise is to teach and demonstrate how the JXTA resolver service can be used:

- *Calendar*—Calendar events are as defined by the XCal standard. In addition to the standard entries defined by the XML specification, the peer group and peer context of creation is also included. Invitation lists of the events will be based on the VCard references in the address book of this application.

- *To Do list*—To Do items are as defined by the XCal standard. In addition to the standard entries defined by the XML specification, the peer group and peer context of creation is also included.

- *Address book*—Address items are as defined by the VCard standard. In addition to the standard entries defined by the XML specification, the peer group and peer context of creation is also included.

- *Application World group*—The world group is a group created as a child to the JXTA world group. This group has a set ID known to all PIP peers. If the group is not found, the peer creates the group using a specific application world group ID. This is required because their ID and not their name are used to index groups and route messages. If new groups were created with different identifiers, messages would be improperly routed.

- *Interest groups*—Interest groups are peer groups that are concerned with a specific subject. These groups may have user-defined sub groups. Examples of interest groups are little league teams, vanpools, organizations, or a specific group of friends. These groups will use specific implementations of authenticators in the peer group membership protocol to ensure that the group members are authorized. Like the application world group, the ID of the interest groups also needs to be maintained to ensure that the groups can be used even though the group advertisement may have expired through lack of use. The ID is also maintained to ensure that the application can be used for long periods of time offline without losing its group context.

- *Group sync*—This is the default group sync and is the first to be implemented in the application. All users that add data to this group are publishing to all groups.

In the future, other features will be added to this project. The following features are not implemented because of the limited scope of this chapter:

- *Advanced group management*—Interest groups should be very flexible. For example, if there was a Van Pool group, how do you ensure that it is just for your group? How do you advertise a group to only those you want to join? How do you share the idea of a Van Pool group to allow other vanpoolers to create their own from your template? These are hard questions and will likely require the creation of new PeerGroup functionality to be added by sub-classing the platform implementation.

- *SyncML support*—SyncML is another XML standard and is used to describe synchronization of data. SyncML support would improve the ability to interoperate with other applications. SyncML may also improve the ability of the application to synchronize by adding a well-known protocol.

- *Device sync*—The device sync is a synchronization of a list of specific peers. This is not group based, but peers are part of the application world group. Information synchronized includes all groups joined and the current data associated with each group. In addition, shared configuration data will be synchronized.

Future Development

We have pointed out several times that JPDA is written as a demonstration of a JXTA resolver application. However, the idea has much merit. The idea of a distributed and secure PDA application can solve many problems if there is an adequate feature set. Important features include the following:

- *Encryption*—When passing information, such as peoples' addresses and their schedules, there is a great need for privacy. This is especially true in a peer-to-peer network where several peers can see the data but were not an endpoint of the communication, only a relay.

- *Ad-hoc membership Designer*—This is the ability to add different membership models on-the-fly. The reason for this is to allow users to create their own groups that have specific criteria. This would allow the user to create a form and contain specific conditions of acceptance into a group. For example, this would allow a softball league to create a membership protocol that would only allow valid members to see the event schedule.

- *Online/Offline*—Capability to be turned on- and offline. This is required for laptops and PDAs that might not always be connected to the network.

- *Commercial integration*—JPDA could run as a synchronizer to other organizer tools, such as Netscape, Outlook, Act, and others. The user would use JPDA to synchronize these applications with other users. JPDA would be used for transport rather than as an organizer itself.

- *Event agents*—Event agents are modules that are used to improve the ease of use of To Do and calendar events. Like a personal secretary, the agent would book events and To-Do tasks depending on a list of criteria and other information. The simplest case would allow other users to automatically book meetings on your calendar. In the case of meetings associated with your job, the agent would only allow meetings to be booked by authorized persons and only during business hours. The agent would also make sure that the meetings would not conflict and that there is time to mix meetings and To Do tasks.

The beginnings of these features and others are currently under development and will be available as the project matures. In fact, your participation is most welcome. The current release of the code and the initial version described in this book can be found at www.samspublishing.com. The project will also be available at www.jxta.org and www.cluck.com.

Design Considerations

Before we start the design, there are a few issues of the implementation that need to be discussed.

Application Startup

When a user starts this application, the application will initialize to a state that was similar to the last session. The first thing that happens is that the Application World Group is joined, and then all other groups that the peer was a member of are joined. The personal information management data (PIM) for each group is created on the display. If there are any missed events or To Do items, these are displayed to the user. If there are other peers in the peer's default user group, these are synchronized.

Because this is just a demonstration and the code is not ready for regular use on the JXTA network, we will not persist any data. The reason is that if enough users begin to use the application before the synchronization is streamlined, the amount of data could flood the network.

Adding PIM Data

PIM data, which includes addresses, To-Do items, and calendar entries, are added by first selecting the group to which the address will belong. The PIM data can only belong to one group, including the application world group. In the future, the application should probably prevent the user from adding data to the world group. The only reason it is allowed in this version is to gain speed.

Synchronization

Synchronization will be by brute force in our example. At any time, a peer can request synchronization to the peer group. The sync will be broadcast to all peers in the JPDA groups. Each peer that receives the synchronization query will broadcast all of its current contents. As was discussed, this could be problematic. Imagine all the PDAs in the world attempting to synchronize with just one peer. Unless the data is properly filtered and reduced to just the required differences, the traffic generated could waste a lot of bandwidth.

Synchronization should only take place if it is actually required. Instead of transmitting the data as it is now done, a checksum could be created of the current data and transmitted first. The other peer can then calculate the checksum for the current data and then only send data if the sums do not match. This would solve part of the bandwidth problem, but synchronization is actually more complex. To create an efficient system, SyncML—an XML standard for synchronization—should be used, along with differentiating algorithms so that only the minimum data is exchanged.

How much data is synchronized between peers? If you were to share all your appointments and tasks, everyone would know all there was about you. You should only share what you are comfortable sharing. You should also not share anything that is worthless to the peer group. If you had a task to pick up a gallon of milk, the juggling club's To-Do list is probably not where you should put the task. This is also related to permission. Remember that a peer can have different credentials. The credential could be used by the application to allow or prevent a peer from posting events or to forward them first to a moderator for final posting. Such functionality is not in this initial version, but something like it would be required.

Group Security and Associations

As the design evolved, groups appeared to be a good choice for compartmentalizing the sharing of data. If you belong to a group, you have access to the data within it. Despite the straightforward nature, there are problems with this approach. Due to schedule concerns, this is how the first JPDA application was designed.

Groups can be problematic for several reasons, the first being ownership. See Figure 9.1, which shows a set of groups. The group root is the world group for the application. Under world, we will have various users and other groups, such as companies. Under the user, there are further compartmentalized groups for home, work, and enemies. In some cases, such as the enemies group, there is a legitimate reason to create a group that limits access. You would not want your enemies to know that they are on your list.

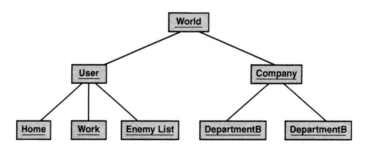

FIGURE 9.1   Simplified view of a tree of peer groups.

The problem here is that the level of security is perhaps too much and worse, as you can see in Figure 9.2, which adds a few contact addresses to the system. Look at the number of times that data on people is repeated. Both Bert, and Luke are in several groups. Note that the user group Anthony has the Anthony address entry. This means that only someone who gains access to the Anthony user group can access Anthony's address. The members of the Anthony group can also see that Anthony has several sub groups. By gaining access to these groups, the user can see any of the addresses underneath. In the case of the enemy list, the group can only be accessed by Anthony.

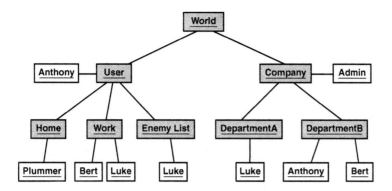

FIGURE 9.2 Peer groups with address data associated. Note that some addresses are repeated. (Peer groups are gray, addresses white).

We can't really maintain this well at the group level. You would need a higher level of abstraction that could make the system operate more like that of Figure 9.3.

In Figure 9.3, the data is divided between address items and ownership of lists that point to addresses. This arrangement also helps account for the fact that not all addresses represent people who are a part of the JPDA network, so the initial owner is the first person to add the address to their group.

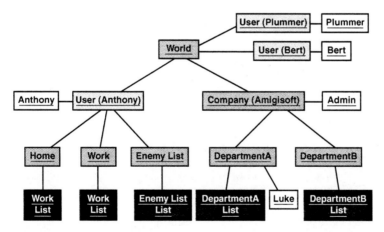

FIGURE 9.3 Peer groups with address data and lists that point to addresses maintained by other groups (lists are in black).

As you can imagine, we could go on with many other scenarios for managing data.

Class Design

Our class design is broken into eight areas:

- Overall Management and PIM concepts

- Group management

- Address classes

- Calendar classes

- To Do classes

- Receiving synchronization messages

- Sending synchronization messages

- Editing and displaying

Each of these concepts will be discussed with UML and some of the code. The key sections of the JXTA code will be covered in detail. The entire set of code and online listings are available at www.samspublishing.com.

The Main Class

The main class for this application is JPDA (see Figure 9.4). This class is used to manage the peer groups, PIM data services, and most of the control of the application via the GUI. There is a circular reference between the main GUI AssistantView class and the JPDA class. The circular reference, although not ideal, reduces the complexity of the application by reducing the number of event listeners that would need to be created to sufficiently isolate the classes from each other.

We will not describe the methods here, but will refer to them as we discuss the other classes.

Group Management

Group management is provided by the code created in Chapter 6. There was a change made to the code to allow groups to be created with a specified group ID. This is done because we need persistent and well-known groups to ensure that if a group is created in the context of the application, the group will be identical, no matter which peer creates the group.

The default behavior had been to associate groups by name. In a development environment, the cache is often destroyed and the group ID is lost. By embedding the ID in code, the peer is guaranteed to be able to create a group that is recognizable to other peers as an identical group.

JPDA
(com.sams.jxta.pda)

+addAddressModel(model : DefaultListModel) : void
+addCalendarModel(model : DefaultListModel) : void
+addEntry(peerGroup : PeerGroup, vCard : VCard) : void
+addEvent(peerGroup : PeerGroup, xCal : XCal) : void
+addGroup(groupName : String, groupDescription : String) : PeerGroup
+addNewgroup(joinedPeerGroup : PeerGroup) : void
+addToDo(peerGroup: PeerGroup, vToDo : VToDo) : void
+addToDoModel(model : DefaultListModel) : void
+getNetPeerGroup() : PeerGroup
+getRootJPA() : PeerGroup
+joinGroup(peerGroup : PeerGroup) : Object
+JPDA()
+main(args : String[]) : void
+serializeDoc(doc : StructuredTextDocument) : String
+startAddressBook(peerGroup : PeerGroup) : void
+startApplication(args : String[]) : void
+startCalendar(peerGroup : PeerGroup) : void
+startJxta() : void
+startServices(peerGroup : PeerGroup) : void
+startToDo(peerGroup : PeerGroup) : void
+synchronize() : void
+synchronizeAddressBookService() : void
+synchronizeCalendaraService() : void
+synchronizeToDoListService() : void
+tests() : void
+updateAddress(peerGroup : PeerGroup, vCard : VCard) : void
+updateEvent(peerGroup : PeerGroup, xCal : XCal) : void
+updateToDo(peerGroup : PeerGroup, vToDo : VToDo) : void

FIGURE 9.4   UML of the *JPDA* class. This is the main class of the application and manages JXTA and the display.

Persistence of identifiers, such as the peer group ID, is a big issue. The problem is that identifiers should be unique. To support unique IDs, a large random number is often used on a canonical name like a Web site URL. Although a canonical name could be used, it was simpler to use the standard ID creation methods and hashtable lookup for our simple example.

XML PIM Class Design

The PIM classes (see Figure 9.5) are broken up into their specific types and given a name that is relative to the XML that they support. There are many methods in these classes, but they are mostly assessors for the data that they represent. Note that the VCard class uses Address and Phone because this data may repeat and we will need to create and manipulate an array of these objects.

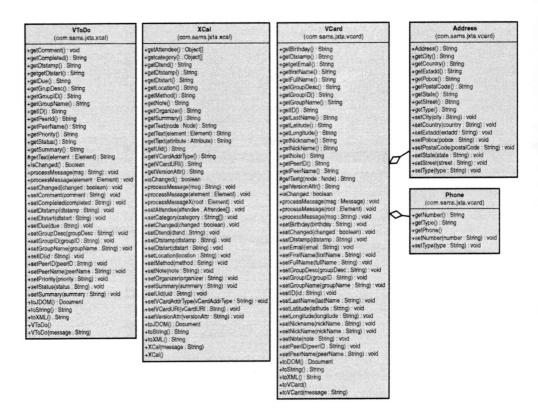

FIGURE 9.5   UML of the PIM classes that are used to represent To Do, calendar events, and addresses. These classes also encode and decode the XML they represent.

A Detailed Look at the VToDo Class

The code for VToDo is relatively straightforward and mostly identical to the code used for VCard, and the event class is decoded by the XCal class. Go to the book's Web site at www.samspublishing.com if you are interested in the specifics of this class.

As was pointed out at the beginning of this chapter, the PIM data will follow well known standards for PIM data as represented as XML. VToDo data is defined as a part of the XCal specification. The DTD and specification document for XCal is available on the Web at various sites. The following is sample XML for XML VToDo that follows the version 3.0 specification.

There are only two methods of consequence. The first is the toXML method used create an XML string (see Listing 9.1). The code simply appends the tags and data.

Note that this may look inefficient because we are not using a `StringBuffer` class. In reality, the compiler and possibly the just-in-time compiler will convert the concatenations into a character buffer, so we do not need to do this by hand. You could have used JDOM to create the XML object directly. An advantage of doing that is that there is less likelihood of a parsing error when decoded. The following code uses strings instead, because it is just quicker to develop our example.

LISTING 9.1   The toXML Method

```
public String toXML(){
    if (changed){
        // Note that many compilers convert this into a
        // series of appends to a StringBuffer, thus
        // making this efficient when written this way.
        valueOfXML =   "<?xml version=\"1.0\" encoding=\"UTF-8\"?> \n"
            + "<icalendar> \n"
            + "<vcalendar method=\""+method+"\" version=\""+supportedVersion
            + "\" prodid=\"-//HandGen//NONSGML vGen v1.0//EN\"> \n"
            +"<vtodo> \n"
            +"  <"+dtstampTag+">"+dtstamp+"</"+dtstampTag+"> \n"
            +"  <"+peerIDTag+">"+peerID+"</"+peerIDTag+">\n"
            +"  <"+peerNameTag+">"+peerName+"</"+peerNameTag+">\n"
            +"  <"+idTag+">"+id+"</"+idTag+">\n"
            +"  <"+groupIDTag+">"+groupID+"</"+groupIDTag+">\n"
            +"  <"+groupNameTag+">"+groupName+"</"+groupNameTag+">\n"
            +"  <"+groupDescTag+">"+groupDesc+"</"+groupDescTag+">\n"
            +"  <summary>"+summary+"</summary> \n"
            +"  <comment>"+comment+"</comment> \n"
            +"  <dtstart>"+dtstart+"</dtstart> \n"
            +"  <due>"+due+"</due> \n"
            +"  <priority>"+priority+"</priority> \n"
            +"  <categories> \n"
            +"     <item>"+category[0]+"</item> \n"
            +"  </categories> \n"
            +"</vtodo> \n"
            +"</vcalendar> \n"
            +"</icalendar> \n";
    }
    return valueOfXML;
}
```

To decode the data, the JDOM library is used to convert the raw string into an XML data model that can then be mined for the data found between the tags (see Listing 9.2). Note that there is very little error handling to catch errors when paring. There should be more code here to recover from parsing errors. For now, the code does nothing to validate the data because this class creates the same code it reads. Therefore, there is no need for too much error handling.

LISTING 9.2   The processMessage Method Used to Populate a VToDo Object from the Contents of an XML Document Supplied in the Element

```
public void processMessage(org.jdom.Element    element) {
        org.jdom.Document doc = element.getDocument();

        XMLOutputter outputter = new XMLOutputter("   ",true);
        id   = getText(element.getChild(idTag));
        dtstamp = getText(element.getChild(dtstampTag));
        summary = getText(element.getChild(summaryTag));
        comment = getText(element.getChild(commentTag));
        due =  getText(element.getChild(dueTag));
        completed = getText(element.getChild(completedTag));
        dtstart =  getText(element.getChild(dtstartTag));
        status =  getText(element.getChild(statusTag));
        category[0] = getText(element.getChild(categoriesTag));
        groupID =  getText(element.getChild(groupIDTag));
        groupName =  getText(element.getChild(groupNameTag));
        groupDesc =  getText(element.getChild(groupDescTag));
        peerID =  getText(element.getChild(peerIDTag));
        peerName =  getText(element.getChild(peerNameTag));
    }// end of processMessage()
```

When this application is integrated with others, more due diligence will need to be applied to ensure the data is valid. Because other applications may not support our extensions, the code will need to be able to deal with the differences.

THE JDOM XML LIBRARY

This chapter has code that uses the JDOM library to decode the XML. JDOM, available at www.jdom.org, is a simplified API for quick and easy manipulation of XML. If you compare the code in this application to others, you should see a marked difference in the readability and ease of use of the code. JDOM was created as a wrapper to traditional XML libraries because the metaphors used were difficult to understand and difficult to code.

JDOM is simpler than other APIs, because it attempts to stay as close to Java programming concepts as possible. JDOM also reduces the number of class casts that would normally be required.

If you are having trouble understanding XML, JDOM should ease the transition, and it will likely create much better and cleaner code as a result.

Extending the XML

We used a non-standard extension in each of the PIM classes. We did this by creating tags with the x- prefix. The added tags included peer and group identification, as well as a unique ID used to index data. The following is an example of an XCal extension:

```
<x-foo-cust-code>1998-ABC Corp-1234</x-foo-cust-code>
```

The ResolverService

For most messages, we will use the ResolverService class to send, receive, and process messages. The model used is a group broadcast. All messages will be broadcast to all members of the peer groups that will be specific to the application.

To understand why we are using the resolver, first look at the UML diagram of Figure 9.6. What you should realize from this diagram is that there is a lot of capability managed by the ResolverServiceImpl class. This class implements the ResolverService interface (both shown in Figure 9.7).

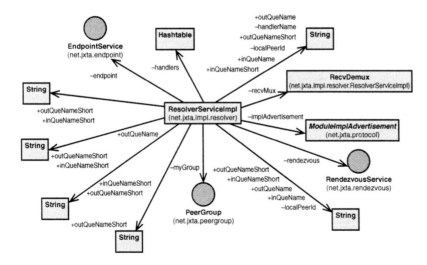

FIGURE 9.6   UML diagram showing the relationship between the ResolverServiceImpl and other parts of JXTA. Note that the resolver uses the RendezVousService.

Using the resolver is simply a matter of registering a handler and sending messages. This is the beauty of the resolver as compared to pipes that require some amount of cooperation from peers during setup.

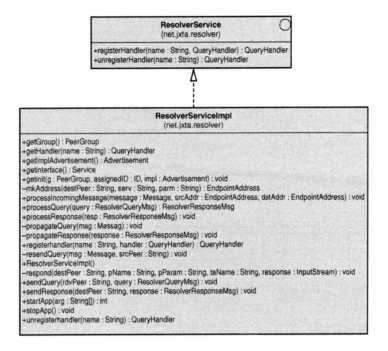

ResolverService
(net.jxta.resolver)

+registerHandler(name : String, QueryHandler) : QueryHandler
+unregisterHandler(name : String) : QueryHandler

ResolverServiceImpl
(net.jxta.resolver)

+getGroup() : PeerGroup
+getHandler(name : String) : QueryHandler
+getImplAdvertisement() : Advertisement
+getInterface() : Service
+getinit(g : PeerGroup, assignedID : ID, impl : Advertisement) : void
−mkAddress(destPeer : String, serv : String, parm : String) : EndpointAddress
+processIncomingMessage(message : Message, srcAddr : EndpointAddress, dstAddr : EndpointAddress) : void
+processQuery(query : ResolverQueryMsg) : ResolverResponseMsg
+processResponse(resp : ResolverResponseMsg) : void
−propagateQuery(msg : Messag) : void
−propagateResponse(response : ResolverResponseMsg) : void
+registerhandler(name : String, handler : QueryHandler) : QueryHandler
−resendQuery(msg : Message, srcPeer : String) : void
+ResolverServiceImpl()
−respond(destPeer : String, pName : String, pParam : String, taName : String, response : InputStream) : void
+sendQuery(rdvPeer : String, query : ResolverQueryMsg) : void
+sendResponse(destPeer : String, response : ResolverResponseMsg) : void
+startApp(arg : String[]) : int
+stopApp() : void
+unregisterhandler(name : String) : QueryHandler

FIGURE 9.7   UML diagram of the `ResolverService` interface and the `ResolverServiceImpl` class.

The disadvantages of the resolver are that messages are always sent in a broadcast mode. All peers in the group that have registered handlers will receive the messages. There is no way to target a specific peer. Even if you specify a specific peer, other peers may still receive the message.

For our application, these negatives are only slightly bothersome. We want all the peers in the group to receive most of the messages. The first version of JPDA suffers a little bit because the sync messages include all the information whether or not the peer wants it all. In the future, the sync message of JPDA should be shorter, because they should only include differences and not the complete database.

Setup of the Resolver Handlers

For the synchronization and update functionality, there will be two resolver handlers for each of the data types. There will be a specific handler for the update messages and a handler for the sync messages.

To manage the group isolation of data, there is an instance of each of the services for each group. This also means that there is also another instance of each of the handlers.

It is possible to use just the two handlers per service. This is possible because the resolver calls the handler by name and the handler name is included in the messages routed to particular handler object. In this particular design, because it needed to be simple for explanation, the design uses a handler per group and particular service. Had we kept with a single handler, the code would have required parsing of the handler name and other processing.

One reason to mention the possibility of reusing handlers is also to point out another possible design. Instead of groups, we could have simply created a different resolver handler and corresponding message names. We might want to do this if the current scheme of using peer groups turns out to be a bad choice. Using a name-based approach is very applicable to other applications that need to route different types of messages but does not worry about a large number of peer groups.

PIM Service classes

There are currently three PIM service classes—AddressBookService, CalendarService, and ToDoListService. The UML for these classes is shown in Figure 9.8. Note that this diagram shows the member variables for reference because there are inner classes that refer to them.

There are several important methods that have identical or similar signatures:

- addModel—Used to add a GUI list model to be updated as new entries arrive.

- addEntry—Called from the JPDA class when a new entry is added. This method takes the corresponding calendar type.

- merge—Used to process a new entry and add it to memory and the GUI display.

- synchronize—Called to send a synchronization query. Called from JPDA in response to the user selecting the synchronize menu item.

We will now discuss the handlers. The example code will be for the inner classes in the ToDoListService class. The three are mostly the same, except for differences in the classes and some of the XML.

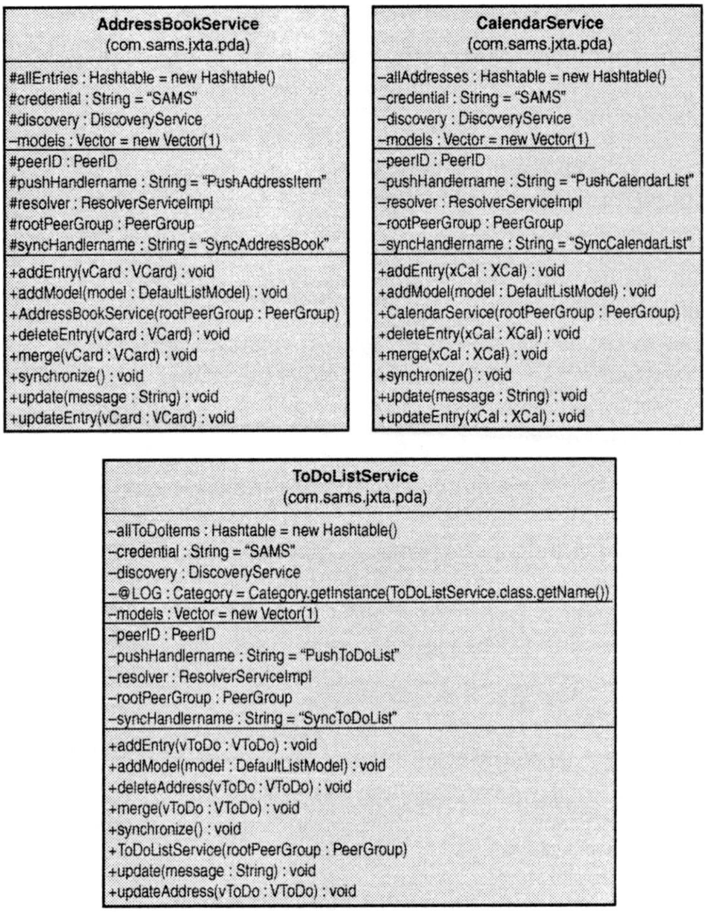

```
┌──────────────────────────────────────┐  ┌──────────────────────────────────────┐
│          AddressBookService          │  │           CalendarService            │
│          (com.sams.jxta.pda)          │  │          (com.sams.jxta.pda)          │
├──────────────────────────────────────┤  ├──────────────────────────────────────┤
│ #allEntries : Hashtable = new Hashtable()│ │ –allAddresses : Hashtable = new Hashtable()│
│ #credential : String = "SAMS"         │  │ –credential : String = "SAMS"         │
│ #discovery : DiscoveryService         │  │ –discovery : DiscoveryService         │
│ –models : Vector = new Vector(1)      │  │ –models : Vector = new Vector(1)      │
│ #peerID : PeerID                      │  │ –peerID : PeerID                      │
│ #pushHandlername : String = "PushAddressItem"│ │ –pushHandlername : String = "PushCalendarList"│
│ #resolver : ResolverServiceImpl       │  │ –resolver : ResolverServiceImpl       │
│ #rootPeerGroup : PeerGroup            │  │ –rootPeerGroup : PeerGroup            │
│ #syncHandlername : String = "SyncAddressBook"│ │ –syncHandlername : String = "SyncCalendarList"│
├──────────────────────────────────────┤  ├──────────────────────────────────────┤
│ +addEntry(vCard : VCard) : void       │  │ +addEntry(xCal : XCal) : void          │
│ +addModel(model : DefaultListModel) : void│ │ +addModel(model : DefaultListModel) : void│
│ +AddressBookService(rootPeerGroup : PeerGroup)│ │ +CalendarService(rootPeerGroup : PeerGroup)│
│ +deleteEntry(vCard : VCard) : void    │  │ +deleteEntry(xCal : XCal) : void       │
│ +merge(vCard : VCard) : void          │  │ +merge(xCal : XCal) : void             │
│ +synchronize() : void                 │  │ +synchronize() : void                  │
│ +update(message : String) : void      │  │ +update(message : String) : void       │
│ +updateEntry(vCard : VCard) : void    │  │ +updateEntry(xCal : XCal) : void       │
└──────────────────────────────────────┘  └──────────────────────────────────────┘

         ┌────────────────────────────────────────────────────────────┐
         │                      ToDoListService                        │
         │                    (com.sams.jxta.pda)                      │
         ├────────────────────────────────────────────────────────────┤
         │ –allToDoItems : Hashtable = new Hashtable()                 │
         │ –credential : String = "SAMS"                               │
         │ –discovery : DiscoveryService                               │
         │ –@LOG : Category = Category.getInstance(ToDoListService.class.getName())│
         │ –models : Vector = new Vector(1)                            │
         │ –peerID : PeerID                                            │
         │ –pushHandlername : String = "PushToDoList"                  │
         │ –resolver : ResolverServiceImpl                             │
         │ –rootPeerGroup : PeerGroup                                  │
         │ –syncHandlername : String = "SyncToDoList"                  │
         ├────────────────────────────────────────────────────────────┤
         │ +addEntry(vToDo : VToDo) : void                             │
         │ +addModel(model : DefaultListModel) : void                  │
         │ +deleteAddress(vToDo : VToDo) : void                        │
         │ +merge(vToDo : VToDo) : void                                │
         │ +synchronize() : void                                       │
         │ +ToDoListService(rootPeerGroup : PeerGroup)                 │
         │ +update(message : String) : void                           │
         │ +updateAddress(vToDo : VToDo) : void                        │
         └────────────────────────────────────────────────────────────┘
```

FIGURE 9.8   UML class diagram of each of the core PIM service classes.

PushHandler **Class**

The PushHandler class is used to send messages to other peers containing new or changed PIM entries (see Listing 9.3). The class is an inner class to the service class for which it is written. There is no need for this class to be an inner class, it was only done for convenience to simplify the code. This does mean that there are variables referenced in the appropriate parent service class (refer to Figure 9.8 for these member variables).

There are two methods and a constructor. The two methods are the implementation of the QueryHandler interface. The processQuery method throws NoResponseException because there is no response expected by the message sender. The method calls the merge method of the parent class to process the incoming PIM data.

We do not have any significant code in the processResponse method, but it is only to log messages. The method should never be called, so you should never see the logger messages.

LISTING 9.3   PushHandler class used to process resolver query messages with new VToDo items.

```
class PushHandler implements QueryHandler{
    protected String handlerName;
    protected String credential;
    protected SimpleDateFormat format;
    format = new SimpleDateFormat("MM, dd, yyyy hh:mm:ss.S");

    public PushHandler(String handlerName, String credential){
        this.handlerName = handlerName;
        this.credential = credential;
    }// end of constructor CalendarHandler()

    public ResolverResponseMsg processQuery(ResolverQueryMsg query)
                                throws NoResponseException
                                    , ResendQueryException
                                    , DiscardQueryException{
        LOG.debug("Received a query");
        LOG.debug(((ResolverQuery)query).toString());
        String xml = query.getQuery();
        // Process the incoming data
        merge(new VToDo(xml));
        throw new NoResponseException("Got the data we were interested in.");
    }// end of processQuery()

    public void processResponse(ResolverResponseMsg response) {
        LOG.debug("Received a ToDo response");
        LOG.debug(((ResolverResponse)response).toString());
    }// End of processResponse()

}// end of class PushHandler
```

SyncHandler class

The SyncHandler class is also an implementation of the QueryHandler interface (see Listing 9.4). In this class, however, the usage is more like what it was intended for. The processQuery method responds to the message by creating a message that contains all of the entries associated with the type and group. The message is then returned. The resolver then takes this message and sends it back to the peer that made the original request. The result is that the processResponse method in the original peer is called.

The processResponse method deserializes the list of entries and calls the merge method of the parent class for each of the items found in the message.

Remember that the response method is only called on the originating query peer, and the processQuery method is only called on a peer that receives the query peer's message.

LISTING 9.4   SyncHandler Class Used to Process Synchronization of PIM Objects

```
class SyncHandler implements QueryHandler{
    protected String handlerName;
    protected String credential;
    protected Hashtable entryBook;
    protected SimpleDateFormat format;
    format = new SimpleDateFormat("MM, dd, yyyy hh:mm:ss.S");


    public SyncHandler( String handlerName
                      , Hashtable entryBook
                      , String credential){
        this.handlerName = handlerName;
        this.credential = credential;
        this.entryBook = entryBook;
    }// end of constructor PullHandler()



    public ResolverResponseMsg processQuery(ResolverQueryMsg query)
                                throws NoResponseException
                                  , ResendQueryException
                                  , DiscardQueryException{
        try{
            LOG.debug("Received a synchronizer query");

            org.jdom.Element root = new org.jdom.Element("todo-list");
            org.jdom.Document doc = new org.jdom.Document(root);
            Enumeration enum = entryBook.elements();
            for(;enum.hasMoreElements();){
                org.jdom.Document d2 =((VToDo)enum.nextElement()).toJDOM();
                org.jdom.Element ele = d2.getRootElement();
                ele.detach();
```

LISTING 9.4   Continued

```
            root.addContent(ele);
        }
        // Return a generic response;
        ResolverResponseMsg message = null;
        XMLOutputter putter = new XMLOutputter("   ",true);
        StringWriter writer = new StringWriter();
        putter.output(doc,writer);

        LOG.debug(" sync messag:"+writer.toString());
        message = new ResolverResponse(handlerName
                                    ,credential
                                    ,query.getQueryId()
                                    ,writer.toString());
      return (ResolverResponseMsg)message;
    }catch(Exception e ){
        e.printStackTrace();
        LOG.error("Error processing query",e);
        throw new NoResponseException("Error processing query");
    }
}// end of processQuery()

public void processResponse(ResolverResponseMsg response) {
    LOG.debug("Received a response");
    String textDoc = response.getResponse();
    if (textDoc ==null)return;
    //System.out.println("Received a response:"+textDoc);

    try{
        ByteArrayInputStream in;
        in = new ByteArrayInputStream(textDoc.getBytes());
        org.jdom.input.SAXBuilder builder;
        builder = new org.jdom.input.SAXBuilder();
        org.jdom.Document doc = builder.build(in);
        org.jdom.Element root = doc.getRootElement();
        //specific to todo
        List book = (List) root .getChildren("icalendar");
        ListIterator lister = book.listIterator();

        LOG.debug("name:"+root.getName());
        while (lister.hasNext()){
```

LISTING 9.4   Continued

```
                org.jdom.Element entry = (org.jdom.Element) lister.next();
                entry = entry .getChild("vcalendar").getChild("vtodo");

                LOG.debug("Received a response:"+entry.getText());
                XMLOutputter putter = new XMLOutputter("   ",true);
                StringWriter writer = new StringWriter();
                putter.output(entry,writer);

                LOG.debug(" sync messag:"+writer.toString());
                String xml = writer.toString();
                merge(new VToDo(xml));
            }

        }catch(Exception je){//org.jdom.JDOMException je){
            je.printStackTrace();
            LOG.error("Error processing incoming message.",je);
        }
    }// End of processResponse()
}// end of class SyncHandler
```

Initializing and Registering Handlers

The code to register both of the handlers starts with the creation of the push handler and the sync handler classes. The following push handler takes the name of the handler and a credential. The credential is not used yet, but is used in the query response method of the response message. The credential should be the same credential created when a group is joined:

```
PushHandler pushHandler = new  PushHandler(pushHandlerName,credential);
```

The creation of the `SyncHandler` class includes a reference to a hashtable called `allToDoItems`. This hashtable contains the To Do items that are managed by the handler.

```
SyncHandler syncHandler = new  SyncHandler( syncHandlerName
                                    , allToDoItems
                                    , credential);
```

Next, the resolver is requested from the current peer group:

```
resolver = (ResolverServiceImpl)rootPeerGroup.getResolverService();
```

With the resolver, the `registerHandler` method is called for each of the handlers. Note that each call has a resolver handler name that is specific to the type of handler:

```
resolver.registerHandler(pushHandlerName, pushHandler);
resolver.registerHandler(syncHandlerName, syncHandler);
```

After these method calls, the resolver is ready to accept any new messages for both synchronization and updates to the particular group with which the `ToDoListService` class was registered. As can be seen, this is a modestly small amount of code to allow a large group of computers to interact.

Sending Update Query Messages

Sending an update message via the resolver is amazingly simple. Most of the work is done in the XML objects `XCal`, `VCard`, and `VToDo`. All that needs to be done is to convert the objects to an XML string, create a message object to store the message, and send the message with the resolver.

To start, Listing 9.5 is the `addEntry` method of the `ToDoListService` class. This is called by the GUI with a `VToDo` object that was built in the GUI. In this method, the context of the peer group and the peer is set for later use. The `merge` method is then called to send the entry to the network.

LISTING 9.5 The `addEntry` and `merge` Methods of the `ToDoListService` Class

```
public void addEntry( VToDo vToDo){
    vToDo.setGroupID(rootPeerGroup.getPeerGroupID().toString());
    vToDo.setGroupName(rootPeerGroup.getPeerGroupName());
    vToDo.setPeerID(rootPeerGroup.getPeerID().toString());
    vToDo.setPeerName(rootPeerGroup.getPeerName());
    vToDo.setGroupDesc(
            rootPeerGroup.getPeerGroupAdvertisement().getDescription());
    merge(vToDo);
    update(vToDo.toXML());
}


    public synchronized void merge(VToDo vToDo){
        VToDo old = (VToDo)allToDoItems.get(vToDo.getID());
        if ( old !=null){
            LOG.debug("To do list already has this message");
            if (!vToDo.getDtstamp().equals(old.getDtstamp()) ){
                LOG.debug("Update because it is newer");
                allToDoItems.put(vToDo.getID(),vToDo);
            }
```

LISTING 9.5   Continued

```
            return;
      }else{
          LOG.debug("New todo  message");
          allToDoItems.put(vToDo.getID(),vToDo);
      }
      // Update displays
      LOG.debug("Updating list in display");
      for (int i =0;i <models.size();i++){
          LOG.debug("Updating list item:"+vToDo);
          ((DefaultListModel)models.elementAt(i)).addElement(vToDo);
      }
}// end of merge()
```

The update method of the ToDoListService is where you actually create and send a
ResolverQueryMsg with the VToDo XML (see Listing 9.6). The message is created by
creating a ResolverQuery object.

LISTING 9.6   The update Method of the ToDoListService Class

```
public void  update(String message){
    LOG.debug("Resolver sending messages");
    ResolverQueryMsg resolverQueryMsg = null;
    resolverQueryMsg
        = new ResolverQuery( pushHandlerName
                           , credential
                           , rootPeerGroup.getPeerID().toString()
                           , message,1);
    ResolverSend resolverSend;
    resolverSend = new ResolverSend(resolver, null, resolverQueryMsg);

    resolverSend.start();
}
```

The ResolverSend class is very simple and is only used to send the actual message
(see Listing 9.7). Oddly, the sendQuery method blocks until it has contacted the
other peers. This is very odd because there is no value returned. The responses arrive
via callbacks to the response method in the resolver handler that we have registered.
Unfortunately, we needed to create this thread so that we can offload the waiting for
this action and return control to the GUI.

Note that we are not being too frugal with our thread. It would be better to maintain a single thread and reuse the same thread object rather than creating and destroying it each time we need to send a message. In addition, we probably need a queue that is also running in a thread to prevent blocking on our single message thread.

Note that the first parameter is null in the sendQuery method call. This could have specified a peer to which to target the query. Remember that the goal in our application is to send updates to all the peers listening, so we set the peer to null, which will propagate the message to the registered peers.

LISTING 9.7 The ResolverSend Class

```
public class ResolverSend extends Thread{
    net.jxta.impl.resolver.ResolverServiceImpl resolver;
    PeerAdvertisement peer;
    ResolverQueryMsg resolverQueryMsg;

    public ResolverSend( ResolverServiceImpl resolver
                       , PeerAdvertisement peer
                       , ResolverQueryMsg resolverQueryMsg){
        this.resolver = resolver;
        this.peer = peer;
        this.resolverQueryMsg = resolverQueryMsg;
    }

    public void run(){
        try{
            resolver.sendQuery(null, resolverQueryMsg);
            System.out.println( "Peer:"+peer
                              + " Message sent:"+resolverQueryMsg);
        }catch(Exception e){
            e.printStackTrace();
        }
    }
}
```

Note that most of the code we have covered to send the message really included few lines associated with the resolver (these lines were bolded in the update and run methods for quick reference). The rest of the code dealt with storage, the GUI, and the thread used to make the GUI more responsive (for example, the GUI accepts inputs again soon after the thread is started and out code returns control to the GUI). The GUI and storage code would have been done in any application, but the resolver code would have been replaced by much more code for equivalent behavior where a group of peers would receive the message.

Sending Synchronization Messages

Sending a synchronization method is almost identical to that of sending an update of a new item. The key difference is that the synchronize method is essentially blank and is only used to trigger the other peers to respond to the request. As was discussed earlier, this part of the application is where we could improve the efficiency greatly. Instead of a blank message, there could be information that describes the state of the data in terms of last updates and perhaps checksums that could be compared to data on other peers to ensure that only the minimum differences would be sent in the reply to the query.

As in the update method, the synchronize method in Listing 9.8 also uses the ResolverSend class to allow the query to operate in its own thread and allow the GUI to resume when control is returned.

LISTING 9.8   The synchronize Method

```
public void synchronize(){
    LOG.debug("Resolver sending synchronize");
    ResolverQueryMsg resolverQueryMsg = null;
    resolverQueryMsg
            = new ResolverQuery( syncHandlerName
                              , credential
                              , rootPeerGroup.getPeerID().toString()
                              , "" // Blank message
                              , 1);
    ResolverSend resolverSend = new  ResolverSend( resolver
                                                , null
                                                , resolverQueryMsg);
    resolverSend.start();
}
```

Edit, Display, and Control

The design of the user interface classes takes a straightforward approach (see Figure 9.9). Most of the code is in the Assistant view class. The JPDA and AssistantView classes work together to manage either data from the user or data from the JXTA network via the resolver. The AssistantView maintains the lists that are used to store PIM data and the peer group objects in use. The AssistantView class also launches the edit classes.

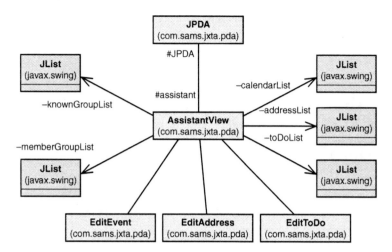

FIGURE 9.9   UML class diagram showing the relationships of the GUI classes to JPDA.

There is also a menu that is used. On the menu is where you will find the Synchronize command as well as Delete, Exit, and About.

Application Layout

The next part of the design is concerned with the layout of the display. Because this is the initial version, the display is very primitive (see Figure 9.10). The screen is divided into right and left sections. The left side contains a list of groups that have been joined.

On the right is a tabbed pane with tabs for the calendar, To-Do list, and address book. Each of these has a simple list that displays the current contents. Each tab also has buttons for adding, viewing, and editing the entries. There is a final tab for adding and joining groups.

The overall design is seen previously in the UML diagram of Figure 9.9. The main program is in the JPDA class which, as discussed, manages most of the operations on the PIM data and JXTA. The AssistantView class is an extension of the Frame class and contains the key components for viewing, editing, and creating PIM data and groups. In addition, there are three dialogs that are used to view and edit all the fields supported by each of the PIM data classes. These dialogs take as arguments the PIM classes of VToDo, XCal, and VCard and display the contents. If the user selects the OK button, the data is updated in the application, and the updated objects are sent out on the JXTA network to other JPDA peers.

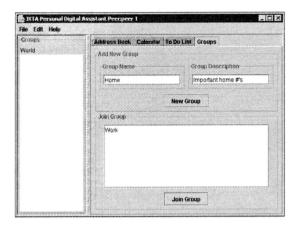

FIGURE 9.10   The initial screenshot of the JPDA application.

Figures 9.11, 9.12, and 9.13 show the address, To-Do item, and calendar entry dialogs. Note that they are also very primitive at this stage. They also do not support the full XML specification they represent.

FIGURE 9.11   Screenshot of the dialog window used to create an address book entry.

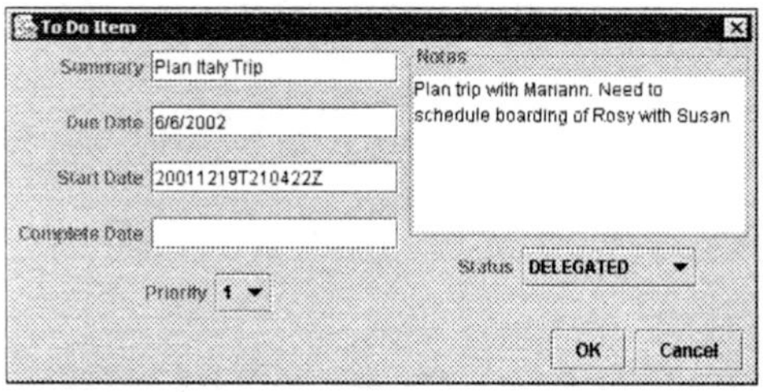

FIGURE 9.12   Screen shot of the dialog used to create a To Do item.

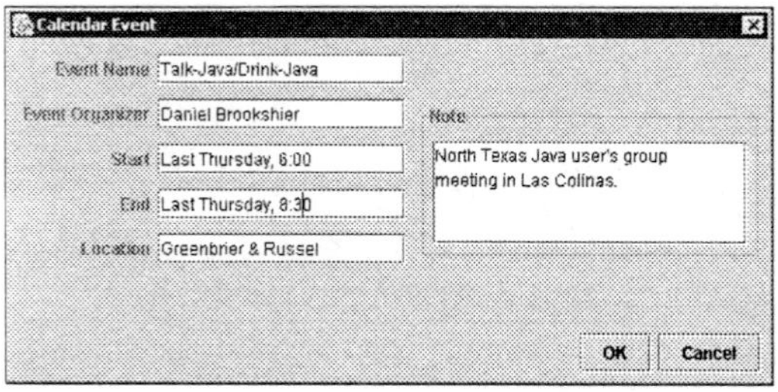

FIGURE 9.13   Screen shot of the dialog used to create a calendar event entry.

Finally, in Figure 9.14, we show the panel used to create and join peer groups. As discussed, the creation of groups should be carefully managed. Groups could be created that are then never used again. In the future, this part of the application should be changed to provide more control of groups and include extra functions to discover groups or invite peers to join groups (like inviting peers to join a club or carpool).

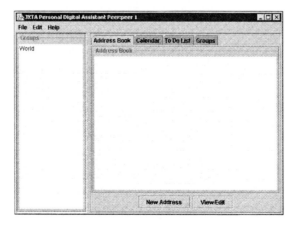

FIGURE 9.14   Screen shot of the panel used create and join peer groups.

Summary

The ResolverService interface and associated classes is one of the simpler JXTA metaphors to use in a distributed peer-to-peer application. The ability to communicate in a query response fashion is a simple matter of implementing and registering the QueryHandler interface with the Resolver Service of the PeerGroup within which you want to operate.

The complexity of applications that use the resolver is another matter. The JPDA application is simplistic in its first version and specifically avoided many issues that are required in a final version. Before this application reaches widespread use, there will be a much greater effort to design both more useful models of use and efficient use of JXTA resources and networking. For example, propagation pipes, though more complex to use, may be more appropriate.

Also, because this chapter has shown that the resolver is simple to use, does not mean it should be used in every application. The resolver should only be used when a query/response model is warranted. In addition, the system needs to be able to withstand failures of the network to deliver messages to all of the peers in the network. In JPDA, we did this by design by having both a broadcast of changes and a synchronize that allowed a peer to search the network for information it may have missed.

In addition to the resolver, we have also shown another model of how a JXTA application can be designed. In this case, there is a manager represented by the JPDA class and data-specific handlers represented by the service classes.

The data we are manipulating is also very important to the design. We specifically chose very well known XML standards for calendars, To Dos, and addresses. This will be expanded in future to include SyncML, a standard for synchronizing data via XML. By using these XML standards, we have saved design time as well as created an opportunity for integration with other applications.

In addition, because we chose to transmit the data as XML instead of a binary format, we have made it possible to write peers in other languages to run on other platforms. This is important because we ultimately would like to communicate to true PIM devices that may not have the capacity to run Java but can run JXTA clients written in C.

In the next chapter, we will discuss an application that uses propagation pipes. The JXTA Chess application from the JXTA.org site will be studied to see how others have dealt with the problems and solutions to a collaborative P2P application.

10

JXTA Chess: Game Programming

By Daniel Brookshier

JXTA Chess (http://chess.jxta.org/) is an application that implements a peer-to-peer chess game. The application manages a chess tournament complete with an audience. Yaroslav Faybishenko created JXTA Chess, with help from others at jxta.org, to create a platform for demonstrating one-to-many pipes, also known as propagation pipes or wire pipes.

We are covering this particular application in this book because it is a great example of a collaborative P2P game. Also, JXTA Chess to date has not had a lot of documentation, and this chapter hopes to document the application to help developers understand how it works.

The game uses XML, pipes, peer groups, and bi-directional pipes. We will cover some of the code and give an overview of important classes. By the time we are done, you should have an idea of how a collaborative P2P application is developed.

The current tournament code supports Blitz Chess. Each game of Blitz Chess is played with a clock with a set time, usually five minutes per game. The points are calculated by pieces captured and who wins the game. If your clock runs out before a king has been captured, you lose the game. You can resign or ask for a draw (tie).

> **NOTE**
>
> JXTA Chess is a proof-of-concept effort and was not written to follow specific guidelines or standards. This means that you may see coding style and techniques that might seem out of place. We have not modified them or modified the listings except for formatting to fit the page. When looking at code like this, try to concentrate on just the JXTA functionality and build an architecture that suits your specific needs.

AN INTERVIEW WITH YAROSLAV FAYBISHENKO, CREATOR OF JXTA CHESS

Daniel Brookshier: Any bodies buried in the code that I should know about?

Yaroslav Faybishenko: Yes, the current code does not create a group per tournament, which would be very desirable because it would help partition the network better.

Daniel: How did your chess example come about? Was it written before JXTA?

Yaroslav: The chess example came about when Eric Pouyoul started working on the jxta-wire project (jxta-wire.jxta.org) and put up a list of applications he would have liked to see use the primitives provided by jxta-wire. Chess was one of them, so I just decided to do it, since I always wanted to write one. The only other jxta-wire example at the time was Eric's group chat app, so I wanted to help him show other programmers the jxta-wire features.

Daniel: How important are propagate pipes to JXTA chess? Would it have been difficult to write otherwise?

Yaroslav: Propagate pipes are essential to JXTA Chess. They essentially provide a broadcast-to-a-subset-of-a-network primitive and so allow observers to watch games and tournaments take place.

Daniel: What was the hardest part of getting your application to work?

Yaroslav: I think the hardest part was actually to make the look of the application clean while exposing as many actual features as possible. So the hardest was the UI, not the networking.

Daniel: Are you happy with the performance?

Yaroslav: Yes, JXTA Chess only exchanges small messages, such as move and game-history encodings, relatively infrequently, so I had no reason to measure performance objectively.

Daniel: Is there anything you would have done different?

Yaroslav: I think I have done everything well. The application is sinkable and pretty modular, so it was easy to swap out the UI for one that uses the J2ME GUI class library. We are presenting this work at JavaOne (November, 2001 conference in Japan) this week and hope that it will excite mobile-device developers.

Daniel: How much did you contribute to propagate pipes?

Yaroslav: I only watched Eric do it.

Daniel: What other areas of JXTA have you contributed to?

Yaroslav: I contributed to advertisement-expiration, advertisement indexing and xpath querying, etc.

Daniel: Why do you think JXTA is important?

Yaroslav: I think JXTA is important because it gives developers a library that they can start using to build applications right away. We are slowly getting there and I hope our pace will accelerate.

Daniel: Any other comments?

Yaroslav: The shorter we can make the time-span between the developer downloading the JXTA code and building apps with it, the better.

Running JXTA Chess

The first step in understanding how JXTA Chess works is to approach the application as a user. Of course, the first thing to do is to download the application and install it. The installation files are available at `http://chess.jxta.org/`, where you should find a link on the front page.

To run the application, run the bat or shell file, which will start Java. If you want to run two copies of JXTA chess on the same machine for experimentation purposes, copy the `bin` directory and use different ports for TCP/IP and HTTP. If you also configure your peers as rendezvous and gateways, the application will run a little bit faster when you are only playing chess on the one machine.

Opening Screen

The first thing you will see when you start JXTA Chess is a dialog window that asks you for a screen name (nickname), as shown in Figure 10.1.

FIGURE 10.1   Example of a nickname dialog.

The screen name is usually a good idea because many people do not name their peers very appropriately or use nonsense names. In an interactive game like chess, you would want to give your users an opportunity to use a name that is more natural. After you've entered your screen name, do the following:

1. The opening screen in Figure 10.2 will appear next. On this screen is a tabbed window for games and tournaments.

2. Select the Tournaments tab so that the application looks like Figure 10.3. On this tab page, start a tournament by pressing the Start a New Tournament button.

3. You will be presented with a dialog to configure the tournament. Type the name of the tournament and parameters about the tournament, such as the number of minutes per round and the number of games played per round (see Figure 10.4).

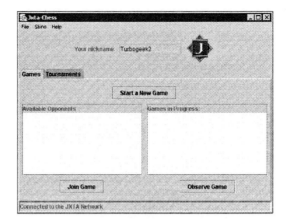

FIGURE 10.2   Opening screen of JXTA Chess with Games tab selected.

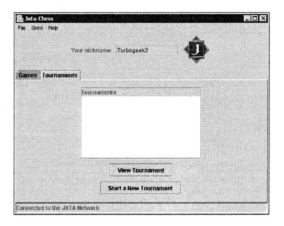

FIGURE 10.3   Main screen with the Tournaments tab selected so that you can start a tournament.

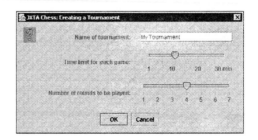

FIGURE 10.4   Tournament definition screen.

4. After you have added a new tournament, you will see a new tab displayed, as shown in Figure 10.5. The display simply shows the participants and a diagram of tournament results.

Notice also that in the upper right there is a parameter called Your Status. In this case, you are a Manager because you created the group. You could also see Observer or Participant. Note also that you have a button to terminate the tournament if required.

The tournament scorecard is the box with all the squares. Scores are shown in each square at the end of each match. The total score for a player is shown on the right of the box. The black squares are positions in the matrix where an opponent could play himself, so we show that as a null game and blank out that spot. The player with the highest score on the right after all games are played is the winner.

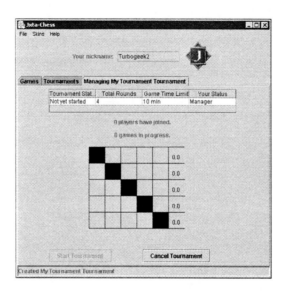

FIGURE 10.5 Manager tab for the new tournament group created earlier.

5. The next thing you are going to do is go back to the Tournaments tab. Notice that your tournament is now in the list box, as shown in Figure 10.6. You can now view the tournament.

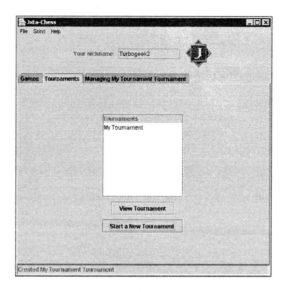

FIGURE 10.6   Tournaments tab showing the new tournament ready for viewing.

6. When you view the tournament, you get yet another tab, shown in Figure 10.7. This time, the Your Status section of the display shows that you are now an Observer.

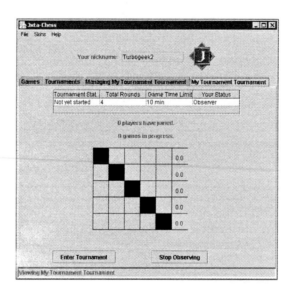

FIGURE 10.7   Tournament tab with Observer state. Note that the manager tab is still available.

7. Now you can officially join the tournament as a player by clicking the Enter Tournament button. When you do this, you will see a change in the tab contents, as shown in Figure 10.8. You can now see that you still need to play up to four rounds and you have 10 minutes for your next game. Also, your status has been changed from Observer to Participant.

Note that your name is now visible on the matrix on the top and bottom. The black box where the vertical and horizontal intersect means you cannot play a game against yourself.

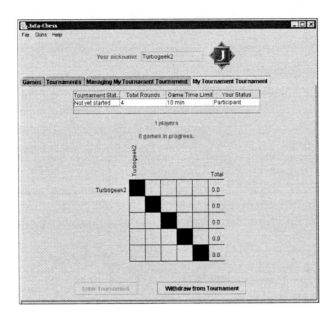

FIGURE 10.8   Tournament tab after Enter Tournament button is clicked.

8. To start a game, go to the Games tab and click the Start a New Game button. Figure 10.9 shows the resulting window.

After another opponent decides to play a game with you, a dialog will ask your permission and then display the dialog shown in Figure 10.10. The dialog has the chessboard, move clocks, and other components.

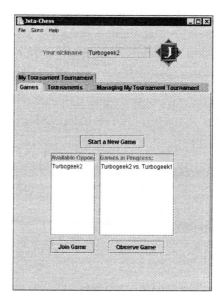

FIGURE 10.9   Resulting Games screen after Start a New Game button is chosen. Note that the Available Opponents list now has your nickname.

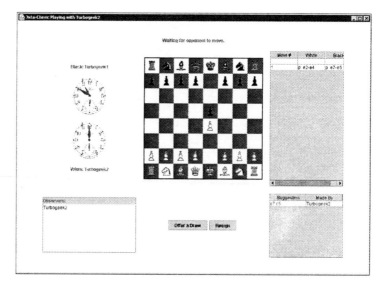

FIGURE 10.10   Chess game screen. Note the Observer's, Suggestion, and Move lists.

At this point, the original dialog on the Games tab now shows that your game is in progress, as shown in Figure 10.11.

FIGURE 10.11   Games display after another peer joins an advertised game.

Figure 10.12 shows the observer dialog. If the game just started is selected, this dialog is displayed. It allows others to view the game in progress and suggest moves. This is an important feature because it shows that multiple peers can view a single game, making this a collaboration-like application.

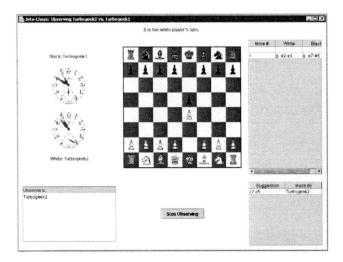

FIGURE 10.12   Chess game as seen by a user when they press the Observe Game button.

Overview of the Classes

At first glance, JXTA Chess looks like a rather simple application. There are only nine active class files in the project. Unfortunately, most of these classes have inner classes used for various purposes, including event listeners and classes that allow the code to create new threads to handle either incoming messages or to prevent blocking of execution while waiting for connections.

The good news is that the bulk of the JXTA code is in the JxtaChessNetwork and Tournament classes. The rest of the classes are primarily for handling the GUI. The following is a list of the top-level classes and what their general responsibilities include:

- Board—Data representation of the chessboard and pieces. There are inner classes for all the pieces that implement the movement rules.

- ChessClockComponent—This is an extension of Component that implements the chess clock used to time moves.

- JxtaChess—This is the main class for the program. This creates the GUI and links the GUI with the JXTA networking class JxtaChessNetwork.

- JxtaChessMenu—This is the menu builder for the application.

- JxtaChessSkins—This class is used to change the look of the chess game.

- JxtaChessUI—An extension of Jpanel, this class integrates the bulk of the main screen and dialogs.

- Tournament—Manages the tournament. Also includes classes that represent a chess match, players, and tournament rounds.

- TournamentUI—GUI for the tournament management interface.

- JxtaChessNetwork—This class has most of the code used to implement chess via JXTA. This class contains multiple inner classes that will be explained in the next section.

JxtaChessNetwork

The JxtaChessNetwork class is a very large collection of classes that collectively implement the JXTA networking for the game. The JxtaChessNetwork class itself is a manager for the system. The class has the following methods:

- createChildGroup—Creates a new group as a child of the current group. This creates a new PeerGroup object that will be used to host the tournament.

- createTournament—Creates a new instance of a tournament.

- createGame—Creates a new game. The game is broadcast. Another peer can join the game by calling the joinGame method it its JxtaChessNetwork object.

- getName—Utility method that converts an advertisement name (retrieved by calling the Advertisement method getName). Advertisement names are used to pass information, and this method is used to find the type.

- getPeerName—Returns the name of the peer from the root peer group. In other words, returns the name of this peer.

- isGame—Utility method that returns true if the string "Game" is in the name of a supplied PipeAdvertisement object. This is used as a simple way to determine what type of pipe advertisement this is without adding custom tags.

- isTournament—Utility method that returns true if the string "Tournament" is in the name of a supplied PipeAdvertisement object. This is used as a simple way to determine what type of pipe advertisement this is without adding custom tags.

- joinTournament—Note that this method is not implemented in the current release (this method may be deleted in future). The TournamentParticipant class's join method is used instead.

- joinGame—Used to join a game by presenting a TournamentParticipant object, the peer name, the opponents peer name, and a GameListener object. This method creates a GameJoiner object with the information and starts the object in a separate thread.

- observeTournament—Creates a TournamentManagerFinder object to locate and register the peer as a tournament participant. The Tournament.Listener interface is used to inform the client of tournament results from games and other events. The listener class has multiple methods to pass specific information about the tournament in progress. The methods include created, observing, joined, playerJoined, roundStart, setMatch, gameStarted, setResult, resultMismatch, tournamentStart, tournamentEnd, needNameChange, and networkIsDown.

- debug—Utility method for printing to the console.

- debugMsg—Prints the contents of a Message to the console.

- quitGame—Removes the peer from a specifically named game.

- stop—Kills the GameDiscoverer thread that was created when the JxtaChessNetwork object was constructed.

In Figure 10.13, we show the UML diagram for the JxtaChessNetwork class. Note that isGame, isTournament, and createChildGroup are private methods, because only this class uses them. Also, although it is not obvious from the UML, the debug and debugMsg methods are package protected (their access scope is default) and are not part of the public interface to the class.

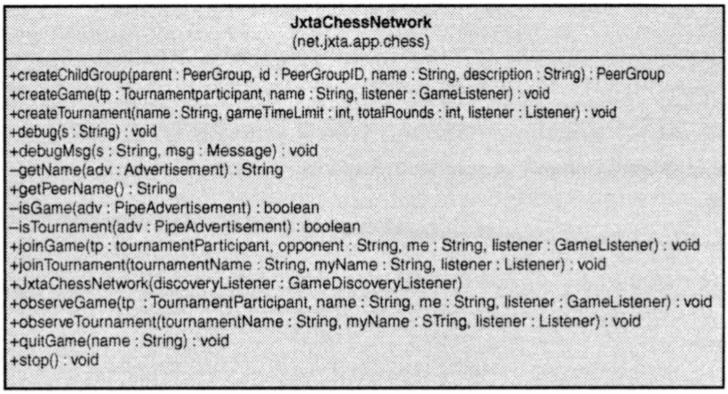

```
                        JxtaChessNetwork
                        (net.jxta.app.chess)

+createChildGroup(parent : PeerGroup, id : PeerGroupID, name : String, description : String) : PeerGroup
+createGame(tp : Tournamentparticipant, name : String, listener : GameListener) : void
+createTournament(name : String, gameTimeLimit : int, totalRounds : int, listener : Listener) : void
+debug(s : String) : void
+debugMsg(s : String, msg : Message) : void
-getName(adv : Advertisement) : String
+getPeerName() : String
-isGame(adv : PipeAdvertisement) : boolean
-isTournament(adv : PipeAdvertisement) : boolean
+joinGame(tp : tournamentParticipant, opponent : String, me : String, listener : GameListener) : void
+joinTournament(tournamentName : String, myName : String, listener : Listener) : void
+JxtaChessNetwork(discoveryListener : GameDiscoveryListener)
+observeGame(tp : TournamentParticipant, name : String, me : String, listener : GameListener) : void
+observeTournament(tournamentName : String, myName : STring, listener : Listener) : void
+quitGame(name : String) : void
+stop() : void
```

FIGURE 10.13   UML diagram of the JxtaChessNetwork class.

Now we will cover a set of inner classes contained in JxtaChessNetwork. Note that the use of inner classes in this case is probably inappropriate. The design was probably slightly quicker to develop, but there is an increased cost to maintain a larger amount of code in a single file (around two thousand lines). Although the compartmentalization of classes is well designed, it is much harder to maintain and document in a production environment. But before you blame the programmer, remember that this game was probably written in a few days, and so it can be pardoned for a few inconsistencies (remember that the design could change in the future because JXTA Chess is an active project at www.jxta.org).

GameDiscoveryListener Interface

The GameDiscoveryListener interface is used to announce when the system locates a game. This interface is implemented by the AllGameDiscoveryListener, which is instantiated in the JxtaChess class to begin the process of discovery. As you can see by the method signatures in the UML diagram in Figure 10.14, there is an event for the discovery of a game and an invalidation of a game. The methods are also used to designate if a game is a tournament and if the game is in progress.

FIGURE 10.14 UML diagram of the `GameDiscovery` interface used to announce new games or changes in state of games.

GameListener Interface

The `GameListener` interface, shown in Figure 10.15, is implemented by the `GameHook` class, which is located in the `JxtaChess` class. The `GameHook` class is used to notify the GUI of changes. For example, when the `addObserver` method is called, the `GameHook` updates the state of the display to show that there is a new observer. `GameHook` is in effect the controller for the display.

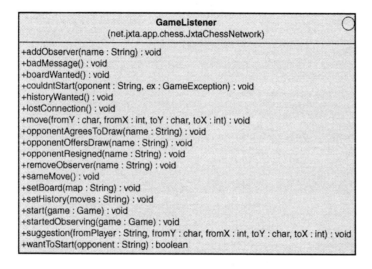

FIGURE 10.15 UML for the `GameListener` interface used to notify a peer of most game events.

The `JxtaChess` class creates a `GameHook` for each of the two players and each observer that is added. The listener is then added to the `ChessNetwork`, which calls the appropriate methods as the games progress. The UML for the `GameHook` is shown in Figure 10.16. Note the constructors of the class that allow for the designation of the type of player (white/black) or observer. The class also adds a set method to define the chessboard (`setBoard` method) for the game and the history (`setHistory` method).

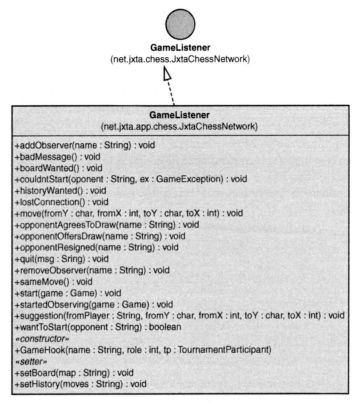

FIGURE 10.16   UML diagram of the `GameHook` class that implements the `GameListener` interface to listen for game events and manipulate the GUI.

AllGameDiscoveryListener Class

The `AllGameDiscoveryListener` is used to process new advertisements that specify a game in progress or a game that is open for joining by a new opponent. The `AllGameDiscoveryListener` class implements the `DiscoveryListener` interface that calls the `discoveryEvent` method each time a remote advertisement is found. The advertisements the implementation method matches are those that announce the existence and state of games. The class maintains two hashtables in the `JxtaChessNetwork` class for in progress games and open games (remember that an open game has only one player). The `GameDiscoverer` class instantiates the `AllGameDiscoveryListener` class and passes it as a listener to the `getRemoteAdvertisements` method of `DiscoveryService`. This may sound a little complicated, and the UML diagram shown in Figure 10.17 may seem even more complex. In reality, the effect is that when an advertisement is found that matches the pattern, the appropriate function based on a hash of the name is initiated.

Passing commands in the advertisement name seems to be a popular method in the JXTA community. Alternatively, a custom advertisement could have been created that contains information as well as the pipe to use. This implementation is simplistic, so encoding information in the advertisement name is appropriate and avoids adding more code to process the XML messages.

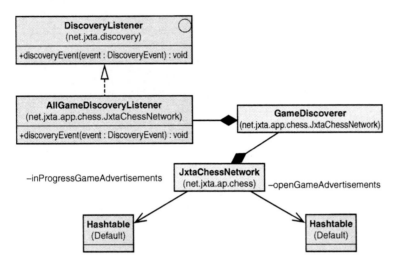

FIGURE 10.17 UML diagram showing the relationships associated with the AllGameDiscoveryListener interface and other classes.

The call to the getRemoteAdvertisements method causes the listener to be called for all advertisements that begin with *"JxtaChess.Game."*

Game **Class**
The Game class (shown in Figure 10.18) is where the guts of pipe messages in the game are found. The following code fragment shows the makeMove method. As can be seen, the only thing done is that an XML message is formed and the message is sent on the game pipe via the sendMessage method:

```
public void makeMove (char fromX, int fromY,
                      char toX,   int toY) throws IOException {

   ++moveCount;
   myLastMoveTimestamp = System.currentTimeMillis ();

   sendMessage ( "<jxta-chess>" +
                 "  <move>" +
                 "    <number>" + moveCount + "</number>" +
```

```
   "    <from>" + fromX + "" + fromY + "</from>" +
   "    <to>"   + toX  + "" + toY   + "</to>"    +
   "  </move>" +
   "</jxta-chess>");

}
```

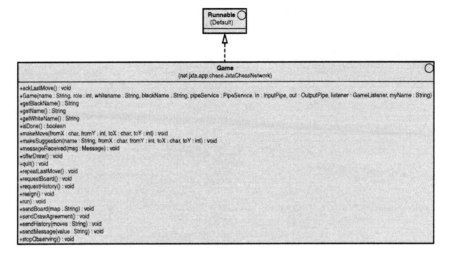

FIGURE 10.18 UML diagram of the Game class used for the peer's management of the current game.

The sendMessage method is extremely simple, as can be seen in the following code fragment from the Game class. There are only three steps to sending the message on the pipe:

1. Get a message container from the pipe service.

2. Set the bytes of the message (from the XML we passed into the method).

3. Send the message via the out pipe's send method:

```
public void sendMessage (String value) throws IOException {
    Message msg = pipeService.createMessage ();
    msg.setBytes ("jxta-chess", value.getBytes ());
    out.send (msg);
}
```

The run method in the Game class is used to process incoming requests to the game's input pipe. The method keeps track of the other player's status and actions both through the message and a timeout on the read. If a read times out, the other peer has either been terminated or the message was never received. The code attempts to resend the message ID if there was an error or a timeout. If there was an IOException, the listener is notified that the connection was lost:

```
public void run () {
    Message msg;
    try {
        int silent = 0;
        while ( ! isDone () ) {
            try {
                msg = in.poll (MSG_READ_TIMEOUT);
                if ( isDone () ) break;
                if (msg == null) {
                    if (silent++ > 6) {
                        silent = 0;
                        repeatLastMove();
                    }
                    continue;
                }
                silent = 0;
                try {
                    messageReceived (msg);
                } catch (IOException e) {
                    listener.badMessage ();
                } catch (InvocationTargetException e) {
                    e.printStackTrace ();
                    break;
                }
            } catch (InterruptedException e) {
                if (silent++ > 6) {
                    silent = 0;
                    repeatLastMove();
                }
            }
        }
    } catch (IOException e) {
        listener.lostConnection ();
    }
}
```

The final method in the Game class we will discuss is messageReceived. This method is called from the run method we just discussed. The following code fragment shows that this method starts by validating the message to see if it contains data. If it does, the XML is extracted. After the XML is extracted, the name is used to match against the various message types that arrive for the game including moves, requests, and messages. We won't get into the specifics of the game processing, but you can see that this method of processing messages can cause a rather long method if many commands are handled this way:

```
void messageReceived (Message msg)
            throws IOException, InvocationTargetException {
  MessageElement el = msg.getElement ("jxta-chess");
  if (el == null) {
    debugMsg ("Received odd message", msg);
    return;
  }

  InputStream in = el.getStream ();

  StructuredTextDocument doc = (StructuredTextDocument)
  StructuredDocumentFactory.newStructuredDocument (textXml, in);

  if (doc.getName().equals("board-wanted")) {
    debug("Received request for a full board.");
    listener.boardWanted();
    return;
  } else if (doc.getName ().equals ("history-wanted")) {
    listener.historyWanted ();
    return;
  }

  debug ("Game.messageReceived: " + doc.getName ());


  boolean isAck = (doc.getName().equals("ack"));
  boolean isBoard = (doc.getName().equals("board"));
  boolean isSuggestion = (doc.getName ().equals ("suggestion"));
  Enumeration children = doc.getChildren ();

  String number = null;
  String from   = null;
  String to     = null;
  String map    = null;
```

```
String name    = null;

if (doc.getName ().equals ("chat")) {
   String fromm   = null;
   String message = null;

   while (children.hasMoreElements ()) {
      TextElement tag = (TextElement) children.nextElement ();
      if (tag.getName ().equals ("name"))
         fromm = tag.getTextValue ();
      else if (tag.getName ().equals ("message"))
         message = tag.getTextValue ();
   }

   if (fromm != null && message != null)
      listener.receivedChatMessage (fromm, message);
   } else if (doc.getName ().equals ("history")) {
      System.out.println ("received history");
      while (children.hasMoreElements ()) {
         TextElement tag = (TextElement) children.nextElement ();
         if (  tag.getName ().equals ("moves")
            && tag.getTextValue () != null)
            listener.setHistory (tag.getTextValue ());
         }
         return;
   } else if (doc.getName ().equals ("observe")) {
      while (children.hasMoreElements ()) {
         TextElement tag = (TextElement) children.nextElement ();
         if (tag.getName ().equals ("name"))
            listener.addObserver (tag.getTextValue ());
         }
         return;
      } if (doc.getName ().equals ("resignation")) {
         while (children.hasMoreElements ()) {
            TextElement tag = (TextElement) children.nextElement ();
            if (tag.getName ().equals ("name"))
               listener.opponentResigned (tag.getTextValue ());
            }
            return;
         } else if (doc.getName ().equals ("draw-offer")) {
            while (children.hasMoreElements ()) {
                TextElement tag = (TextElement) children.nextElement ();
```

```
                    if (tag.getName ().equals ("name"))
                        listener.opponentOffersDraw (tag.getTextValue ());
                }
            return;
        } else if (doc.getName ().equals ("stop-observing")) {
            while (children.hasMoreElements ()) {
                TextElement tag = (TextElement) children.nextElement ();
                if (tag.getName ().equals ("name")) {
                    debug("name tag from stop-observer: " + tag.getTextValue ());
                    listener.removeObserver (tag.getTextValue ());
                }
            }
            return;
        } else if (doc.getName ().equals ("draw-agreement")) {
            TextElement tag = (TextElement) children.nextElement ();
            if (tag.getName ().equals ("name"))
                listener.opponentAgreesToDraw (tag.getTextValue ());
        }

        while (children.hasMoreElements ()) {
            TextElement tag = (TextElement) children.nextElement ();

            if (tag.getName ().equals ("number"))
                number = tag.getTextValue ();
            else if (tag.getName ().equals ("from"))
                from = tag.getTextValue ();
            else if (tag.getName ().equals ("to"))
                to = tag.getTextValue ();
            else if (tag.getName ().equals ("map"))
                map = tag.getTextValue ();
            else if (tag.getName ().equals ("name"))
                name = tag.getTextValue ();
        }

    if (number == null) return;

        int receivedCount = Integer.parseInt(number);

        if (isSuggestion) {

            debug ("Received suggestion from " + from + " to " + to);
            listener.suggestion (name,
```

```
            from.charAt (0), from.charAt (1) - '0',
            to.charAt (0), to.charAt (1) - '0');
         return;
   }

   if (receivedCount < moveCount) {
      debug("Received old information.");
      return;
   }

   debug ("move count = " + moveCount +
      ", received count = " +  receivedCount);

   if (receivedCount == moveCount) { // ack business or ignore.
      if (isAck) {
         debug("Received ack of move number "
            + receivedCount);
         lastMove = null;
      } else {
         if (isBoard) {
            debug ("redundant board; don't care");
           return; // redundant board; don't care.
         }

         // Redundant move. Therefore, we received it before as
         // a new move, therefore we have cleared our own last move.
         // Unless this is our own move, in which case we must not
         // ack it.
         // Also, listener shall not ack if it is an observer.
         if (lastMove == null) {
               debug("Received repeat of move number "
                  + receivedCount);
            listener.sameMove();
         }
      }
      return;
   }

   if (isBoard) {
      // All maps showing a moveCount more recent than
      // ours are good to take.
      try {
```

```
            debug ("Setting board to " + map);
          listener.setBoard(map);
            moveCount = receivedCount;
        } catch (Throwable t) {
        debug("Received broken board map.");
        t.printStackTrace();
        moveCount = 0;
    }
    return;
}


// Could be a hack of some move we missed, or could be a
// move. If it's ahead of us either way, it's time to
// ask for an update.
if (receivedCount > moveCount + 1) {
    debug("Hey, we missed some moves here..."
            + "asking for an update.");
    requestBoard();
    return;
}


// Now it has to be a regular, in-sequence move or suggestion
if (from == null || to == null ||
    from.length () != 2 || from.length () != 2) {
    debug("Received broken move.");
    return;
}

debug("Received move from " + from + " to " + to);

lastMove = null; // we can stop repeating our last move; we've just
// received a valid countermove from the opponent.
lastAck = null;  // This is a new move; we'll need a new ack.

listener.move (from.charAt (0), from.charAt (1) - '0',
to.charAt (0),   to.charAt (1) - '0');
moveCount = receivedCount;
```

GameCreationRunner **Class**

Whenever the GameManager receives a connection and a message for a join, a GameCreationRunner is created and its thread started. The GameCreationRunner class then creates the game. In the UML diagram in Figure 10.19, it should be noted that the process method is package protected and only called by the run method when the thread is started.

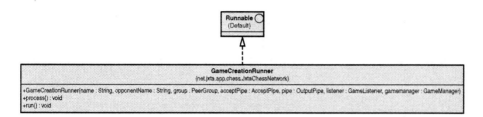

FIGURE 10.19   UML of the GameCreationRunner class used to create new games. Note that only the constructor is used external to the class.

GameDiscoverer

We have already mentioned GameDiscoverer (shown in Listing 10.1), but now we will look at the code. As can be seen in the UML diagram in Figure 10.20, the class implements the Runnable interface, which means that this class is a thread. The thread is used to periodically cause the discovery service to look for our advertisements again. The reason we need the thread is that requests by the discovery service only propagate through the network once. So, if we ask for an advertisement, we get all the advertisements known at the time of the query. New advertisements are not known until you cause another discovery query.

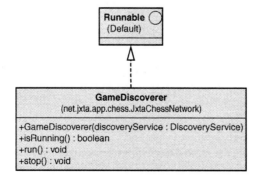

FIGURE 10.20   UML for GameDiscoverer class. The class manages discovery of games to update the display.

The amount of time between queries is important. Too many queries, and we could clog the P2P network. Too few, and the user stares at a static screen and believes that the system is not responding or that no one is interested in playing a chess game.

JXTA Chess has a discovery update interval specified by the static final variable REMOTE_DISCOVERY_INTERVAL. The interval is thirty seconds. This may be too short and should probably be changed to something on the order of several minutes. Lengthening the interval up to a few minutes may behave nearly like that of thirty seconds. The reason is that the discovery process could take several minutes to propagate through the network.

Most of the discovery in this application could be redesigned to reduce traffic and improve user feedback by allowing the user to request discovery by clicking a button. Alternatively, instead of advertisements, the application could be redesigned to distribute new game announcements via a propagation pipe to which all tournament participants belong.

One last thing to mention in the GameDiscoverer class is a slight problem with the code. The set of the isRunning variable in the constructor is in the wrong place. If you create a new instance of a GameDiscoverer and then do not start the thread, the isRunning boolean is true, even if in fact it's false (not running).

LISTING 10.1   Inner Class GameDiscoverer

```
class GameDiscoverer implements Runnable {
   DiscoveryService discoveryService;
   boolean isRunning;

   GameDiscoverer(DiscoveryService discoveryService) {
      this.discoveryService = discoveryService;
      this.isRunning = true;
   }

   synchronized boolean isRunning() {
      return isRunning;
   }

   synchronized void stop() {
      isRunning = false;
   }

   public void run() {

      while (isRunning()) {
```

LISTING 10.1   Continued

```
        discoveryService.getRemoteAdvertisements(null
                            , DiscoveryService.ADV
                            , "Name"
                            , JXTA_CHESS + "Game.*"
                            , 100
                            , new AllGameDiscoveryListener());

        discoveryService.getRemoteAdvertisements(null
                            , DiscoveryService.ADV,
                            , "Name"
                            , JXTA_CHESS + "Tournament.*"
                            , 100
                            , new TournamentDiscoveryListener());
        try {
          Thread.sleep(REMOTE_DISCOVERY_INTERVAL);
        } catch (InterruptedException ex) {
          stop();
        }
      }
    }
}
```

GameJoiner
The GameJoiner class (shown in Figure 10.21) is a Runnable class used to initiate games. The class is created and the thread started by the joinGame method of the JxtaChess class. When the thread starts, the run method calls the sendJoinMessage method (shown in Listing 10.2) to create a bidirectional pipe to the other chess player's peer.

The process of opening the pipe is shown in Listing 10.2 for the sendJoinMessage method. The process starts by looking up the opponents peer's pipe advertisement from the openGameAdvertisements variable that was populated with a pipe advertisement by the AllGameDiscovery class. Next, a bidirectional pipe is created with the advertisement. If there are any errors creating the pipe, exceptions are thrown and the game is destroyed because it is invalid probably due to pipe expiration or the opponent's peer is not listening for pipe messages.

After the pipe is created, a message with the name of jxta-chess:join-game is sent to the opponent. The waitForJoinResponse method is then called. When waitForJoinResponse returns a Game object, the game is registered to the system and the Game object's thread is started to begin processing game events.

LISTING 10.2   The sendJoinMessage Method from the GameJoiner Class

```
public void sendJoinMessage() throws GameException {
    PipeAdvertisement adv;
    Message         msg;
    BidirectionalPipeService.Pipe pipe;
    adv = (PipeAdvertisement) openGameAdvertisements.get(opponent);
    try {
        pipe = bidirPipeService.connect(adv,
        MSG_READ_TIMEOUT);
        // PipeService.PropagateType);
    } catch (IOException e) {
        discoveryListener.invalidated(opponent, false, false);
        openGameAdvertisements.remove(opponent);
        throw new GameException("Unable to resolve pipe…", e);
    }
    try {
        debug("Sending join request for " + me);
        msg = pipeService.createMessage();
        msg.setString("jxta-chess:join-game", me);
        pipe.getOutputPipe().send(msg);
        Game game = waitForJoinResponse(pipe.getInputPipe(),
        opponent + " vs. " + me);
        games.put(game.getName(), game);
        listener.start(game);
        new Thread(game).start();
    } catch (IOException e) {
        discoveryListener.invalidated(opponent, false, false);
        openGameAdvertisements.remove(opponent);
        throw new GameException( "Could not communicate with "
                        + "opponent.", e);
    }
}
```

A bidirectional pipe is really a façade that manages two pipes. The initial pipe creation is a process that creates both the input and output pipes. However, the pipe is not really created until the other peer has created the complementary connections. When this is done, the input and output pipes are retrieved for later use. In the waitForJoinResponse method of Listing 10.3, the pipe is created when the connections are complete. The pipes are used to build a new Game object.

LISTING 10.3 The waitForJoinResponse Method

```
Game waitForJoinResponse( InputPipe in
                        , String gameName) throws IOException {
   Message          msg;
   String           val;
   PipeAdvertisement wirePipeAdv;
   OutputPipe       out;
   try {
      msg = in.poll(90 * 1000);
      if (msg != null) {
         if (((val = msg.getString("jxta-chess:join-game")) != null)
            && val.equals("accepted")) {
            wirePipeAdv = (PipeAdvertisement)
                  AdvertisementFactory.newAdvertisement (
                  new MimeMediaType("text/xml")
                , msg.getElement("jxta-chess:wire-pipe-adv").getStream());
            in  = pipeService.createInputPipe(wirePipeAdv);
            out = pipeService.createOutputPipe( wirePipeAdv
                                              , 10*MSG_READ_TIMEOUT);
            return new Game( gameName,Board.BLACK,opponent
                           , me,pipeService,in,out,listener,null);
         }
      }
   } catch (InterruptedException e) {
      // no message arrived before timeout expired
   }
   throw new IOException("Opponent " + opponent +
             " failed to respond to your request "+
             " to play with him or her in 90 " +
             " seconds.");
}
```

GameManager

GameManager is the focal point for processing messages during a game. This class, shown in Figure 10.22, has two modes that are controlled by the constructor's isAccepting parameter. If it is true, this is the opponent's peer and we are accepting the other end of the pipe. The pipe is created with the GameManager as a listener to the input pipe's messages. The thread that is created is really only viable for the time it takes to make the connection.

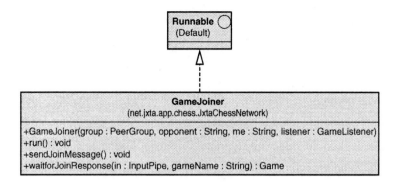

FIGURE 10.21   UML diagram of GameJoiner class used by an opponent to join an advertised game and initialize the game.

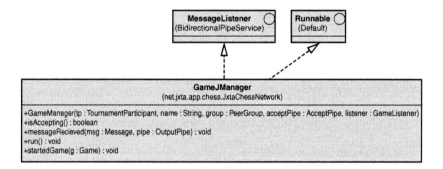

FIGURE 10.22   UML diagram of GameManager showing its implementation of Runnable and MessageListener interfaces.

TournamentDiscoveryListener

The TournamentDiscoveryListener class is nearly identical to the AllGameDiscoveryListener class, except that this class is used to maintain the tournamentAdvertisements hashtable that holds all of the tournament advertisements received. The UML for the class is shown in Figure 10.23.

TournamentManager

The TournamentManager class is used to update information to all of the participants and observers of a tournament. The class, shown in Figure 10.24, is added as a listener to a tournament pipe. As the game progresses, tournament information is received via the pipeMsgEvent method. The class then updates the display and tables. The peer can broadcast information using the broadcast method, which sends out a message on the tournament's wire pipe to all of the peers listening to the wire.

When a round is complete, the sendRoundInfo is called.

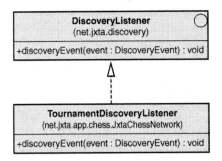

FIGURE 10.23 UML diagram of TournamentDiscoveryListener used to handle tournament messages.

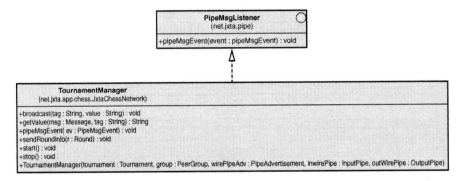

FIGURE 10.24 UML diagram of TournamentManager class that listens to the tournament pipe (via PipeMsgListener interface).

To further help explain the TournamentManager, let's look at the other classes involved. As can be seen in Figure 10.24, the TournamentManager is created with an object of the Tournament class. Figure 10.25 shows the Tournament class and its three inner classes—Round, Match, and Player.

The Tournament class contains all the information about the tournament including the players (Player class), the games (Match class), and the results (Round class).

TournamentManagerFinder

TournamentManagerFinder (see Figure 10.26) is similar to GameFinder with the exception that the pipes that are created are wire pipes instead of a bidirectional pipe. The class implements both the DiscoveryListener and Runnable interfaces. The constructor of this call allows you to specify the group, the name of the tournament, your participant name, and the tournament listener.

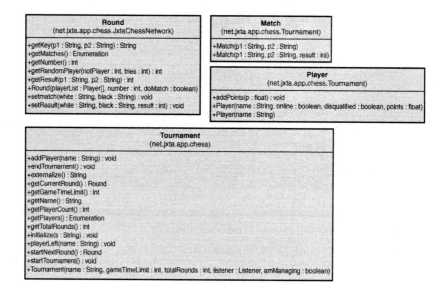

FIGURE 10.25   UML diagram of the `Tournament` class and its inner classes `Round`, `Match`, and `Player`.

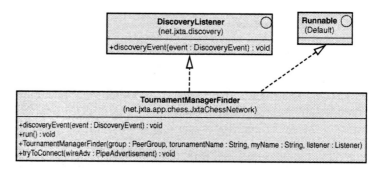

FIGURE 10.26   UML diagram of `TournamentManagerFinder` class, used to locate peers that manage tournaments.

TournamentParticipant

The `TournamentParticipant` (see Figure 10.27) is used as the focal point for a tournament member. The class is a thread and waits for tournament messages from the network. The class also provides several methods for sending messages to the tournament network, as well as for joining or resigning from the network.

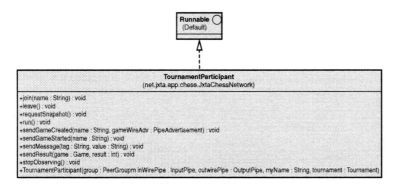

FIGURE 10.27 UML diagram of `TournamentParticipant` class used to process messages for the user.

Summary

JXTA Chess is a reasonably complex program using pipes both as an advertisement medium as well as a communications medium. The software also uses bidirectional pipes as well as propagation pipes (wire pipes). JXTA Chess is also a true collaborative application that allows an audience to view the game and interact with the participants.

As often pointed out, you should be careful about using the exact implementation. Besides a preference for the use of inner classes, the software also creates a lot of threads.

Threads can be dangerous, so be careful to synchronize your methods or used synchronized blocks when accessing multiple items. The number of threads generated could also be problematic for smaller devices because of the higher cost of instantiating thread objects.

JXTA Chess is definitely a great resource for learning JXTA. JXTA Chess also gives several patterns for JXTA development, for example, using the pipe name as part of a message or the manager classes used to resolve the pipes. JXTA Chess should be a premium example for a collaborative application. Remember to check the `jxta.org` site for updates to JXTA Chess.

In the next chapter, we will get back to some code written exclusively for this book. We will next write an application that allows you to browse the XML advertisements that are flowing on the JXTA network.

11

JXTA Explorer

By Daniel Brookshier

Advertisements in the JXTA network are critical to most operations. However, advertisements are also relatively complex because contents vary and are sometimes also created or interpreted incorrectly. In this chapter, we present a small tool to explore the XML of these advertisements. The tool, called Explorer, can be used for debugging and simply for the general examination of advertisements available on the JXTA network.

Designing an Advertisement Explorer

Advertisements in JXTA are located by a query to the Discovery Service. As discussed in earlier chapters, the advertisements are in the context of peer groups. So, in addition to searching and displaying advertisements, the application will also need to join groups it finds to discover further advertisements.

The operation of the application should be simplistic. The display of advertisements will be hierarchical by group. Each group node will have three nodes for sub-groups, peers, and general advertisements.

Because there are many groups, they will not be joined and searched until the user selects a specific advertisement.

Design Goals

The goals for the application are as follows:

- Display a list of advertisements discovered in each group. The starting group will be the net peer group.
- Display the contents of advertisements as formatted XML.

- The display will have a tree view that will display the group advertisement as a root with advertisements as children to the group. Sub-groups will be shown as a further child with its advertisements as further children.

- Advertisements will be added to the tree view as they are discovered, and the XML will be displayed when the node is selected.

- Groups, when selected, will be initialized, and child advertisements will be displayed in the same manner as the net peer group.

This is the initial version of Explorer. The code will be available in its entirety at www.samspublishing.com and at www.jxta.org. Future versions will add to the functionality, so please check for the latest version. Also, because the code is at jxta.org, feel free to participate in the advancement of the code.

Operation

This program is a simple utility. It should be easily operated. Most of the functionality is operated from the tree that displays the hierarchical representation of groups and advertisements.

When you select a node in the tree, one of two things will happen:

- If the node is a group and the group has not been opened, the group is instantiated and initialized. The subnodes for peer, group, and advertisements will be created. Finally, a remote search for advertisements will be initiated.

- If the node is an advertisement (including a group that is also an advertisement), the XML of the advertisement will be displayed in the pane to the right of the tree.

Design Overview

The design has just three main elements—the JXTA discovery mechanism, group joining, and the hierarchical display of groups and advertisements. We also show the text of advertisements in a simple scrollable text viewer. Remember that groups in the reference JXTA platform are hierarchical. You need to join a group to see advertisements from the group, so we must have code to join groups. Because discovery has three different types (groups, peers, and everything else), it makes sense to use the JFC JTree component to show the parent-child relationship of a group to its child types and the advertisements found.

Of all the code in this book, this application is probably the simplest. The only JXTA code is the startup of the JXTA platform, a discovery thread class, and code used to properly print an advertisement. In addition, there is group join code. The group code will be minimalistic, because we will not support custom membership protocols. Instead, the group will just be created and initialized. For most peer groups, there is no need to join the group explicitly to use its discovery service. If you want to add such behavior, you will need to add the code as needed.

The Explorer Class

The Explorer class is the main class of the application and is a subclass of Jform, so it is the display GUI. The UML class for Explorer is shown in Figure 11.1. The bulk of the code in Explorer is concerned with creation of the GUI, but there are a few methods that are used to interact with JXTA.

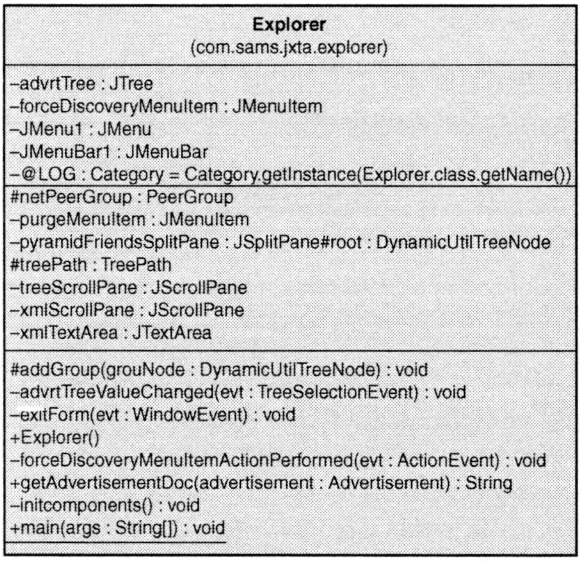

```
                        Explorer
                   (com.sams.jxta.explorer)

–advrtTree : JTree
–forceDiscoveryMenuItem : JMenuItem
–JMenu1 : JMenu
–JMenuBar1 : JMenuBar
–@LOG : Category = Category.getInstance(Explorer.class.getName())
#netPeerGroup : PeerGroup
–purgeMenuItem : JMenuItem
–pyramidFriendsSplitPane : JSplitPane#root : DynamicUtilTreeNode
#treePath : TreePath
–treeScrollPane : JScrollPane
–xmlScrollPane : JScrollPane
–xmlTextArea : JTextArea

#addGroup(grouNode : DynamicUtilTreeNode) : void
–advrtTreeValueChanged(evt : TreeSelectionEvent) : void
–exitForm(evt : WindowEvent) : void
+Explorer()
–forceDiscoveryMenuItemActionPerformed(evt : ActionEvent) : void
+getAdvertisementDoc(advertisement : Advertisement) : String
–initcomponents() : void
+main(args : String[]) : void
```

FIGURE 11.1 UML of the Explorer class.

The source code for the Explorer class is shown in Listings 11.1 through 11.7. The first section of the code in 11.1 shows the imports and member variables. The only JXTA classes in this application are imported first. The only member variable is NetPeerGroup used to hold the net world group.

LISTING 11.1 Explorer Class—Imports and Member Variables

```
package com.sams.jxta.explorer;
import net.jxta.document.Advertisement;
import net.jxta.peergroup.PeerGroup;
```

LISTING 11.1   Continued

```
import net.jxta.peergroup.PeerGroupFactory;
import net.jxta.exception.PeerGroupException;
import com.sams.swing.AdvertisementTreeCellRenderer;
import net.jxta.document.StructuredTextDocument;
import javax.swing.JTree;
import javax.swing.JFrame;
import javax.swing.tree.DefaultTreeModel;
import javax.swing.tree.DefaultMutableTreeNode;
import javax.swing.tree.TreePath;
import net.jxta.protocol.PeerGroupAdvertisement;
import java.io.IOException;
import java.io.StringWriter;
import org.apache.log4j.Category;
import java.util.Hashtable;
import javax.swing.JTree.DynamicUtilTreeNode;
public class Explorer extends JFrame {
    private static final Category LOG
                = Category.getInstance(Explorer.class.getName());
    protected PeerGroup netPeerGroup;
    protected TreePath treePath;
    protected JTree.DynamicUtilTreeNode root;
```

The constructor in Listing 11.2 initializes the components first and then initializes the netPeerGroup. The NetPeerGroup is then used to create a DynamicUtilTreeNode node for the JTree and sets it as the tree's root.

The node is then used to call the addGroup method that will add the child nodes for advertisements, groups, and peers and start the discovery process.

LISTING 11.2   Explorer Class—Constructor

```
public Explorer() {
    initComponents();
    // Initialize discovery tree
    advrtTree.setCellRenderer(new AdvertisementTreeCellRenderer());
    try{
        netPeerGroup = PeerGroupFactory.newNetPeerGroup();
        root = new JTree.DynamicUtilTreeNode(netPeerGroup,new Hashtable());
        ((DefaultTreeModel)advrtTree.getModel()).setRoot(root);
        addGroup((JTree.DynamicUtilTreeNode)root);
    } catch (Exception e) {
```

LISTING 11.2 Continued

```
     LOG.error("fatal error : group creation failure",e);
     System.exit(-1);
  }
}
```

The addGroup method in Listing 11.3 is used to create a PeerDiscoveryThread object that will populate the tree with advertisements found for the group specified by the node. After the object is created, a thread is created and started to begin the process. Note that netPeerGroup and advrtTree are member variables in the object and are passed to the thread so that they can be used for group context and manipulating the display.

LISTING 11.3 Explorer Class—addGroup Method

```
protected void addGroup(JTree.DynamicUtilTreeNode groupNode){
   PeerDiscoveryThread peerDiscoveryThread;
   peerDiscoveryThread = new PeerDiscoveryThread( advrtTree
                                               , netPeerGroup
                                               , groupNode);
   Thread discoThread = new Thread(peerDiscoveryThread);
   discoThread.start();
}
```

The next part of the Explorer listing is the initComponents method in Listing 11.4. The interface was created using NetBeans from www.netbeans.org, so the code is verbose and uses fully-qualified classnames. An important part of the code is bolded to show where the NetBeans tool has created an anonymous inner class. This class is added to the JTree and is used to direct selection events to the handler. The handler will be used to open groups and display the advertisements represented by the nodes.

LISTING 11.4 Explorer Class—initComponents Method

```
private void initComponents() {
   pyramidFriendsSplitPane = new javax.swing.JSplitPane();
   treeScrollPane = new javax.swing.JScrollPane();
   advrtTree = new javax.swing.JTree();
   xmlScrollPane = new javax.swing.JScrollPane();
   xmlTextArea = new javax.swing.JTextArea();
   jMenuBar1 = new javax.swing.JMenuBar();
   jMenu1 = new javax.swing.JMenu();
   forceDiscoveryMenuItem = new javax.swing.JMenuItem();
   purgeMenuItem = new javax.swing.JMenuItem();
```

LISTING 11.4   Continued

```
setDefaultCloseOperation(javax.swing.JFrame.EXIT_ON_CLOSE);
addWindowListener(new java.awt.event.WindowAdapter() {
    public void windowClosing(java.awt.event.WindowEvent evt) {
        exitForm(evt);
    }
});
pyramidFriendsSplitPane.setDividerLocation(225);

advrtTree.addTreeSelectionListener(
    new javax.swing.event.TreeSelectionListener() {
    public void valueChanged(javax.swing.event.TreeSelectionEvent evt){
        advrtTreeValueChanged(evt);
    }
});
treeScrollPane.setViewportView(advrtTree);
pyramidFriendsSplitPane.setLeftComponent(treeScrollPane);
xmlScrollPane.setViewportView(xmlTextArea);
pyramidFriendsSplitPane.setRightComponent(xmlScrollPane);
getContentPane().add( pyramidFriendsSplitPane
                    , java.awt.BorderLayout.CENTER);
jMenu1.setText("File");
forceDiscoveryMenuItem.setText("Force Discovery");
purgeMenuItem.setText("Purge Advertisements");
jMenu1.add(purgeMenuItem);
jMenuBar1.add(jMenu1);
setJMenuBar(jMenuBar1);
pack();
}
```

The advrtTreeValueChanged method shown in Listing 11.5 is where we begin the process of opening a group and viewing advertisements. After we have the node, we access the value returned by the getUserObject of the node. If the value is an instance of the Advertisement class, it is converted to text by the getAdvertisementDoc method and displayed in the XML text area of the display. If the node has no children and is a group node, we initialize the group by calling the addGroup method.

LISTING 11.5   Explorer Class—advrtTreeValueChanged Method

```
private void advrtTreeValueChanged(TreeSelectionEvent evt) {
    Object testNode;
    // Get the node so that we can get the object it represents.
    testNode = ((JTree)evt.getSource()).getLastSelectedPathComponent();
    if(testNode == null){
```

LISTING 11.5 Continued

```
    return;
  }
// Synchronize the node so that we block further actions.
  synchronized(testNode){
  DefaultMutableTreeNode node = (DefaultMutableTreeNode)testNode;
  Object nodeInfo=null;
  if (node != null) {
    nodeInfo = node.getUserObject();
    // If it is an advertisement, display it.
    if (nodeInfo instanceof Advertisement){
       Advertisement advertisement = (Advertisement)nodeInfo;
       String data = getAdvertisementDoc (advertisement);
       xmlTextArea.setText(data);
    }
  }
  // If it is a group, open it.
  if (nodeInfo instanceof PeerGroupAdvertisement  ){
    if (node.isLeaf() || node.getChildCount() ==0){
       System.out.println("Opening group");
       addGroup((JTree.DynamicUtilTreeNode)node);
    }
  }
}
}
```

Listing 11.6 contains more code necessary for running the application. Here we add the exit and main methods and the variables created by the NetBeans GUI design tool.

LISTING 11.6 Explorer Class—exitForm, main Methods and Member Variables

```
    private void exitForm(java.awt.event.WindowEvent evt) {
        System.exit(0);
    }

    public static void main(String args[]) {
        new Explorer().show();
    }


    private javax.swing.JSplitPane pyramidFriendsSplitPane;
    private javax.swing.JMenuItem forceDiscoveryMenuItem;
    private javax.swing.JScrollPane treeScrollPane;
    private javax.swing.JTree advrtTree;
```

LISTING 11.6   Continued

```
    private javax.swing.JScrollPane xmlScrollPane;
    private javax.swing.JTextArea xmlTextArea;
    private javax.swing.JMenuBar jMenuBar1;
    private javax.swing.JMenu jMenu1;
    private javax.swing.JMenuItem purgeMenuItem;
```

The last method of the Explorer class is getAdvertisementDoc and is shown in
Listing 11.7. The getAdvertisementDoc method converts an advertisement to a
textual string. The process is to create a string writer and create the string.

LISTING 11.7   Explorer Class—getAdvertisementDoc Method

```
public String getAdvertisementDoc (Advertisement advertisement) {
  try {

      // display the advertisement as a plain text document.
      net.jxta.document.MimeMediaType type;
      type = new net.jxta.document.MimeMediaType("text/xml");

      // Convert the advertisement to a document
      StructuredTextDocument doc ;
      doc = (StructuredTextDocument)advertisement.getDocument(type);

      // Write the advert text to a string.
      StringWriter out = new StringWriter();
      doc.sendToWriter(out);

      //Write the doc to a string.
      String docString = out.toString();

      // cleanup the writer.
      out.close();

      return docString;

  }catch(IOException ioe) {
    ioe.printStackTrace();
    return "Error: IO exception  thrown by StringWriter";
  }catch(Exception jle) {
    jle.printStackTrace();
    return "Error: Exception  thrown by getDocument()";
  }
}//end of printServiceAdvertisement();
```

PeerDiscoveryThread **Class**

The PeerDiscoveryThread class is where most of the real work is done. The class creates all of the child nodes of a peer group and also populates these nodes as discovery events are received. The UML for this class is shown in Figure 11.2. The class implements both the Runnable and DiscoveryListener interfaces. We are using this class as a thread for two reasons. First, even though the time it takes to create the group and initial leafs is relatively quick, there was still a noticeable lag from the time the user selected the tree node to the time that the process completed and returned control to the GUI. By placing this functionality in the thread, the application is more responsive. Secondly, this is a thread because the class needs to call the remote discovery methods over time to get new advertisements that may have been generated after the system was started.

The code for the PeerDiscoveryThread class is in Listings 11.8 through 11.11. The first part in Listing 11.8 shows the imports and member variables. Note that we need to keep track of the hashtables, the group, and the tree nodes that are specific to the peer group that this object is managing. The JTree object is also here to allow us to send messages to the tree that nodes have changed.

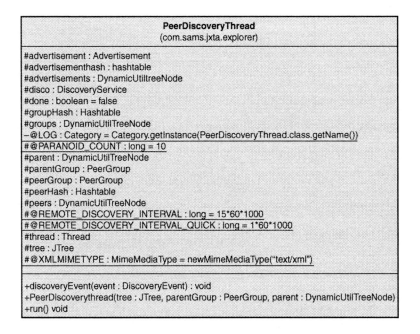

PeerDiscoveryThread
(com.sams.jxta.explorer)

#advertisement : Advertisement
#advertisementhash : hashtable
#advertisements : DynamicUtiltreeNode
#disco : DiscoveryService
#done : boolean = false
#groupHash : Hashtable
#groups : DynamicUtilTreeNode
−@LOG : Category = Category.getInstance(PeerDiscoveryThread.class.getName())
#@PARANOID_COUNT : long = 10
#parent : DynamicUtilTreeNode
#parentGroup : PeerGroup
#peerGroup : PeerGroup
#peerHash : Hashtable
#peers : DynamicUtilTreeNode
#@REMOTE_DISCOVERY_INTERVAL : long = 15*60*1000
#@REMOTE_DISCOVERY_INTERVAL_QUICK : long = 1*60*1000
#thread : Thread
#tree : JTree
#@XMLMIMETYPE : MimeMediaType = newMimeMediaType("text/xml")

+discoveryEvent(event : DiscoveryEvent) : void
+PeerDiscoverythread(tree : JTree, parentGroup : PeerGroup, parent : DynamicUtilTreeNode)
+run() void

FIGURE 11.2   UML for the *PeerDiscoveryThread* class.

LISTING 11.8 PeerDiscoveryThread Class—Imports and Member Variables

```
package com.sams.jxta.explorer;
import java.util.Enumeration;
import java.util.Hashtable;
import org.apache.log4j.Category;
import net.jxta.document.Advertisement;
import net.jxta.document.MimeMediaType;
import net.jxta.document.AdvertisementFactory;
import net.jxta.peergroup.PeerGroup;
import net.jxta.exception.PeerGroupException;
import net.jxta.protocol.DiscoveryResponseMsg;
import net.jxta.protocol.PeerGroupAdvertisement;
import net.jxta.protocol.PeerAdvertisement;
import net.jxta.protocol.ModuleImplAdvertisement;
import net.jxta.discovery.DiscoveryEvent;
import net.jxta.discovery.DiscoveryService;
import net.jxta.discovery.DiscoveryListener;
import javax.swing.JTree.DynamicUtilTreeNode;
import javax.swing.JTree;
import javax.swing.tree.DefaultTreeModel;
import javax.swing.tree.DefaultMutableTreeNode;
import java.io.ByteArrayInputStream;

public class PeerDiscoveryThread implements Runnable, DiscoveryListener {
    private static final Category LOG;
    LOG = Category.getInstance(PeerDiscoveryThread.class.getName());
    // Interval to search when looking for advertisements the first time.
    protected static final long REMOTE_DISCOVERY_INTERVAL_QUICK
                                = 1*60 * 1000;
    // Interval to search after the number of paranoid searches
    // has been reached.
    protected static final long REMOTE_DISCOVERY_INTERVAL = 15*60 * 1000;
    // Number of times that we search at the quick interval.
    protected static final long PARANOID_COUNT = 10;
    protected final static MimeMediaType XMLMIMETYPE
                                = new MimeMediaType("text/xml");
    protected boolean done=false;
    protected Thread thread;
    protected DiscoveryService disco;
    protected DynamicUtilTreeNode peers;
    protected DynamicUtilTreeNode groups;
    protected DynamicUtilTreeNode advertisements;
```

LISTING 11.8   Continued

```
protected Hashtable peerHash  ;
protected Hashtable groupHash  ;
protected Hashtable advertisementHash ;
protected JTree tree;
protected DynamicUtilTreeNode parent;
protected PeerGroup parentGroup;
protected PeerGroup peerGroup;
protected Advertisement advertisement;
```

The constructor for PeerDiscoveryThread is shown in Listing 11.9. The constructor just sets the variables we need to keep track of. The constructor also adds the initial advertisement class nodes to the tree.

LISTING 11.9   PeerDiscoveryThread Class—Constructor

```
public PeerDiscoveryThread( JTree tree
                          , PeerGroup parentGroup
                          , DynamicUtilTreeNode parent){

   this.parentGroup = parentGroup;
   this.tree = tree;
   this.parent = parent;

   peerHash = new Hashtable();
   groupHash = new Hashtable();
   advertisementHash = new Hashtable();

   groups = new DynamicUtilTreeNode("groups",groupHash);
   peers = new DynamicUtilTreeNode("peers",peerHash);
   advertisements = new DynamicUtilTreeNode("adverts",advertisementHash);

   parent.add(groups);
   parent.add(peers);
   parent.add(advertisements);
   ((DefaultTreeModel)tree.getModel()).reload(parent) ;

   if (parent.getUserObject() instanceof Advertisement){
      this.advertisement = (Advertisement)parent.getUserObject();
   }else{
      peerGroup = parentGroup;
   }
}
```

In Listing 11.10, we see the run method that is called when the thread is started. First, the group advertisement is retrieved and a group is created from it. If the group fails, another node is added to the tree to give the user visual feedback that the group failed and why.

When the group is available, three different remote discovery calls are made. You need to call the remote discover for each type of advertisement you want located. In our case, we want all three. We also specify nulls as parameters to obtain all advertisements available.

LISTING 11.10   PeerDiscoveryThread Class—run Method

```
public void run() {
   if (advertisement != null){
      try{
         peerGroup = parentGroup.newGroup(advertisement);
      }catch(PeerGroupException pge){
         parent.add(new DefaultMutableTreeNode( "Cannot open group:"
                                            + pge.getMessage()));
         LOG.error("Unable to initialize peer group.",pge);
         return;
      }
   }
   int i =0;
   int counter = 0;
   long time = 0;
   disco = peerGroup.getDiscoveryService();

   while( !done) {
      disco.getRemoteAdvertisements( null, DiscoveryService.GROUP
                               , null,null, 100, this);
      disco.getRemoteAdvertisements( null, DiscoveryService.PEER
                               , null,null, 100, this);
      disco.getRemoteAdvertisements( null, DiscoveryService.ADV
                               , null,null, 100, this);
      try {
         if ( ++counter < PARANOID_COUNT){
            time = REMOTE_DISCOVERY_INTERVAL_QUICK;
         }else{
            time = REMOTE_DISCOVERY_INTERVAL;
         }
         Thread.currentThread().sleep(time);
      } catch (InterruptedException e) {
```

LISTING 11.10   Continued

```
            LOG.debug("Discovery Sleeping thread Interrupted");
            done = true;
        }
    }
}
```

Listing 11.11 shows the implementation of the DiscoveryListener interface's discoveryEvent method. This method is called whenever a message is received by the discovery mechanism. Note that this is not done per query or by query type. The listener is called for any response from remote peers to this group's requests. Because of the group, rather than query nature, you need to resolve the type of message to determine if it is a peer, group, or general advertisement.

Another interesting note about how this system works is that there may be more than one response received. You usually receive a list of peers, groups, or general advertisements that a rendezvous has cached. Very often, you will see several nodes added to the tree each time this method is called.

After the type has been determined, we check to see if a copy of the advertisement has already been received. If this is a new advertisement, a tree node is created and added to the appropriate parent.

After the lists of advertisements have been added to the tree, the tree is notified that changes have occurred. This completes the process.

LISTING 11.11   PeerDiscoveryThread Class—discoveryEvent Method

```
public void discoveryEvent(DiscoveryEvent event) {
   DiscoveryResponseMsg msg  = event.getResponse();
   Enumeration enum = msg.getResponses();
   String str = null;
   boolean changedGroup = false;
   boolean changedPeer = false;
   boolean changedAdvertisement = false;
   while (enum.hasMoreElements()) {
   try {
      str = (String) enum.nextElement();
      if (str == null) continue;
        // Create Peer(Group)Advertisement from response.
        ByteArrayInputStream stream;
        stream = new ByteArrayInputStream(str.getBytes());
        Advertisement adv;
        adv = AdvertisementFactory.newAdvertisement( XMLMIMETYPE
                                        , stream);
```

LISTING 11.11   Continued

```
        String type = "";
        if (adv instanceof PeerGroupAdvertisement ){
            if (groupHash.get(adv.getID()) == null){
                groupHash.put(adv.getID(),adv);
                JTree.DynamicUtilTreeNode node;
                node = new JTree.DynamicUtilTreeNode(adv,new Hashtable());
                groups.add(node);
                System.out.println(">>>>> added group");
                changedGroup = true;
            }
        }else if (adv instanceof PeerAdvertisement ){
            if (peerHash.get(adv.getID()) == null){
                peerHash.put(adv.getID(),adv);
                DefaultMutableTreeNode node;
                node = new DefaultMutableTreeNode(adv);
                peers.add(node);
                changedPeer = true;
            }
        } else {
            if (adv.getID() != null){
                if ( advertisementHash.get(adv.getID()) == null){
                    advertisementHash.put(adv.getID(),adv);
                    DefaultMutableTreeNode node = new DefaultMutableTreeNode(adv);
                    advertisements.add(node);
                    changedAdvertisement = true;
                }
            }else{
                if (adv instanceof ModuleImplAdvertisement){
                    if ( advertisementHash.get(
                            ((ModuleImplAdvertisement)adv).getModuleSpecID()
                          )== null){
                        advertisementHash.put(
                            ((ModuleImplAdvertisement)adv).getModuleSpecID()
                            ,adv);
                        DefaultMutableTreeNode node;
                        node = new DefaultMutableTreeNode(adv);
                        advertisements.add(node);
                        changedAdvertisement = true;
                    }
                }else  if ( advertisementHash.get(
                            new Long(adv.getLocalExpirationTime()))
```

LISTING 11.11   Continued

```
                        == null){
                advertisementHash.put(
                        new Long(adv.getLocalExpirationTime())
                        ,adv);
                DefaultMutableTreeNode node;
                node = new DefaultMutableTreeNode(adv);
                advertisements.add(node);
                changedAdvertisement = true;
            }
        }
    }
    } catch (Exception ex) {
        LOG.error("Error processing a new advertisement:\""+str+"\"",ex);
    }
    if (changedGroup){
        ((DefaultTreeModel)tree.getModel()).reload(groups) ;
    }
    if (changedPeer){
        ((DefaultTreeModel)tree.getModel()).reload(peers) ;
    }
    if (changedAdvertisement){
        ((DefaultTreeModel)tree.getModel()).reload(advertisements) ;
    }
    }// end while
}// end of discoveryEvent()
```

AdvertisementTreeCellRenderer **Class**

The final class in the Explorer application is the AdvertisementTreeCellRenderer
class in Listing 11.12. This class is used to change the value of the JTree node,
depending on the type of data stored in the node. The object of this class is to make
the display more informative. Many different types are checked here, but not all are
actually sent as raw advertisements.

This class could be used for other applications because of this. Checking for another
advertisement type can also extend the class.

LISTING 11.12   AdvertisementTreeCellRenderer Class—Imports and Constructor

```
package com.sams.swing;
import net.jxta.document.*;
import net.jxta.service.*;
import net.jxta.protocol.*;
import net.jxta.endpoint.*;
import net.jxta.peer.*;
import net.jxta.impl.protocol.*;
import net.jxta.platform.*;
import net.jxta.peergroup.*;
import net.jxta.id.*;
import net.jxta.pipe.*;
import net.jxta.exception.*;
import javax.swing.*;
import javax.swing.tree.*;
import java.awt.*;
public class AdvertisementTreeCellRenderer extends DefaultTreeCellRenderer{

    /** Creates new AdvertisementTreeCellRenderer */
    public AdvertisementTreeCellRenderer() {
    }
    public Component getTreeCellRendererComponent( JTree tree
                                        , Object node
                                        , boolean sel
                                        , boolean expanded
                                        , boolean leaf
                                        , int row
                                        , boolean hasFocus) {
        super.getTreeCellRendererComponent( tree, node, sel, expanded
                                        , leaf, row, hasFocus);

        Object value =((DefaultMutableTreeNode)node).getUserObject();
        String text = value.getClass().getName()+":  ";

        if (value instanceof   PeerAdvertisement){
            text = ((PeerAdvertisement)value).getName() ;
        }else if (value instanceof   PeerGroup){
            text = ((PeerGroup)value).getPeerGroupName();
        }else if (value instanceof   PeerGroupAdvertisement){
            text = ((PeerGroupAdv)value).getName();
        }else if (value instanceof   PeerInfoAdvertisement){
            text += "SourcePID = "
```

LISTING 11.12   Continued

```
                + ((PeerInfoAdvertisement)value).getSourcePid();
        }else if (value instanceof   ModuleClassAdv){
            text += "Name = "+((ModuleClassAdv)value).getName();
        }else if (value instanceof   ModuleImplAdv){
            text += "Code = "+((ModuleImplAdv)value).getCode();
        }else if (value instanceof   ModuleSpecAdv){
            text += "Name = "+((ModuleSpecAdv)value).getName();
        }else if (value instanceof   RdvAdvertisement){
            text += "Name = "+((RdvAdvertisement)value).getName();
        }else if (value instanceof   EndpointAdvertisement){
            text += "Name = "+((EndpointAdvertisement)value).getName();
        }else if (value instanceof   TransportAdvertisement){
            text += "Type = "
                + ((TransportAdvertisement)value).getAdvertisementType();
        }else if (value instanceof   PipeAdvertisement){
            text += "PipeName = "+((PipeAdvertisement)value).getName();
        }else if (value instanceof   HTTPAdv){
            text += ((HTTPAdv)value).getProtocol()+" Addrr = "
                + ((HTTPAdv)value).getServer()+":"
                + ((HTTPAdv)value).getPort() ;
        }else if (value instanceof   TCPAdv){
            text += ((TCPAdv)value).getProtocol()+" Addr = "
                +((TCPAdv)value).getInterfaceAddress()+" port"
                + ((TCPAdv)value).getPort() ;
        }else if (value instanceof BeepAdv){
            text += ((BeepAdv)value).getProtocol()+" Addr = "
                +((BeepAdv)value).getPublicAddress()
                +" & local="+((BeepAdv)value).getLocalAddress()
                +" port"+ ((BeepAdv)value).getPort() ;
        }else if (value instanceof   String){
            text = (String)value;
        }else {
            text += " NOT EVALUATED";
        }
        if (text.length() == 0){
            text = "none";
        }
        setText(text);
        return this;
    }// end of getTreeCellRendererComponent()
}// End of class AdvertisementTreeCellRenderer
```

Running Explorer

Running the Explorer is very simple. Just start the application and start selecting and expanding nodes on the advertisement tree. The application looks like that shown in Figure 11.3. The advertisement tree is on the left and the advertisement display is on the right.

Be aware that the discovery process is very slow. If you select and then open a group leaf, you will see the sub-folders, but the sub-folders may not be populated with advertisements.

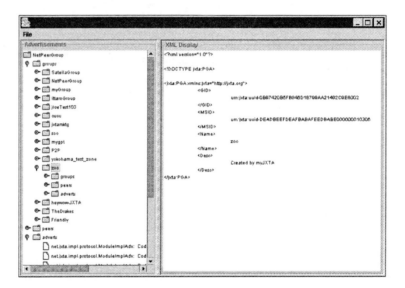

FIGURE 11.3   Screen shot of Explorer. The peer group *Zoo* is selected and its XML advertisement is shown on the right panel.

Sometimes, you will be looking at a folder's contents, like groups, and the system will suddenly add new groups. The reason is that the discovery process is receiving a different set of groups from another rendezvous. This is normal. By now, you should understand that P2P computing rarely gives you exactly what you want all at once.

Learning about JXTA

There are a few things to learn about the JXTA network. First is the response of the discovery mechanism. The remote discovery is very inconsistent as to when it begins to return data to the requesting peer. Sometimes you will see several minutes go by before the advertisement tree begins to populate. The delay is very important when the user is waiting. You should have a way to inform the user that the discovery mechanism is working.

Another aspect of the discovery service is in the code. We use hashtables to store advertisements. Depending on the type, we use the ID of the advertisement. Because some advertisements do not have identifiers, we use other means. The reason we are using hashtables and some type of unique identifier is that remote discovery will return duplicate advertisements. In practice, duplicates are a problem because you do not want to act on duplicate responses. Any process that depends on the event handler for remote discovery must take duplicates into account.

Volume Advertisements

Another problem with remote discovery, especially in this type of application is that the process needs to be repeated at intervals. In this application, the remote search is repeated to ensure that it finds advertisements from peers as they come online. There is one problem with this type of discovery; it takes up resources as rendezvous peers respond. This would not be too bad except for the duplicates returned.

To pinpoint the problem, all incoming messages have advertisements that are processed by the cache manager and stored. In the current version of JXTA, each advertisement is written to the hard disk. The cache manager (CM) may also rewrite the duplicate advertisements as they are received (depending on the version of the CM). As a minimum, new advertisements are written to the hard disk. Your computer's resources will begin to be lost to new and duplicated advertisements that must be processed by core JXTA and your application.

Avoid doing remote discovery. If you do need remote discovery to be repeated over time, reduce the search scope to specific groups and advertisements.

You may also see many pipe advertisements or others, such as temporary groups with the same names but different identifiers. One of the problems with developing JXTA is that pipes and other constructs are meant to be longer lived than they are in development. This often means that an application is started, advertisements published, and then the application is stopped. When the application is restarted, new advertisements with new identifiers are created. To avoid this, you may want to force identifiers for some of these advertisements, especially groups, so that you will not discover stale advertisements that can hamper execution or result in the need to write code to purge the advertisements.

Summary

The Explorer application is both useful and an informative example of how the discovery mechanism works. You should now understand how to request and manage remote advertisements.

You should understand that remote discovery has pitfalls, such as duplicate messages, and cause an increased use of your peer's resources. Remember that the cache manager is also processing these messages and saving new and updated data to the local storage.

Doing remote discovery is inconsistent in its timing. Messages in response to queries can arrive at any time.

You can now discover messages that are currently available on the JXTA network. This is very informative and can even show you a lot about your applications and others. Please explore the network and learn about what is out there. You might want to do this from time to time to see what is going on in the world of JXTA.

APPENDIX A

The Project JXTA Community

By Daniel Brookshier

JXTA, as has been stated many times in this book, is a community. This is evident in the number and variations of projects that are currently registered on the jxta.org site. Both companies and individuals maintain their projects on the site and can utilize a workforce of volunteers from the community.

Like any community, project owners need to manage their projects on a regular basis. The volunteers also need to contribute various amounts of their time to ensure that things get done. What this means is that some projects, though listed at jxta.org, may not be active.

Contributing to a Project

Developer roles are not granted lightly. If you submit changes or new code to the developer lists or via e-mails to project owners or developers, your request for a change in status is more likely.

In some projects, you may only gain access to the bug reporting system and never be given a right to submit or modify the CVS repository. This is because some groups may choose to limit membership to just a few people for more efficient collaboration.

Although this is a community, there are sometimes cliques. We all have the right to use code because of open-source licensing, but we don't always get to contribute. In some groups, you may need to prove yourself. You need to do this for the same reasons that you have to prove yourself at work.

Because of the nature of open-source collaboration, be careful. It is very easy to submit a change to code that causes the application or service to fail to compile. Be sure to test all of your code before committing it to the Web site repository.

Also, before making radical or seeping changes, discuss your ideas with your fellow developers. This is a collaboration and not a selfish monarchy. Just because you have the right to change code, does not mean the rest of the community will like your code or your changes. Tread carefully or your rights will be revoked.

Submitting a New Project

Submitting a project is relatively simple. After joining project JXTA and submitting a contract that basically binds you to the open-source rules of the Web site and a relationship with Sun, you only need to submit your proposal to the main discussion group. If there is no large dissention, a JXTA community manager will grant you rights as a project owner and create a project area for you.

Be sure that you research the existing projects before submitting a proposal. There are already projects that may have all or most of what you need. Be thorough in your searches. You may just need to volunteer in an existing project to add your ideas.

It is also recommended that you create a good set of starting documentation laying out goals, requirements, and design. By doing this and posting it on your project page, you can help ensure that volunteers will understand your goals.

In addition to good documentation, try to start a project with existing code. This is not always possible with large projects, but if you can create at least a framework, your volunteers are going to be more likely to participate.

JXTA.ORG Development Environment

The jxta.org site was developed and is manage by CollabNet. CollabNet was created by the same people who created the Web site for Apache.org. The site includes management of documents, code, managers, contributors, and developers.

If you have ever worked on an open-source project, such as Apache or those managed by CollabNet, you should already be familiar with how the system works. The system uses remote CVS to download files and has an error reporting system used to submit bugs and feature requests. There are also list groups for discussing development or user issues and Web space for descriptions, downloads, and documents.

If you have developed using tools available on the SourceForge tools and Web site, another Open Source community, there are a few differences. For example, SourceForge has a different user management scheme. SourceForge supports remote CVS access, as does CollabNet, but SourceForge requires a different authentication mechanism and supports encrypted access via SSL.

jxta.org **Projects**

This section lists all the projects listed at jxta.org as of January, 2002. Not all of these are active, and some may have code but are slow to change. If you feel a project is slow but you are interested in the result, e-mail the project owner and volunteer your services. You can also submit yourself for a role on a project.

Applications

Applications are projects that either have a user interface or are standalone programs that perform or operate a service:

- AllHands—Event notification application.
- Brando—P2P Java source code sharing tool.
- Configurator—A GUI configuration tool for the JXTA platform.
- dfwbase—P2P network with a database at each peer.
- gnougat—Fully decentralized file caching.
- jnushare—A file-sharing application of GISP.
- juxtaprose—A Web discussion and content sharing application.
- jxauction—Auction software using JXTA.
- jxta-httpd—Set of service and tools for Web publishing.
- myjxta—JXTA Demonstration Application (InstantP2P). The features include chat and file sharing.
- parlor—Application framework for creating collaborative P2P spaces.
- project2p—A peer-to-peer solution to share project documents.
- rosettachat—Localized JXTA Peer Text Messaging.
- shell—JXTA command-line shell for interactive access to the JXTA network.
- www—A project for HTML documents and information.

Core Projects

The core projects are projects that are basic to the JXTA network. These include implementations of JXTA on specific platforms and the development of services that will be a part of the reference platform:

- DI—Distributed Indexing.
- jxme—JXTA for J2ME (CLDC / MIDP).

- jxta-c—C language binding for JXTA core.
- JxtaPerl—An implementation of the core JXTA protocols in Perl 5.
- JxtaRuby—Ruby implementation of the core JXTA protocols.
- Objc-jxta—An Objective-c binding for the JXTA platform.
- Platform—JXTA platform infrastructure and protocols for Java 2 SE.
- PocketJxta—Porting the JXTA platform to the PocketPC.
- Security—JXTA P2P Security Project.
- TINI—TINI binding for JXTA platform.

Services

Services are peer-group–based programmatic services that can be used in JXTA applications. Think about services like Java packages, but instead the services specialized to operate via the JXTA network:

- CAService—Peer service that can validate certificate chains (Certificate Authority).
- CMS—CMS, Content Management Service, is a JXTA service that provides sharing across peers in a peer group. It implements simple searching across all peers in a peer group.
- compute-power-market—Economics-driven P2P computing platform and marketplace.
- Edutella—RDF-based metadata infrastructure for P2P applications.
- GISP—Global Information Sharing Protocol.
- IPeers—Artificial intelligence in P2P networks.
- JXRTL—XML language allowing Active Networks to be implemented in JXTA.
- JXTA-RMI—RMI API on top of JXTA.
- JXTA-Wire—Provide a set of tools to allow many to many JXTA pipes.
- JXTA-XML-RPC—JXTA transport binding implementation for XML-RPC.
- JxtaSpaces—A distributed shared memory service for JXTA.
- JxtaVFS—JxtaVFS organizes JXTA network resources as virtual file system.
- Monitoring—Monitoring and metering of peers and services.
- NetworkServices—Integrate Web Services concepts into JXTA.
- P2P-Email—P2P e-mail group discussions using JXTA PeerGroup technology.

- Payment—Implement anonymous and secure financial transactions.

- Replication—Replication/sync engine.

- RRS—Service for local and remote administration of rendezvous peers.

- RVManager—RendezVous Manager used to remotely control and manage peers acting as a RendezVous.

- Search—Distributed search service for JXTA and Web content and services.

Other

The "Other" section of JXTA is simply what it sounds like. Here you will find a random collection of subjects that cover subjects that are not necessarily directly associated with programming with JXTA:

- Download—JXTA download area.

- JXTA-CAD—A community effort to adopt JXTA in Computer Aided Design (CAD).

- JxtaBeans—JavaBean JXTA components.

- NPProtocol—A place to work on the protocols for establishing new projects.

- People—Work Area for jxta.org Members Project Committers and Owners. This is a place to read about other developers.

- Spec—Project JXTA Specifications. All of the core specifications are available here.

Details on Select Projects

During the writing of this book, several interesting JXTA projects came to our attention. We took the time to talk to the project members to get some insight to what their projects were about and why they used JXTA.

JuxtaProse

Robin Johnson of Mendota Heights submitted the following information on JuxtaProse. Its purpose and goals are as follows:

- To create a user-moderated, self-organizing decentralized discussion network that is resistant to spam.

- To integrate other JXTA services into the HTML pages that are used as a display medium for discussion postings.

- To provide an efficient way to search for discussions pertinent to a certain topic or topics, regardless of the context.

The application should be capable of meeting the first objective by the beginning of 2002.

Johnson said the following, "JXTA is the only completely open source peer-to-peer networking framework and API that I know of. Although I could have gotten by using Gnutella or Mojo Nation as a platform to run JuxtaProse on, the resulting application would not have the potential to do everything I wanted it to do."

JuxtaProse runs on top of the content management service. The service has a very simple interface and saved Johnson the trouble of having to write yet another file sharing application to do relatively light file transfers.

Johnson also stated, "JXTA is important to the developer of JuxtaProse because the Internet is controlled by the hardware. Traditionally, most of this control belonged to governments, universities, or large corporations that own servers. However, the gold rush during the late 1990s left consumers with far more hardware than they typically need. Not until recently have we begun to realize that all this extra computing power can empower everyday people not just by letting them use the Internet, but by allowing them to steering its evolution their way. By choosing what their computer is used for, a user is able to express their opinions. If they know of an artist that they like, they can help promote the artists' works by sharing (legally reproduced) copies of them. If they see cancer as one of mankind's most serious problems, they can donate CPU cycles and disk space towards finding a cure. With an application like JuxtaProse, they would be able to share their opinions with others, as well as amplify and focus arguments that they deem important."

An early application of distributed networking let Carl Sagan fans everywhere pitch-in on humanity's search for extraterrestrial intelligence (SETI@Home). Where JXTA fits into all of this is that it is a very promising attempt at a framework that would make it easy to write software that allows all of these things to happen.

Security Project

The purpose and goal of the security project is to insure that JXTA has state-of-the-art security. The initial security implementation is done. This implements the "Poblano, A Distributed Trust Model for Peer-to-Peer Networks" by William Yeager and Rita Chen of Sun Microsystems (http://www.jxta.org/project/docs/trust.pdf) security model with TLS (rfc2246) as a reliable, end-to-end, virtual transport on the Project JXTA Virtual Network. It uses X509.v3 certificates as are required by TLS, and offers zero dollar cost security as the Poblano entry level0. Here, every peer is its own certificate authority. The model is implemented to scale and to support traditional certificate authorities currently used on the Internet.

The security implementation is a virtual TLS transport (VTLS) implemented at the endpoint. As such, it is bi-directional, and multiple pipes will multiplex all of their data on the same VTLS connection between two peers. If TCP/IP is the underlying real transport, only one connection is used for multiple secure pipes over the VTLS connection.

The developers on the project believe that we have arrived at a point in time where there is more than enough power in typical home and mobile computing systems to support true P2P networks. The Project JXTA protocols are ideal because they provide an appropriate abstraction so as to be independent of the underlying real transports and physical layers and are self-adapting. As such, they do enable peers on the JXTA virtual network (JVN) to create self-organizing peer groups as a natural evolution of their presence on the JVN. The Project JXTA protocols work!

Rita Chen, a Senior Software Engineer at Sun, co-authored the Poblano paper with Bill Yeager, and helped to write the full implementation of the current Project JXTA security code.

JXTA-CAD

JXTA-CAD is a community effort to merge JXTA into Computer Aided Designing (CAD). This project assess the benefits of JXTA in Core Industrial Sector, such as heavy engineering, manufacturing, architectural, and aeronautical fields. Basically, it will be an application-cum-service that brings consultants, designers, and customers together by allowing them to share the best designs in their own fields and exchange their views online and offline.

Various CAD product manufacturers have their own file extensions (AutoCad having `*.drg`, Unigraphics having `*.prt`, and so on). The project's initial task is to interact and collect all the CAD product manufacturers' file extensions and classify them into groups according to their extensions and field of use.

JXTA-CAD was in the team building and specification definition stage at the time this book went to press. This is an example of a project at `jxta.org` that started simply with an idea and created a community of developers.

Commercial Projects

Internet Access Methods, Inc. has been developing P2P applications for many years (both products and professional services) and is doing a lot with JXTA. A PDF version of a talk at Sun at their JXTA Developer Briefing, describing their efforts is available at `www.sdc.sun.com/briefings`.

They have an entire suite of JXTA-based component libraries, centralized services, and applications, including a real-time collaborative IDE that are downloadable at www.iam-there.com.

The company is also submitting additional projects to JXTA in the application level pipe system (both API related and libraries). The contributions to project JXTA include the following:

- Greater control of message delivery (queue control)

- Production quality "Connection" (also known as bidirectionalPipe/SocketPipe)

- Utility classes

- Debugging monitors and tools

They have been developing these for a while internally and have decided to open source them. The changes/additions greatly simplify JXTA application development. You can get some information about what they are doing at http://www.iamethods.com and http://www.iam-there.com.

The company is also sponsoring a JXTA SIG in NYC. The SIG information is available at www.jxtasig.com/www.jxtasig.org.

Contact information:

Internet Access Methods, Inc.

200 West 72nd Street Suite 48

New York, NY 10023

(212) 580-2700 x130

seidman@iamx.com

VistaRepository—Vista Portal Software, Inc.

VistaRepository (www.ivistaportal.com) is software that provides distributed or centralized storage with scalable, flexible, secure, and unified access to resources.

VistaPortal Software Inc. has two projects that utilize JXTA Technology:

- VistaRepository software provides distributed or centralized storage and scalable, flexible, secure, and unified access to resources (objects of different kinds). VistaRepository supports different storage types (file system, LDAP, and RDBMS), using framework that allows plug-in Services.

- VistaDataProvider software provides scalable, flexible, secure, and unified access to data and enables querying different data sources (RDBMS, spreadsheets, LDAP, XML, and so on).

VistaRepository software is a Java program that turns every computer into a peer of VistaRepository. The system blends networking, versioning, access, security, and other aspects using XML, LDAP, databases, Web Services, and others into a P2P framework for creating applications.

VistaRepository is based on several concepts:

- Peer-to-peer architecture (based on JXTA technology) provides a distributed repository.

- Mount Point services provide unified interface of access to heterogeneous storage types (file system, LDAP, database).

- DWAs (Distributed Working Areas) provide flexible grouping of resources and adaptable, yet powerful, security mechanisms.

The company sees P2P technology and JXTA as a base for the emerging next generation of Internet applications.

Currently, most Internet applications still utilize a client/server approach. Clients retain a passive role in the computing. The new generation of Internet applications, in our opinion, will enable clients to be active in the process of computations. It means that clients (desktop computer, PDA, and so on) will share their resources (data/CPU).

The JXTA technology provides a powerful and flexible platform for implementation of the next generation of Internet applications because:

- It is created on the right protocol-based architecture.

- It is programming language–independent.

- It is platform-independent.

Contact information: www.ivistaportal.com

Reptile

Kevin A. Burton submitted information to us as we were putting the final touches on this book. Kevin's software is at http://reptile.openprivacy.org and is called Reptile. Reptile is a content exchange mechanism, based on P2P and Web technologies, that enables users to manage information in a distributed yet uniform environment.

Reptile provides a distributed and secure mechanism for finding, accessing, and selectively sharing information. Reptile integrates the concept of pseudonymous reputation, which we believe has the potential to enhance the value of the Internet as much as the Web browser did.

Reptile integrates the Sierra Reputation Framework
(`http://sierra.openprivacy.org/`) that provides a simple and powerful mechanism
for measuring the quality of information. This is very important in a distributed
environment. The reputations of authors are important when there is no central
authority or publisher to ensure the quality and accuracy of content.

Kevin noted that JXTA was used for this project because it provides a great way to
distribute content, get through firewalls, and provides a distributed search framework. JXTA is important because it provides a stable API, great framework, and a
great community. All of this is important for a P2P network to succeed.

B

XML Primer

By Daniel Brookshier

Extensible Markup Language (XML) is a way to format data. The closest thing to XML is HTML. In fact, if you look at an XML document, it looks a lot like HTML. What XML provides is the ability to describe any type of data that makes it easy for another computer to understand. Because it is easy to read, XML is ideal when many different languages, devices, and operating systems need to communicate. Consequently, XML is a great standard for a peer-to-peer system.

Simply put, XML is a language meant to mark differences between chunks of data. XML is language agnostic because most languages can interpret XML and convert data represented to the languages' native types and create more complex types, such as objects.

XML is also often referred to in terms of displaying data. For example, instead of sending a text version of a formatted date, we send a standard date value that is then rendered on the display according to formatting rules.

Another common use for XML is similar but removes parts of the XML document to be transmitted before sending it to particular devices. For example, the complete XML representation of data for an article would be sent to a desktop browser, while only the headline of the article will be transmitted to a small cell phone browser.

XML Basics

If you are unfamiliar with XML, we can cover the basics in just a few moments. There are two key aspects of XML. The first is that it is all text based, and the second is that the data items are separated by tags.

Text

XML is text based because text is the one thing that most computer scientists agree is the most standard between computers. Despite text being standard, there are two ways of representing text on computers—ASCII and Unicode. The text we are most familiar with is ASCII. ASCII is a standard that maps a binary representation to a letter, symbol, or number in the alphabet. ASCII characters are 8-bits wide.

Unicode was created to account for the many different languages in the world that could not be represented in ASCII's 8 bits or 256 possible characters. Unicode characters are 16-bits wide to allow for a much larger number of unique characters and symbols.

ASCII is compatible to Unicode because the first 256 characters of Unicode are the same ASCII characters. As long as there is no use of foreign languages that would not work in ASCII, you can just use the last 8 bits of data. Most communication should be done via Unicode, because that is what most consumers of XML messages are expecting.

Tags

XML tags are exactly like tags in HTML. The following is an example tag:

```
<Sample> data </Sample>
```

The preceding is a custom tag that defines a tag called `Sample`. The tag consists of two parts, a start tag and an end tag. The end tag is the one with the slash (/) character preceding the tag name. The space between the start and end tags is your data.

Tags can also have parameters. The form of parameters is exactly like those used in HTML. The parameter(s) is only used in the start tag and not in the end tag. The following is an example tag with parameters:

```
<Sample color="red" style="bold"> data </Sample>
```

The parameters are separated from the tag name by one space. Note that the parameter consists of a name, an equal sign, and then the parameter value, which is in quotes. Also, if there are multiple parameters, each parameter is separated from the next by a space.

Tags can also be of a slightly different form. The following is an example of this shorter form:

```
<Sample/>
```

The shorter tag is used to mark a point in an XML document or to convey a setting or other information. Settings can be represented by the presence of the tag itself or via parameters in the tag. The following is an example of a shortened tag with parameters:

```
<Sample debug="true" />
```

Self-Describing

One very nice feature of XML is that the tags describe data. XML is self-describing because of its tags. This feature makes it quite easy to understand the contents and match them to concepts. Electronic Data Interchange (EDI) is another standard for data exchange that is not self-describing, because the packets of data only contain data, not the names of the data. With EDI, you cannot tell if data is in a message; with XML you can not.

Strong Typing and Syntax Validation

XML is capable of being strongly typed and a custom syntax can be enforced and validated. However, not all XML implementations, including JXTA, take advantage of these capabilities.

At the time of this writing, the XML of JXTA advertisements are not validated. The Java code does fail at times and, thus, gives the appearance of strong syntax validation. Validation may be provided in the future, or you could add validation yourself at various points. You will need a Data Type Definition file (DTD). The DTD describes the typing and the syntax of an XML specification. DTD files are available at JXTA.org. Alternatively, you can use an XML schema definition file to verify that the XML messages are correct.

Validation of syntax has marginal value depending on how well the code is written. When an application is able to generate valid advertisements, there is little need for a DTD and the overhead of processing. Also, because advertisements are converted to objects or other constructs, it is pretty obvious when the XML has something unexpected.

Problems with XML

XML is pretty verbose. One of the worst problems is with the way that tags are used. By duplicating the tag name in the end tag, XML begins to waste as much space as there are tags in an XML document.

In addition, XML data is formatted as text. Text data can be much larger than its binary equivalent. This is especially true of numbers, which waste more space as they increase in the size of significant digits.

Another problem with XML is compression. Sticking with the raw Unicode compared to the same thing as a compressed equivalent, you could see a difference of size. Unfortunately, compression requires CPU capacity as well as the extra memory required for encoding and decoding the compression. JXTA does not use compression because the extra resources may prevent JXTA from being used on smaller systems. Despite the resources required, JXTA may support some form of compressed XML in the future.

Index

Symbols

A